Dedication

*For Paula, Torianna, and Tyler,
the highpoints of my life*

CALIFORNIA
County Summits

A Guide to the Highest Point
in Each of the 58 Counties

Gary Suttle

WILDERNESS PRESS
BERKELEY

Copyright © 1994 by Gary D. Suttle
Maps by the author
PHOTO CREDITS:
  Gary Suttle—ii, 5, 9, 10, 13, 29, 77, 99, 100, 126, 148, 199
  Bill Broeckel—16, 41, 60, 86, 112 bottom, 117, 139, 143, 147, 166 top and bottom,
    184, 186
  Pete Yamagata—xii, 36, 47, 64, 69, 91, 105, 112 top, 173, 193
  Dinesh Desai—53, 97
  Joy Desai—133
Design by Thomas Winnett and Kathy Morey
Cover design by Larry B. Van Dyke
Cover photo by E.C. Rangé

Library of Congress Card Catalog Number 93-46432
ISBN 0-89997-164-4

Manufactured in the United States of America
Published by **Wilderness Press**
            2440 Bancroft Way
            Berkeley, CA 94704
            (510) 843-8080

          Write or call for free catalog

Library of Congress Cataloging-in-Publication Data

Suttle, Gary.
      California County Summits / Gary Suttle
          p.   cm.
      Includes bibliographical references (p.   ) and index.
      ISBN 0-89997-164-4
      1. Hiking--California--Guidebooks. 2. California--Guidebooks.
  I. Title
  GV199.42.C2S88 1994
  796.5'1'09794--dc20   93-46432
                                                                 CIP

Cover photo: Mt. Whitney (14,492'), the highest point in Inyo and Tulare Counties, the state of California and the continental United States.

Acknowledgments

An all-encompassing thank you to the dozens of county, state, and federal public servants who contributed information to this volume. Thanks specifically to Scott Adams, Greg Mangan, and Robert Beehler (Bureau of Land Management), Charles Smay, Charles McFadin, and Karen Shimamoto (Forest Service), Barry Breckling and Douglas Kauffman (California Department of Parks and Recreation), Isa Dempsey and David Soho (California Department of Forestry), Dan Reasor (East Bay Regional Park District), and Jack Mottram (United States Geological Survey).

For inspiration and encouragement, thanks to Kent, Elsie, and Joanie Suttle, Jamshid Khajavi, Jack Robertson, David Rawlins, Mary Dixon, and Richard and Peggy Whittaker. For various contributions I am grateful to Teri Astle, Ed Caster, Joy Desai, Bill Hauser, Ira Heinrich, Don C. Johns, Frederick Johnson, Duncan McPherson IV, and John Sarna. Major thanks to V.K. Leary and to Andy Martin for leading me to higher points. Andy also supplied valuable map data. Special gratitude goes to Warren Johnson and to Weldon Astle for accompanying me on steep climbs. Weldon's support throughout the project buoyed my efforts. I give particular credit to Dinesh Desai, whose search for highpoints reaped rewards. Dinesh and I shared friendship, findings, and high adventures; he spearheaded the first group outings for county-summit seekers and contributed vital information to this work. Thanks to Dinesh and to Pete Yamagata for sharing their fine mountain photography.

I warmly appreciate the assistance of my wife, Paula, for her review of the draft and for her always uplifting words. I am grateful to Dr. Douglas H. Strong, who read the entire manuscript and made innumerable suggestions to clarify ideas and enhance readability. Many thanks to the staff of Wilderness Press and especially to Tom Winnett for his editorial acumen and his kind guidance throughout the course of the project. I extend my deepest gratitude to Bill Broeckel. Bill generously shared his detailed highpoints journal, his quality photography, and his mountaineering skills; he guided me up North Palisade. The help and camaraderie of fellow highpoint enthusiasts added much to the pleasure of writing this book.

Despite the many contributions and my striving for accuracy, errors may occur and conditions do change. I welcome corrections and additional information on California county highpoints. Please address letters to the author in care of Wilderness Press.

Gary D. Suttle
San Diego, California
January, 1994

California County Highpoints

County	Summit	Elevation
Alameda	DISCOVERY PEAK	3840+
Alpine	SONORA PEAK	11,459
Amador	THUNDER MOUNTAIN	9410
Butte	LOST LAKE RIDGE	7120+
Calaveras	CORRAL RIDGE	8170
Colusa	SNOW MTN. EAST	7040+
Contra Costa	MT. DIABLO	3849
Del Norte	BEAR MOUNTAIN	6400+
El Dorado	FREEL PEAK	10,881
Fresno	NORTH PALISADE	14,242
Glenn	BLACK BUTTE	7448
Humboldt	SALMON MOUNTAIN	6956
Imperial	BLUE ANGELS PEAK	4548
Inyo	MOUNT WHITNEY	14,491
Kern	SAWMILL MTN.	8818
Kings	TABLE MOUNTAIN	3473
Lake	SNOW MTN. EAST	7056
Lassen	HAT MOUNTAIN	8737
Los Angeles	MT. SAN ANTONIO	10,064
Madera	MOUNT RITTER	13,143
Marin	MT. TAMALPAIS	2571
Mariposa	PARSONS PEAK RIDGE	12,040+
Mendocino	ANTHONY PEAK	6954
Merced	LAVEAGA PEAK	3801
Modoc	EAGLE PEAK	9892
Mono	WHITE MOUNTAIN PEAK	14,246
Monterey	JUNIPERO SERRA PEAK	5862
Napa	MT. ST. HELENA EAST	4200+
Nevada	MOUNT LOLA	9148
Orange	SANTIAGO PEAK	5687
Placer	GRANITE CHIEF	9006
Plumas	MOUNT INGALLS	8372
Riverside	SAN JACINTO PEAK	10,804
Sacramento	CARPENTER HILL	828
San Benito	SAN BENITO MTN.	5241
San Bernardino	SAN GORGONIO MT.	11,502
San Diego	HOT SPRINGS MOUNTAIN	6533
San Francisco	MT. DAVIDSON	927
San Joaquin	MT. BOARDMAN N	3626
San Luis Obispo	CALIENTE MTN.	5106
San Mateo	LONG RIDGE	2600+
Santa Barbara	BIG PINE MTN.	6800+
Santa Clara	COPERNICUS PEAK	4360+
Santa Cruz	MT. MCPHERSON	3231
Shasta	LASSEN PEAK	10,457
Sierra	MOUNT LOLA NORTH	8844
Siskiyou	MOUNT SHASTA	14,162
Solano	MT. VACA	2819
Sonoma	COBB MTN. WEST RIM	4480+
Stanislaus	MT. STAKES	3804
Sutter	SOUTH BUTTE	2120+
Tehama	BROKEOFF MTN.	9235
Trinity	MOUNT EDDY	9025
Tulare	MOUNT WHITNEY	14,491
Tuolumne	MOUNT LYELL	13,114
Ventura	MT. PINOS	8831
Yolo	LITTLE BLUE PEAK	3120+
Yuba	SUGAR PINE PEAK	4825+

California County Summits—Elevation Profile

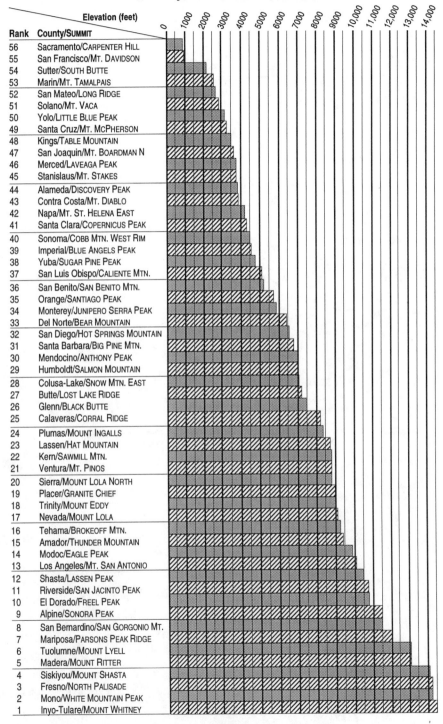

Rank	County/SUMMIT
56	Sacramento/CARPENTER HILL
55	San Francisco/MT. DAVIDSON
54	Sutter/SOUTH BUTTE
53	Marin/MT. TAMALPAIS
52	San Mateo/LONG RIDGE
51	Solano/MT. VACA
50	Yolo/LITTLE BLUE PEAK
49	Santa Cruz/MT. MCPHERSON
48	Kings/TABLE MOUNTAIN
47	San Joaquin/MT. BOARDMAN N
46	Merced/LAVEAGA PEAK
45	Stanislaus/MT. STAKES
44	Alameda/DISCOVERY PEAK
43	Contra Costa/MT. DIABLO
42	Napa/MT. ST. HELENA EAST
41	Santa Clara/COPERNICUS PEAK
40	Sonoma/COBB MTN. WEST RIM
39	Imperial/BLUE ANGELS PEAK
38	Yuba/SUGAR PINE PEAK
37	San Luis Obispo/CALIENTE MTN.
36	San Benito/SAN BENITO MTN.
35	Orange/SANTIAGO PEAK
34	Monterey/JUNIPERO SERRA PEAK
33	Del Norte/BEAR MOUNTAIN
32	San Diego/HOT SPRINGS MOUNTAIN
31	Santa Barbara/BIG PINE MTN.
30	Mendocino/ANTHONY PEAK
29	Humboldt/SALMON MOUNTAIN
28	Colusa-Lake/SNOW MTN. EAST
27	Butte/LOST LAKE RIDGE
26	Glenn/BLACK BUTTE
25	Calaveras/CORRAL RIDGE
24	Plumas/MOUNT INGALLS
23	Lassen/HAT MOUNTAIN
22	Kern/SAWMILL MTN.
21	Ventura/MT. PINOS
20	Sierra/MOUNT LOLA NORTH
19	Placer/GRANITE CHIEF
18	Trinity/MOUNT EDDY
17	Nevada/MOUNT LOLA
16	Tehama/BROKEOFF MTN.
15	Amador/THUNDER MOUNTAIN
14	Modoc/EAGLE PEAK
13	Los Angeles/MT. SAN ANTONIO
12	Shasta/LASSEN PEAK
11	Riverside/SAN JACINTO PEAK
10	El Dorado/FREEL PEAK
9	Alpine/SONORA PEAK
8	San Bernardino/SAN GORGONIO MT.
7	Mariposa/PARSONS PEAK RIDGE
6	Tuolumne/MOUNT LYELL
5	Madera/MOUNT RITTER
4	Siskiyou/MOUNT SHASTA
3	Fresno/NORTH PALISADE
2	Mono/WHITE MOUNTAIN PEAK
1	Inyo-Tulare/MOUNT WHITNEY

California County Summits—
General Location and Rank*

*See **California County Summits—Elevation Profile**, page vii, for key to rank, county, and name of summit.

California's 58 Counties

Contents

Freel Peak (El Dorado County)

Introduction

*Go where you may within the bounds of California, mountains are ever in
sight, charming and glorifying every landscape.*
—John Muir
The Mountains of California

California's 58 counties contain a diversity of mountains unequaled in any other
state in the nation or in any comparably sized place on Earth. Within each county,
one mountaintop rises above all others—the **County Highpoint**. This guide leads
you to these special and often extraordinary summits.

County Highpoint Attractions

The county highpoints encompass an astounding variety of landscapes, including every major mountain region in California. The highpoints range from a
modest 828-foot hill to the tallest peak in the contiguous 48 states, and include four
of California's six highest mountains. The summits rise within four national parks,
thirteen wilderness areas, twelve national forests, three state parks, and one city
park. Other county tops rest on Bureau of Land Management acreage, private
ranchland, a University of California scientific reserve, and an Indian reservation.

These summits command some of the best natural scenery in the state. They
overlook lush, moss-draped forests near Oregon, picturesque pinyon woodlands
along the Mexican border, expansive seascapes in central California, and glacier-
carved peaks in the High Sierra. Except on a few highly visited peaks, hikers can
enjoy the varied geology, flora, and fauna in peaceful communion with nature.
Quiet paths let county-highpoint seekers rise above the lowland throng, to a world
apart from crowds and complexity.

Each county highpoint has its own character and personality. Each represents
not just another peak but the absolute county zenith. This singularity gives the
summits an aura, a mystique all their own, and makes them more fun to climb. Most
can be climbed in a day and require no fancy gear or elaborate preparation. With
few exceptions, the highpoints are accessible by anybody in good condition, from
youthful hikers to active retirees. The climbs range from a mere five-minute walk-
up to a demanding multiday backpack. Most routes follow maintained trails, dirt
roads, or easy cross-country terrain.

As the highest point in the county, most of the summits afford breathtaking views and leave unforgettable impressions. Hikers recall the peaks and views years after experiencing them. To stand atop California, county by county, brings a sense of accomplishment and joy. Striding to a summit takes time and energy, but amid the state's unparalleled natural grandeur, how could time be better spent? We feel most alive when engaged in pulse-quickening activity. We love to soar, and climbing islands in the sky lets us ascend. For this reason alone the upward trail brings good feelings and fulfillment—and more. From time immemorial, humans have climbed mountains to gain renewal, perspective, and enlightenment. In the lowlands, we manipulate the environment; on a mountain, nature has control and we adapt to the natural surroundings. In touch with elemental forces, we gain a feeling of oneness with nature and recapture a vital bond too often weakened by the distractions of modern life.

Many county summits make good side trips en route to other destinations, as from Los Angeles to San Francisco, or from the Bay Area to Lake Tahoe. Other tops lie in remote, out-of-the-way corners of California, such as Eagle Peak in Modoc County and Blue Angels Peak in Imperial County. Just the scenic drives on backcountry roads to approach the highpoints provide great pleasure. Rural landscapes, small-town stores, and real country radio add spice to the hike's adventure.

Climbing the county summits not only acts as a springboard to exploration of the Golden State, but also provides observant hikers with a field course in California geography. County boundary signs become meaningful and place names become solid realities. News from anywhere in California takes on a new dimension for anyone who has explored the 58 counties.

Explanation of Entries

This guide presents the highpoints alphabetically by **county**; each description begins with a summit **name**, **elevation**, and **elevation rank** among the highpoints. While most highpoints have well-established names, the author and fellow county-summit seekers labeled unnamed highpoints informally, often with names based on adjoining geographic features. Many county tops also bear United States Geological Survey benchmarks. Imprecise elevations are flagged with a "+" mark. Unless otherwise noted, elevation figures are derived from the latest available USGS topographic maps.

Uncertainty necessarily surrounds the elevation of some highpoints. Even benchmarked elevations fall short of total accuracy. Some elevations based on older surveys done with unsophisticated equipment lack certainty. Earthquakes, erosion, and crustal-plate movements also subtly alter the elevations. Newer survey equipment and satellite geodesy make all elevations subject to revision.

Beginning in 1989, the author studied topographic maps and sifted through other sources to catalog county summits and to determine the location of unknown highpoints. Sources included county surveyors' offices, various small- and large-scale maps, reference works, and the USGS Earth Science Information Center in

Menlo Park. An initial compilation of county summits went through several revisions as some higher points came to light. Considerable research and field work, aided substantially by other highpoint enthusiasts, resulted in the current list, completed in 1993.

The **Location and Maps** entry places the highpoint within the county and lists USGS topographic quadrangles as well as other useful maps. A topographic map accompanies each description, either a 7½-minute map (1:24,000 original scale) or a 15-minute map (1:62,500 original scale), depending on the length of the hike. Some topo maps required photo reduction to fit the page. On every map a scale gives the correct 1-mile equivalent. The "**P**" indicates trailhead parking. A solid black line marks the main route, while dashed lines show alternate routes. All maps have north at the top.

The **Distance** entry gives round-trip mileage, from the trailhead to the top and back again. The **elevation gain** is total vertical footage gained on the hike. Some routes lose and recover altitude on the way to a summit. For these, all uphill segments figure in the total vertical climb, so the elevation gain exceeds the simple elevation difference between trailhead and summit.

The **Grade** assesses the physical demand of hiking to the highpoint as *easy, moderate,* or *strenuous.* The grade refers to physical exertion, not to technical climbing difficulty. Mountaineers commonly use a rating system to describe the technical difficulty of a climb. Class 1 is walking on a trail. Class 2 entails hiking rough cross-country terrain, such as boulders or talus, sometimes using the hands for balance. Class 3 requires climbing steep rock and talus, employing handholds and footholds, and facing "exposure" (a climbers' term for vulnerability to a fall measured by the distance a climber would plummet in an accident; most everyday hikers find exposure scary, and some prefer a rope for security in Class 3 climbing). Class 4 involves very steep to vertical terrain with great exposure, necessitating ropes and other equipment for safety. Class 5 comprises high-angle rock climbing open only to skilled climbers. By this system the vast majority of county highpoints rate Class 1 or easy Class 2. Several summits require short Class 3 segments, and one ranks Class 4. Individual descriptions detail the nature of the hike and any difficult climbing.

Hiking Time includes slightly above a 2-miles-per-hour pace with extra time added for steep, rugged, and/or high-altitude terrain. Your time may well be slower or faster, depending upon your gait, number of rest stops, and so forth. After a few trips you can predict your hiking time in relation to the figures given.

The **Season** brackets the normal range of months that a highpoint is accessible for hiking. Actual beginning dates vary from year to year based on mountain snowpack, road-grading contracts, and other factors. Before making a trip early or late in the season, you should call the phone number given at the end of a description to check on accessibility. Many lower-elevation summits, while open year-round, sizzle with heat in summer; it's best then to head for the highlands.

Trailnotes describe the highpoint in general terms. The entry explains policies of government agencies that manage the land, such as a requirement for a wilderness permit.

The **Approach** gives explicit directions from major regional highways to reach the trailhead.

Directions to Summit provide specific information on the route to the highpoint. The described route usually covers the most popular, direct, and recommended way to the summit. Many highpoints have more than one possible approach via formal trail or use trail. (A use trail is an unofficial path created by hikers through repeated use.)

The View provides a preview of the vista awaiting hikers who reach the mountaintop. Air pollution may reduce potential panoramas, but even on hazy days the view from most county summits exceeds expectations.

The Environment delves briefly into the highpoint's natural surroundings. Excellent field guides now survey most regions of California, and these books cover many highpoint areas in detail. Turn to the titles found at the end of a description for a wealth of information.

The **Nearby Campgrounds** entry lists developed car campsites close to a highpoint. Most Forest Service campgrounds operate on a first-come, first-served basis although some popular Forest Service campgrounds, as in the Lake Tahoe Basin, take reservations at (800) 280-2267. Campers can make state-park reservations through MISTIX at (800) 444-7275. For national-park reservations call (800) 365-2267.

This guide encourages car camps and dayhikes for several reasons. Car camping and dayhiking impact the environment less than backpacking. Most county summits lend themselves to dayhikes. Dayhiking also takes less preparation than backpacking, seldom requires a wilderness permit, allows for carrying water rather than having to find and purify it, and lets hikers bear a lighter pack for easier climbing.

The County entry gives the origin of each county's name and presents geographical highlights to illuminate California's 58 counties*.

The **Additional Sources of Information/Recommended Reading** entry lists agencies to contact and books to read for advice on alternate routes. In a few cases, dirt or paved roads provide motor-vehicle access to the summit, and in other instances a tram or a ski lift can reduce trail mileage. The guide mentions these options for those who prefer or require them (see Appendix 5 for highpoints accessible to persons with limited mobility) but recommends walking routes for three reasons:

1. To respect the mountain and to gain its view.
2. To experience most fully the highpoint's ambiance.
3. To use human power rather than horsepower, since approaching the highpoints from urban centers entails enough driving already.

Highpoints on Private Property

Private property hinders access to nine county summits. In four of these counties, public access reaches from within a few hundred feet to within a mile of

---

*Two highpoints (Mount Whitney and Snow Mountain East) are each shared by two counties (Inyo/Tulare and Colusa/Lake), making a total of 56, not 58, highpoints.

the highpoint, allowing hikers a close approach to their goal. In one county, a paid guide offers a way to the summit. In the remaining four counties, the highpoints lie within the confines of fenced cattle ranches. The guide explains the situation case by case under the separate county descriptions.

The author sent letters to landowners requesting permission for highpoint seekers to cross private property en route to county summits. Letters included a copy of Section 846 of the California Civil Code, which gives immunity from liability to landowners who permit members of the general public to enter their property for recreational purposes. With notable exceptions, owners failed to respond or responded unfavorably. In several cases, owners allowed one-time individual access to the author but they would not grant *carte blanche* public entry.

This book seeks to strike a balance between the public interest to celebrate county highpoints and the private landowner's interest to protect property rights. While the book identifies private highpoints, entries *exclude* explicit directions to those summits to discourage trespass. Please respect private property. Perhaps one day, under the auspices of a club, highpointers can arrange once-a-year group trips to private summits. The county highpoints deserve some form of public access, given their unique standing in the geography of California.

READ THIS

Hiking in the backcountry entails unavoidable risk that every hiker assumes and must be aware of and respect. The fact that a trail is described in this book is not a representation that it will be safe for you. Trails vary greatly in difficulty and in the degree of conditioning and agility one needs to enjoy them safely. On some hikes routes may have changed or conditions may have deteriorated since the descriptions were written. Also, trail conditions can change even from day to day, owing to weather and other factors. A trail that is safe on a dry day or for a highly conditioned, agile, properly equipped hiker may be completely unsafe for someone else or unsafe under adverse weather conditions.

You can minimize your risks on the trail by being knowledgeable, prepared and alert. There is not space in this book for a general treatise on safety in the mountains, but there are a number of good books and public courses on the subject and you should take advantage of them to increase your knowledge. Just as important, you should always be aware of your own limitations and of conditions existing when and where you are hiking. If conditions are dangerous, or if you are not prepared to deal with them safely, choose a different hike! It's better to have wasted a drive than to be the subject of a mountain rescue.

These warnings are not intended to scare you off the trails. Millions of people have safe and enjoyable hikes every year. However, one element of the beauty, freedom and excitement of the wilderness is the presence of risks that do not confront us at home. When you hike you assume those risks. They can be met safely, but only if you exercise your own independent judgment and common sense.

Preparations
and Precautions

The easy county summits require little preparation, but the moderate and strenuous highpoints call for planning and prudence. Inexperienced hikers should consult books such as *Wilderness Basics: The Complete Handbook for Hikers and Backpackers*, edited by Jerry Schad and David Moser. The following suggestions will get you started.

- Have your vehicle in good condition. Many county summits require long approach drives on remote roads far from gas stations and mechanical assistance. Check all tires, including the spare. Check your battery (the greatest single cause of vehicle breakdown), and your radiator (water boils at a lower temperature in higher altitudes and the coolant may have to be replenished, so bring an extra jug). Fill your gas tank before heading into the outback. Use the motor's compression, either second or low gear, to reduce brake fade on steep downgrades. If the motor fails to start at high elevation, you may have vapor lock; remove the air filter to increase air intake and/or place a damp cloth over the fuel pump for a few minutes.
- Get in good condition. Exercise actively and regularly. Walking, hiking, jogging, swimming, biking, and aerobic dancing are excellent to condition your body for uphill rigors. Start with low-mileage highpoints and build up to the taxing climbs. Hiking to highpoints brings fitness.
- Obtain necessary permits. Some county summits within wilderness areas require wilderness permits for entry. Rangers may levy fines for noncompliance. Application procedures vary; the **Trailnotes** entry provides necessary details. In addition to wilderness permits, national-forest rangers ask you to fill out a free campfire permit if you plan to build a fire.
- Bring ample food and water. Some highpoints have water, but others do not. Hiking requires a minimum of one pint of fluid per hour, so always carry plenty. Purify trailside water sources. Pack high-energy snacks to fortify you on your outings.

- Wear comfortable shoes. Running shoes or lightweight hiking boots work well for most county summit hikes. Only the highest, most rugged peaks require heavy-duty bootwear. Be sure to break-in new footgear before your trip.
- Protect your skin and eyes. Ultraviolet radiation intensifies with elevation. Apply sunscreen liberally. Wear a Hat. Use sunglasses to shield your eyes from bright sun reflecting off snowfields and rocky highlands.
- Acclimate to higher altitudes. Almost half of the county summits rise above 7000 feet, and 13 top 10,000 feet. The higher the elevation, the less oxygen in a lungful of air. Most people need a day or two to adapt to thinner air. If possible, spend time at a halfway elevation and take light warm-up hikes before your major ascent. Doing so will help avoid symptoms of altitude sickness, such as headache, nausea, rapid pulse, shortness of breath, and insomnia. Most symptoms subside with rest, fluids, and acclimatization, and descending always works. Never push yourself. Your body will let you know when to climb. Serious, if rare, forms of altitude sickness called high-altitude pulmonary edema (excess fluid in the lungs) and high-altitude cerebral edema (excess fluid in the brain) require immediate descent and medical attention. People vary in susceptibility to ordinary altitude sickness. Healthy people who find difficulty in adapting to elevation may obtain prescription medication to help alleviate the problem.
- Guard against hypothermia. Rapid loss of body heat caused by cold temperature, wetness, and wind is the number-one killer of outdoor recreationists. Wear proper clothing, preferably wool or synthetics like polypropylene, which maintain warmth even when wet. Carry good-quality raingear. Hypothermia often occurs at *above* freezing temperatures without the victim realizing it. Symptoms include shivering, slurred speech, loss of coordination, and drowsiness. Treat hypothermia by actively rewarming the person. Find shelter, remove wet clothing, and replace with dry clothing. Give the victim warm drinks and energy foods. In severe cases, restore body temperature by placing the victim in a sleeping bag skin to skin with another person.
- Plan for emergencies. Let friends or relatives know your itinerary; if you don't call or return on schedule, they can notify authorities. Hike with a partner when possible so that one may seek help if needed (a threesome is safest, so one person can stay with the victim). Carry a small first-aid kit as well as other essential items: map, compass, waterproof matches, flashlight, whistle, thermal "space blanket," toilet paper, extra clothing, extra food, insect repellent, pain reliever, pocket knife, and moleskin or equivalent for blisters.
- Watch the weather. Expect the unexpected. Snow occasionally falls in mountains above the 7000-foot level during the summer, and afternoon thunderstorms frequently occur. If lightning threatens, get off peaks, ridges, and other exposed areas. Find shelter among dense small trees; crouch between low rocks in a boulder field or in the open, if the area is quite flat. Remove metal-frame packs. Wait out thunderstorms; they usually don't last long.

- Remember hunting season. The Forest Service, Bureau of Land Management, and private ranch owners often permit hunting in the fall, centered around the months of September and October. During this time you may wish to choose among the many county highpoints located within parklands where hunting is prohibited.
- Keep oriented. Most county highpoint trails are easy to follow, and the cross-country routes traverse mostly open terrain. The maps in this guide, and others you may carry, should keep you from getting lost. If you become confused, don't panic. Use your maps, a compass, and the lay of the land to reorient yourself and backtrack to familiar ground. When in doubt, head downhill to where you are more likely to cross a road or a trail.
- Dispose of waste material properly. Carry out all garbage. Select a spot at least 100 feet away from water sources for a toilet. Dig a hole 8–10 inches across and 6–8 inches deep. Cover after use. Make the site indistinguishable from its surroundings.
- Avoid injury from insects, animals, and plants. Use repellent to ward off mosquitoes and ticks. Give a rattlesnake plenty of room and allow it to move on. If a bear approaches, make a lot of noise. If the bear fails to retreat, you should. Watch for stinging nettle along watercourses and avoid poison oak— "Leaves in three, let it be." (While scouting the 58 county summits, the author encountered occasional mosquitoes, no ticks, no rattlesnakes, several bears, little stinging nettle, and infrequent poison oak.)
- Know your limits. The highpoint hobby tends to take you farther than you might otherwise go, to longer and steeper ascents than you might have envisioned. Turn back if the climbing exceeds your ability or if bad weather descends. It is hard to turn back, especially if close to your goal, but the mountain will always be there for a later try. When you're perched on a peak, the saying "better safe than sorry" rings particularly true.

Lyell Canyon footbridge

Overview

The Golden State contains a greater land area and a larger population than many countries of the world. California extends 825 miles in length, stretches 350 miles at its maximum width, and covers 158,693 square miles. The state's rapidly growing population (31 million in 1993) far surpasses that of any other state in the union. Abundant natural resources support an economy larger than the economies of all but seven nations worldwide. An ecological treasure trove, California boasts more native plants, animal species, national forests, wilderness areas, and variety of mountains than any other state. California's 113 named mountain ranges evolved from forces working over eons of time.

Mountain Provinces

The county highpoints are scattered over eight major montane provinces. The *Klamath Mountains* extend across northwest California, low and rounded near the ocean, high and glaciated inland, as in the Trinity Alps. Volcanic cones and lava flows mark the south end of the *Cascade Range*, where Mount Shasta and Lassen Peak dominate the skyline. The *Basin and Range* province extends as far west as eastern California, represented by the Warner Mountains in the northeast corner of the state, and by the White Mountains east of the Owens Valley. The *North Coast Ranges* and the *South Coast Ranges* cover two thirds of western California with rugged, moderately elevated, north-south trending mountains and valleys. The aptly named *Transverse Ranges* file east to west, as dictated by a bend in the San Andreas fault and related fissures. South of the Transverse Ranges, the *Peninsular Ranges* run north to south from the San Jacinto Mountains to the Jacumba Mountains and continue into Mexico. The world-renowned *Sierra Nevada* extends for 400 miles to form the eastern backbone of California. Lastly, standing apart from the eight provinces and unique to themselves, the volcanic *Sutter Buttes* rise up in the heart of the Sacramento Valley. Individual highpoint descriptions elaborate on the provinces, and *California Mountain Ranges* by Russell B. Hill offers a fine description of each province.

Climate, Vegetation, and Wildlife

California's mountains have colder temperatures and greater precipitation than the adjacent lowlands. Temperatures decrease with elevation, about 3.5 degrees

11

per thousand feet. Prevailing winds from the Pacific Ocean push moist air masses upslope; the moisture cools and condenses, and you have rain or snow. The mountains so completely wring moisture from the clouds that dry belts extend over the lee sides of the ranges. In fact, California's mountain chains produce desert or semiarid conditions over the entire eastern length of the state. A rainshadow created by the Sierra Nevada and lesser ranges led to 760 rainless days in Bagdad, Death Valley, the longest rain-free period ever recorded in the United States. Besides the storms, mountains often generate their own weather in the form of summer thundershowers.

Mountain moisture and temperature patterns produce vertical zonation of native vegetation. Plants with similar moisture and temperature requirements tend to cluster in bands on a mountainside. For example, a hike up Junipero Serra Peak, the highpoint of Monterey County, passes through zones of riparian woodland, oak woodland, mixed chaparral, and coniferous forest. Local influences like slope exposure (shady north slopes versus sunny south slopes), wind, soil type, and drainage patterns modify vertical zonation, but every mountain range displays the phenomenon to one degree or another.

California's mountains shelter many rare and endemic species, as well as countless beautiful and unusual ones. Spear-shaped red snowplant pokes up through forest duff. Delicate orange tiger lily graces shady mountain creeksides. Hardy blue sky pilot brightens barren talus slopes far above treeline. Most of all, forests dominate the scene. Trees cover one fifth of the state, from Port Orford cedar and weeping spruce on Bear Mountain, highpoint of Del Norte County, to white fir and Coulter pine on Hot Springs Mountain, the highest spot in San Diego County. More kinds of pine (over 20 species) grow in California than in any other state. Like other mountain vegetation, the pines display marked vertical zonation. On the west slopes of the central Sierra Nevada, Digger pine and knobcone pine grow at lower elevations; ponderosa, sugar, and Jeffrey pines dominate at middle elevations; and western white, lodgepole, foxtail, limber, and whitebark pines appear at higher elevation.

The highpoint ranges pulsate with animal life. Woodpeckers tap, jays squawk, and squirrels chatter. Termites reduce fallen logs to sawdust. Butterflies flit about in flowery meadows. Deer nibble tender herbs. Dippers dive into swift-moving streams to feed along the bottom. Trout jump for insects in subalpine lakes. Pikas and marmots skitter over talus slopes at 12,000 feet. At night, bats careen through the air and black bears forage for edibles, including the food of unwary campers. Many species depend upon mountain habitat for their survival, including puma, spotted owl, fisher, marten, and bighorn sheep.

Human Impact

Native Americans who hunted and gathered in the mountains left little evidence of their passing. But pioneers blazed immigrant wagon trails, trapped furbearing animals, and shot game, depleting wildlife. Ranchers grazed sheep and cattle, trampling meadows and causing erosion. Gold seekers denuded hillsides by hydraulic mining and felled countless trees to provide timber for mineshafts and to build boomtowns. Lumber companies later clear-cut forests, and engineers dammed rivers to supply water and power for lowlanders. Fire-suppression practices led to unchecked growth in vegetation and consequent conflagrations. Residential developments advanced up the foothills. Ski resorts degraded pristine highlands. Railroads and highways spanned many California ranges, and side roads infiltrated the backcountry.

Today's urban problems adversely affect faraway mountains. Metropolitan smog drifts to the highest ranges, harming trees and sullying scenic views. Skyrocketing population, traffic jams, rising crime rates, toxic wastes, cultural clashes, crumbling infrastructures, and government fiscal woes all affect the highlands. For example, budget cutbacks decrease funds for trail maintenance and parkland acquisition, waste managers look to mountain canyons to dump solid waste, and the deterioration of cities spurs immigration to more inhabitable ground. (Sierra foothill counties are among the fastest growing in the state.)

On a positive side, California has the strongest environmental movement in America and ranks first among all states for its pro-environment policies. Thousands of professionals and grassroots volunteers work to protect, preserve, and restore California's natural splendor.

Even if current degradation of the environment continues, California's mountains will ultimately prevail. Highlands resist human development because of their harsh weather and rugged topography. Damage to ecosystems or even the collapse of civilization will not affect how the peaks etch the horizon. The mountains don't rely on us; we rely on the mountains, for water, wood, recreation, and so much more.

County-highpoint seekers experience the mountains' might and majesty, and enjoy much of the natural beauty that remains in California. The highlands' strength and serenity fill the being of those who identify with wildness and with the mountains. They return to the lowlands refreshed and revitalized.

Hike the county summits, then, to get their good tidings. And join one or more conservation groups in the spirit of John Muir, who helped start the Sierra Club "to do something for wildness and make the mountains glad."

Alameda

Discovery Peak   3840+'   **#44**

Location and Maps: South-central edge of the county
USGS 7½-minute *La Costa Valley, Mendenhall
Springs, Mt. Day:* Ohlone Wilderness Regional
Trail Map
Distance: 15 miles round trip/4200' elevation gain
Grade: Strenuous/Class 1
Hiking Time: 9 hours
Season: Year round, best in spring and fall, hot in summer

Trailnotes: The Alameda County Surveyors Office lists Rose Peak as the highest point in the county at 3817 feet. But in 1991 county summits trailblazer Dinesh Desai studied maps and made a "discovery": a higher point rises about 1 mile east of Rose Peak. A spot elevation on the same ridgeline 1.7 miles southeast of "Discovery Peak" measures 3841 feet, but the 3840-foot contour line at Discovery Peak implies a higher elevation than 3841. Thus Discovery Peak stands as the tentative highest point.

Rose Peak lies within the East Bay Regional Park District's Ohlone Regional Wilderness; Discovery Peak lies just outside the Wilderness boundary. The EBRPD holds only partial ownership of the land near Discovery Peak (a printing error on the current EBRPD Trail Map marks the entire Section 12 as public property). EBRPD plans to restrict public access to the land until they acquire full ownership. When allowed, hikers can follow the northeast Rose Flat Road spur off the Ohlone Trail for 0.6 mile to Section 12's east boundary. Discovery Peak, a small, rounded oak- and antenna-decked hilltop, sits on private ranchland just 180 yards beyond the fence line.

With Discovery Peak legally inaccessible, benchmarked Rose Peak remains the attainable highpoint, herein described. Both peaks have two trailhead options:
Del Valle Regional Park Trailhead
   To Discovery Peak, 15 miles round trip/4200' elevation gain
   To Rose Peak, 19 miles round trip/5000' elevation gain
Sunol Regional Wilderness Trailhead
   To Discovery Peak, 22.5 miles round trip/3600' elevation gain
   To Rose Peak, 19 miles round trip/3500' elevation gain
Similar distance but less elevation gain favors a Sunol approach to Rose Peak.

The Sunol route follows old ranch roads, fire roads, and footpaths. It can be done as a long dayhike or an overnight backpack; start early for the dayhike. Obtain a required hiking permit from the entrance kiosk or by mail. Send one dollar with your name, address, and phone number to "Ohlone Wilderness Trail," care of the EBRPD address below; the permit stays valid for a year from the purchase date and includes a descriptive brochure with a fine trail map (to avoid redundancy, this guide's map illustrates only the highpoints area). The park gates open at 7 A.M. and close at dusk. The park is subject to closure during the fire season, May through October.

The Sunol and Ohlone "wildernesses" actually embrace undeveloped pasture land, but this in no way diminishes their value. They preserve a part of the fast-dwindling natural countryside, and their combined 12,000+ acres give hikers an opportunity to experience serene and secluded landscapes, all the more valuable because of their proximity to urban centers. Rose Peak commemorates Antonio and Manual Rose, former landowners and ranchers of Portuguese descent.

Approach: From the Oakland-Berkeley area, go east on Interstate 580, and then south on I 680 to the Calaveras Road exit. The exit is approximately 7 miles south of Dublin and 5 miles north of Fremont. Drive 5 miles south on Calaveras Road, then turn left on Geary Road which leads directly into the park. From the entrance kiosk, go straight ahead, past the service yard on the right and park headquarters on the left, to a sign-in panel. Sign in, and proceed south to a parking area and the trailhead gate.

To reach the Del Valle Regional Park trailhead, take I 580 to Livermore, take the North Livermore exit, and go south on Livermore Avenue, which becomes Tesla Road, then turn right on Mines Road (3.8 miles from the freeway), and right again on Del Valle Road. From the park entrance kiosk, drive 1.3 miles and then turn left at an intersection just after crossing a bridge. Continue 0.3 mile to where a sign says END OF PUBLIC ROAD, TURN AROUND AHEAD. Proceed 0.1 mile beyond the sign to an Ohlone Trail parking area on the right.

Directions to Summit: Walk around the Sunol trailhead gate and across a bridge, heading south and then east on a dirt road that parallels the riparian greenery of Alameda Creek. At about 0.6 mile an inviting side road slants down toward the creek. Stay on the main road, passing the Little Yosemite area (named for its unusual rock outcrops) and Canyon View Trail tie-ins, to reach a trail junction at 1.8 miles. Go left (north) out of the canyon, ascending through oak-strewn grasslands, to an Ohlone Wilderness Trail link and the fenced boundary of the backpack camping area. From this point, small red disks mark the Ohlone Wilderness Trail and guide you toward Rose Peak. (This 29-mile trail connects four regional parklands—Mission Peak, Sunol, Ohlone, and Del Valle; you could have hooked up with the trail at Sunol headquarters, but the route would have added a mile and some rollercoaster topography to the hike, of which plenty lies ahead.)

Go through the first of several squeaky green gates and follow a footpath that climbs steeply under a canopy of oaks, past several trail spurs leading to backpack sites and overlooks with colorful names (Hawk's Nest, Eagle's Eyrie, Star's Rest, Sky Camp). After passing a water faucet, horse trough, and fence line, the trail splits, but either branch takes you up to a gate delineating the boundary of land leased from the San Francisco Water Department. From the gate, the trail contours across grassy meadows. Follow the trail markers carefully to avoid being derailed by interconnecting cow paths and fire roads. Another gate, 2 miles from the last one, signals your entry into Ohlone Regional Wilderness. The trail shortly winds down to a dirt-road junction and then repeatedly climbs, levels off, dips, and climbs again. At the biggest dip, a private inholding forces the trail to veer sharply north from its eastward course, down a small canyon to the south fork of Indian Creek and up the other side. From here, the peak lies just 2 miles ahead and a thousand feet higher.

The surrounding hills and ridges finally fall away as you near the summit knoll. Watch for a faint jeep trail rising up the last hill to the left of the main road. Follow it 0.1 mile and near the apex take one of the dim paths to the right (south) for about a hundred yards to a rock cairn on top. Find a cylindrical black trail-register canister wedged in the rocks.

The View: A bird's-eye view of untrammeled ridges, valleys, and peaks encircles the summit, giving hikers a real sense of being away from civilization. Mount Diablo rises in the north, Copernicus Peak and Mount Hamilton in the south, the Santa Cruz Mountains in the west. In the east, less than 2 miles away, a transmitting tower marks Discovery Peak. Rose Peak lies only 32 feet lower than the famous nearby landmark, Mount Diablo, yet few people have heard of it. The peak's obscurity stems from isolation, lack of paved-road access, and the fact that it's but a topographic nub on Valpe Ridge, one of many high ridges in the area. It's also quite a climb.

The Environment: The surrounding hills and ridges, a northern segment of the Diablo Range, consist of geologically recent sedimentary formations and older metamorphic rocks. Alameda Creek cascades over these rocks and forms pools among the enormous boulders. The largest stream in Alameda County once flowed strongly, before Calaveras Reservoir was built, supporting sizable runs of trout and salmon. The creek still sustains a healthy riparian plant community of sycamore, willow, alder, cattails, and sedges. Coast live oak, the most common oak in the East

Discovery Peak from Rose Flat

Bay, graces the hillsides, as do lesser numbers of blue oak, black oak, valley oak, Digger pine, elderberry, bay, and buckeye. The bordering ranches and watershed lands combine with the parkland to create a substantial preserve for wildlife. Bobcats, coyotes, foxes, and mountain lions prowl the hills. Acorn woodpeckers, black phoebes, belted kingfishers and dozens of other species flit through the trees along Alameda Creek.

Nearby Campgrounds: Sunol Regional Wilderness has four family walk-in campsites near the park headquarters and seven backpack campsites about 3 miles from headquarters. Several backpack sites are available in Ohlone Regional Wilderness. All of these sites may be reserved. Campers must be at least 18 years old or be accompanied by a parent, guardian, or leader who is 21 or older. Del Valle Regional Park has 150 developed campsites. For reservations call (510) 636-1684 between 8:30 A.M. and 4:00 A.M., Monday through Friday.

The County: In the late 1700s the region's early Spanish explorers came upon a sizable watercourse fringed by a lush riparian woodland. It reminded them of the *Alamedas*, the tree-lined roadways of Spain (from *alamo*, the Spanish word for cottonwood or poplar), so they named it Rio de Alameda—Alameda Creek—from which the county took its name.

Alameda County extends from tidal flats and an alluvial plain facing San Francisco Bay to interior hills and valleys and the higher rugged hills of the Diablo Range along its eastern and southern boundaries. The Oakland-Berkeley Hills, rising behind the coastal plain, often prevent marine fog from advancing inland. The Caldecott Tunnel on Highway 24 bores through the hills, allowing commuters to experience a dramatic transition, going from grey overcast to bright sunshine or vice versa as they travel through the tunnel.

Running along the base of the western foothills, the Hayward fault zone—and others in various locations—give the county an infelicitous potential for strong earthquakes. But tremors have not deterred population growth; Alameda County is one of the most densely populated counties in the state. Oakland, its largest city, has a melting-pot population of over 350,000 residents where 34 different languages are spoken. Berkeley, home of the University of California, ranks as one of the world's leading intellectual centers. In recent years, suburban towns like Dublin, Fremont, Pleasanton, and Livermore have added more inhabitants than the central cities have added, at the expense of former agricultural lands.

Additional Sources of Information/Recommended Reading:

East Bay Regional Park District
2950 Peralta Oaks Court
P.O. Box 5381
Oakland CA 94605
(510) 635-0138

Sunol-Ohlone Regional Wilderness
P.O. Box 82
Sunol, CA 94586
(510) 862-2244

Margolin, Malcolm. *The East Bay Out: A Personal Guide to the East Bay Regional Parks,* Heyday Books, 1988.

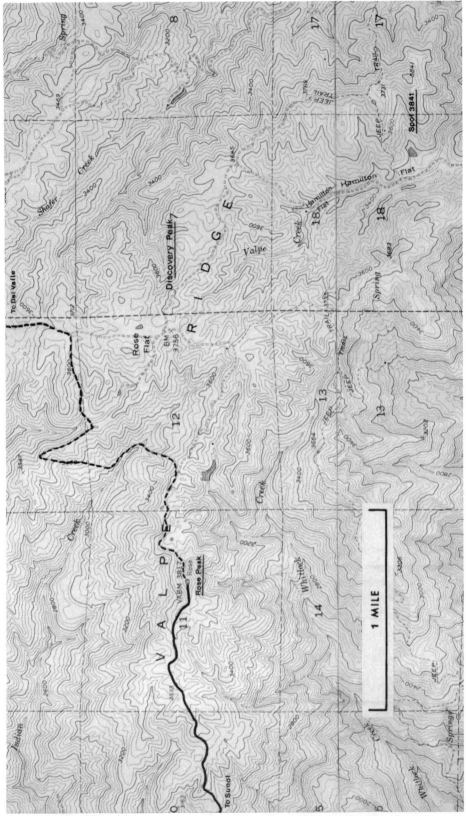

Alpine

Sonora Peak 11,459' #9

Location and Maps:	South end of the county
	USGS 7½-minute *Sonora Peak;* USFS *Toiyabe*
	National Forest, South Sierra Division
Distance:	4.5 miles round trip/2100' elevation gain
Grade:	Moderate/Class 2
Hiking Time:	3 hours
Season:	Late July to mid-September

Trailnotes: A sublime high-country dayhike. From a trailhead at 9430 feet, you follow a segment of the historic Sonora Pass route to a saddle, and then tramp cross-country to the peak amid volcanic crags, summer snowfields, and wildflowers galore. Sonora Peak straddles the boundary between Toiyabe and Stanislaus national forests at the south end of Carson-Iceberg Wilderness. Backpackers require wilderness permits. Bring warm garb; the wind often whips up around the pass. Miners from the northern Mexican state of Sonora, drawn to California mines during the Gold Rush, established a settlement called Sonora in 1848. The peak and the pass take their name from the town, located 66 miles southwest.

Approach: From U.S. 395, 17 miles north of Bridgeport and 43 miles south of Carson City, take SR 108 15 miles to Sonora Pass. From I 5 in Stockton, drive State Routes 4, 49, and 108 for 127 miles to Sonora Pass. From Sonora Pass, go 0.8 mile west and watch for a ST MARYS PASS TRAILHEAD sign on the north side of the road. Park along the roadside or follow a bumpy dirt road to a parking area.

Directions to Summit: From the information board and wilderness boundary sign, stride north up a moderately steep jeep road for about 0.6 mile until the road peters out. A trail continues sharply up a gully, crossing boggy creeklets on the way to a saddle named Saint Marys Pass. (This 1.3 mile stretch of the hike traces part of the first pioneer trail over the pass, opened in 1862.) At the pass (the USGS map label is in the wrong place), turn right (east) to begin a cross-country ramble. Scale the foreground hill and see your destination. Then diagonal across an open bench and up the southwest flank of Sonora Peak, aiming for the tall rock pillars along the ridgeline. Many vague paths ascend steeply over the loose talus and tufted grasses. A good "use trail" parallels the right side of the ridgeline all the way to the summit. Semicircular rock wind shelters are atop the peak.

The View: A stunning, snow-filled panorama. Snow patches often blanket Sonora Peak and many surrounding mountains, especially on shaded north slopes. Nearby Stanislaus Peak pierces the sky in the northwest, and White Mountain stands out in the northeast. The Dardanelles profile the western skyline. Tower Peak and Leavitt Peak rise in the south. High Sierra peaks fill the background, including Mount Lyell, Mount Ritter, and Banner Peak, some 50 miles down-range.

The Environment: Red and brown volcanic rocks overspread Sonora Peak. Long ago volcanoes east of the present Sierra erupted over the youthful range, burying the granite. Glaciers later scoured away most of the overlying deposits in much of the higher Sierra. However, around unglaciated Sonora Peak, the volcanic rock remains. Plants thrive in the rich volcanic soil. Lodgepole pine and whitebark pine grow along the trail until thwarted by cold at timberline. Abundant wildflowers brighten the grassy slopes: lupine, alpine buckwheat, phlox, creeping penstemon, saxifrage, scarlet gilia and many more. Prominent as a headwater, Sonora Peak directs runoff into five different drainages.

Nearby Campgrounds: Developed campgrounds line State Route 108 on both sides of Sonora Pass. The closest sites include Deadman and Upper/Lower Baker west of the pass and Leavitt Meadow and Sonora Bridge to the east. Backpackers have unlimited prospects in Carson-Iceberg Wilderness north of the pass and in Emigrant Wilderness to the immediate south.

The County: Aptly named Alpine County bestrides the crest and the eastern slopes of the "California Alps," the Sierra Nevada. Alpine has the lowest population of any county in the state. Between 1980 and 1990, net population gain numbered 100 persons, bringing the total to around 1200 residents. Government-owned land encompasses 93 percent of the county, mostly in national forests. Tiny Markleeville, the county seat, caters to recreationists and serves as a gateway to Grover Hot Springs State Park. Ski resorts offer downhill and cross-country skiing, as at Bear Valley/Mount Reba. Nearby Tamarack has recorded the state's heaviest month's snowfall (390 inches), the highest seasonal total (884 inches), and the greatest depth on the ground at one time (454 inches)—nearly 38 feet of snow!

Additional Sources of Information/Recommended Reading:

Summit Ranger District
Star Route 1295
Sonora, CA 95370
(209) 965-3434 (for permits west
    of Sonora Pass)

Carson Ranger District
1536 S. Carson St.
Carson City, NV 89701
(702) 882-2766 (for permits east of
    Sonora Pass)

Ferguson, Gary, *Walks in California,* Crown Brooks, 1987.
Schaffer, Jeffrey P., *Carson-Iceberg Wilderness,* 2nd ed., Wilderness Press, 1992.
Schifrin, Ben, *Emigrant Wilderness and Northwestern Yosemite,* Wilderness Press, 1990.

Alpine

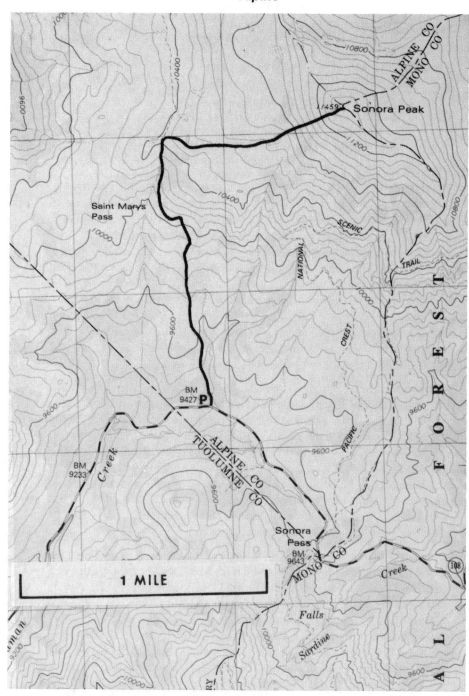

Amador

Thunder Mountain   9410'   #15

Location and Maps:	East edge of the county
	USGS 7½-minute *Caples Lake;* USFS
	Mokelumne Wilderness
Distance:	2.5 miles round trip/1700' elevation gain
Grade:	Moderate/Class 2
Hiking Time:	3 hours
Season:	Mid-July to October

Trailnotes: An imposing jagged volcanic highland, Thunder Mountain occupies a ridgetop between Silver Lake and Kirkwood Meadows in Eldorado National Forest. The mountain's sheer, slightly concave west wall forms a topographic echo chamber for booming thunderclaps that resound over Silver Lake's campgrounds, cabins, and resorts. The highpoint is readily accessible from State Route 88. Short, medium, and long routes branch off along a 4-mile stretch of the highway. The primary short route goes beneath a ski tram and then follows a brief cross-country course. The tram makes a winter cross-country ski ascent possible. The medium route (5.4 miles round trip/2000-foot elevation gain) is cross-country. The long route (8 miles round trip/2300-foot elevation gain) has both trail and off-trail segments. The longer outings offer greater scenic rewards.

Approach: From I 5 in Stockton, take SR 88 east 98 miles to Silver Lake. From U.S. 395 in Bridgeport, go north 41 miles to a junction with SR 89, then follow SR 89 and SR 88 for 46 miles to Silver Lake. From the junction to Kit Carson Resort at the north end of the lake, go north on SR 88 for 0.8 mile (0.2 mile beyond the Oyster Creek Roadside Rest) to a small sign on the right indicating the pullout for the Horse Canyon Trail, the long route. Go another 0.9 mile from the pullout to the Martin Meadow roadside departure point from the medium route. Proceed 3.3 more miles to arrive at the turnoff for the short route at Kirkwood Meadows. From this turnoff, go 1.2 miles to a large parking lot on the right. Park at the south end of the lot near the first ski lift, labeled "Cornice 6."

Directions to Summit: Strike off upslope to the left of the trees lining the Cornice 6 ski lift. In about 0.3 mile you intersect a dirt road. Amble over the road to the lift and then head up ever-steepening slopes beneath the tram. Faint trails parallel the tram line. A stiff slog brings you to the ridgeline. From the ridge, hike west, cross a gently sloping sagebrush- and grass-filled saddle, and then clamber up crusty rock to the upmost crags, where you will find a small register on top. You can work your way southwest along the ridge about 0.3 mile to reach a slightly lower west peak. Boy Scouts from a camp near Silver Lake frequently climb to this overlook, as evidenced by a large container stuffed with their signatures.

The medium-length route begins from a point about 200 yards south of a creeklet in Martin Meadow. Traverse southeast across a meadow and then upward to the large spur projecting northwest from Thunder Mountain. Steep climbing brings you to a ridgecrest near the west summit. Curve northwest and proceed 0.3 mile to the highest point. The long route follows the Horse Canyon Trail as it threads through a shady forest and past unusual lava formations. The trail meets a spur to Silverado Scout camp (marked by a NO MOTORCYCLES sign), shortly crosses a creek, and later crosses larger Thunder Creek, about 2.7 miles from the start. Continue 0.2 mile past the Thunder Creek ford and then watch for a use trail branching north from the main trail. Follow the use trail 0.2 mile to where it crosses Thunder Creek. Cross the creek and tread north up moderately steep canyon slopes. Pass a solitary thumblike outcrop en route to the highest point on the scraggy ridgeline. A use trail from the west overlook descends the southeast ridge of Thunder Mountain back to Thunder Creek.

The View: Pyramid Peak and the Crystal Range rise in the north. Freel Peak caps the Carson Range in the northeast. A startling dropoff plunges to Silver Lake directly below from the west overlook, with the Central Valley and Mount Diablo distantly visible. Multi-saddled Squaw Ridge extends to the south, backed by majestic Mokelumne Peak. Snow-capped Sierra peaks glisten in the southeast. Caples Lake and Thimble Peak appear in the east and between them looms bulky Round Top, at 10,381 feet the highest point in Mokelumne Wilderness.

The Environment: Between 20 and 7 million years ago, volcanoes covered the landscape with vast lava flows and ash deposits. Disgorged andesite lava mixed with water to form hot mudflows and conglomerates. Later erosion removed much volcanic material. But remnant lava flows persist on high drainage divides like Thunder Mountain, and resistant vent cores endure as regional highpoints like Thimble Peak and Round Top. Thunder Mountain's black, lichen-encrusted rock weathers into phantasmagorical shapes and breaks down into rich soil. The soil nurtures the surrounding flower-filled meadows and mixed coniferous forests. The adjacent 105,000-acre Mokelumne Wilderness holds an unusually varied flora.

Nearby Campgrounds: Two Forest Service campgrounds sit just north of Silver Lake beside SR 88. A primitive campground at Martin Meadow lies 3 miles up the road from Silver Lake, and another nearby campground borders Caples Lake.

The County: The county's name pays tribute to Josef Maria Amador (1794–1883), a local rancher and miner who founded a successful gold-mining camp near the present town of Amador. Old gold camps stud the county's rolling foothills and mountainous interior. Deep mine shafts around Jackson, the county seat, produced gold until 1950. Today, lumbering, stock raising, agriculture, and tourism sustain the economy. About 10 miles from Jackson, at Indian Grinding Rock State Historic Park, a large rock shaded by huge oak trees contains almost 1200 mortar holes. Local Miwok tribes held seasonal gatherings at the site. The grounds also feature petroglyphs and replica native dwellings, preserved in California's only state park devoted primarily to Indian culture.

Additional Sources of Information/Recommended Reading:

Amador Ranger Station
26820 Silver Dr.
Pioneer, CA 95666
(209) 295-4251

Grodin, Joseph R., and Sharon Grodin, *Silver Lake,* 3rd ed., Wilderness Press, 1983.

Amador

1 MILE

Butte

Lost Lake Ridge 7120+ **#27**

Location and Maps:	Northeast corner of the county
	USGS 7½-minute *Humboldt Peak, Jonesville*;
	USFS *Lassen National Forest*
Distance:	8 miles round trip/1050′ elevation gain
Grade:	Moderate/Class 1–2
Hiking Time:	5 hours
Season:	July to October

Trailnotes: The famed Pacific Crest Trail (PCT), which passes 14 county highpoints, comes closest to the Butte County summit. A tranquil, lightly trod segment of the PCT reaches to within a few hundred yards of the highpoint, located in Lassen National Forest. A short, well-graded dirt road accesses the trailhead. Snow patches may linger among the area's alternately timbered and brush-covered slopes until mid-July. Lost Lake Ridge, ascertained by highpointer Andy Martin, takes its name from a lake nestled on the northeast flank of the ridge.

Approach: From US 99 at Chico, take SR 32 east for 22 miles to reach inconspicuously signed Humboldt Road on your right, 13.5 miles past Forest Ranch. Drive 11.7 miles along Humboldt Road, passing a large, white two-story structure at Jonesville before arriving at pavement's end and a fork in the road. Drive up the left fork for about 2 miles to a signed PCT crossing at Humboldt Summit. Park off to the left (west) side of the road.

An approach to the highpoint from the south, rather than the north, entails a little less trail mileage, but substantially more dirt-road driving. For this approach, take the right fork at the aforementioned pavement's end (signed Road 26N27). Travel 3.1 miles to a junction. Keep right and stay on the main road, passing several spurs to reach another junction at 5.0 miles, where a sign reads HUMBUG SUMMIT 2 MILES. Steer left at the junction and continue for 1.2 miles to the posted PCT crossing. Park on the north side of the road, adjacent to Cold Springs. Follow the PCT north for about 3 miles to reach the off-trail highpoint described below.

Directions to Summit: From Humboldt Summit embark eastward on the PCT. After just 55 yards, a use trail branches off to the right. (This use trail climbs for 0.7 mile to 7087-foot Humboldt Peak, the highest *benchmarked* point in Butte County; you may wish to visit the peak on your return to see a fine view of Lost Lake Ridge.) Follow the PCT as it winds around the north side of Humboldt Peak, gently descending and then ascending through the forest. You emerge from tree cover to see open views, pinnacle formations, and prominent Eagle Rocks to the northeast. About 1.4 miles from the start, your route shifts southward and shortly re-enters a forest. The trail dips and rises along ridgecrest saddles before breaking out onto a brush-lined path. The path merges with an old jeep track and soon passes a road spur to Lost Lake on the left, 3.6 miles from the trailhead.

From the road spur, continue on the PCT, climbing moderately for 0.3 mile to a point where the trail bends southeastward (this point lies directly on the county line). Leave the trail here and tramp due south amid brush, trees, and rocks, for about 350 yards to reach the highpoint area. The area consists of a 0.2-mile-long sliver of ridge slope. Until surveyed, the exact highpoint along here remains undeterminable.

The View: Where views can be had, forest-cloaked uplands unfurl to the south and to the west. The Sacramento Valley blends into the hazy horizon. Brush-decked Colby Mountain rises in the west and tree-topped Humboldt Peak elevates in the northwest. The ascending ridge blocks views of Lake Almanor to the east, but the lake, and Lassen Peak, can be seen by ambling a short distance farther along the PCT to an open flat atop Lost Lake Ridge.

The Environment: The Pacific Crest Trail stretches 2550 miles between the Canadian and Mexican borders. The California section, the most geologically diverse, runs for 1706 miles. The reddish-brown earth, dark grey rock, and pinnacled landforms seen along this leg of the trail indicate a volcanic origin. Just a few miles south of the highpoint, along Chips Creek, granite bedrock prevails. Lost Lake Ridge borders the great geologic divide between the granitic Sierra Nevada and the volcanic Cascade Range. Red fir, lodgepole pine, pinemat manzanita, and huckleberry oak predominate along the route, and hikers often see mule deer and black bear in the forest.

Nearby Campgrounds: Informal car-camping areas sit adjacent to the trailheads at Humboldt Summit and Cold Springs. Creekside campgrounds at Butte Meadows and Cherry Hill lie along Humboldt Road between Highway 32 and Jonesville. West Branch and Philbrook Lake offer additional sites south of Butte Meadows. Pretty campgrounds line Deer Creek on SR 32 north of the Humboldt Road turnoff.

The County: Sutter Buttes, which lay within the boundaries of the county at its inception, inspired the county's name. In 1990 Butte narrowly avoided the nation's first county bankruptcy. The agriculturally-based economy generated insufficient taxes to fund state-mandated health and welfare programs for the poor, a growing problem in other counties as well. The main communities include Chico, interior California's largest town north of Sacramento; Paradise, an apple-growing region where orchards are falling to residential development; and Oroville, a famous Gold Rush town. The 16,000-acre Oroville State Recreation Area showcases Oroville dam, the tallest earthen dam (770 feet) in the United States. At nearby Feather River Falls, water plummets down a 690-foot granite cliff, the highest falls in California outside of Yosemite.

Additional Sources of Information/Recommended Reading:

Almanor Ranger District
Box 767
Chester, CA 96020
(916) 258-2141

Schaffer, Jeffrey P. *et al., The Pacific Crest Trail, Volume 1 : California*, 4th ed., Wilderness Press, 1989.

Butte

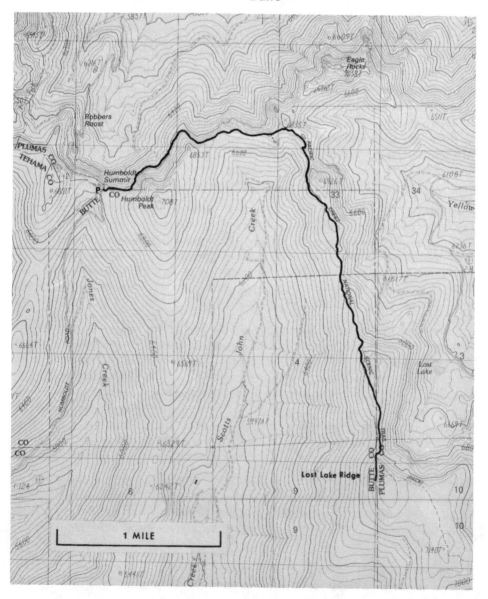

Calaveras

Corral Ridge　　　　　　　　　8170′　　　　　　　　　　#25

Location and Maps:	Eastern edge of the county USGS 7½-minute *Tamarack;* USFS *Stanislaus National Forest*
Distance:	6 miles round trip/1070′ elevation gain
Grade:	Moderate/Class 1–2
Hiking Time:	3 hours
Season:	Late June to early October

Trailnotes: This unheralded county summit sits high in the central Mother Lode country of Stanislaus National Forest. Corral Ridge affords wide-ranging views into Mokelumne Wilderness to the north and Carson-Iceberg Wilderness to the south. Jeep trails lead close to the highpoint, and a short cross-country jaunt brings you to your goal. Corral Ridge lies near the Bear Valley/Mount Reba Ski Area; skimobilers and cross-country skiers sign the register in winter. Nearby Corral Hollow and Corral Gulch lent their name to the highpoint.

Approach: From I 5 in Stockton take SR 4 approximately 98 miles to Tamarack. Two miles east of Tamarack, watch for a sign demarking the Alpine County line, and 0.6 mile beyond the sign, a packtrail sign signals your arrival at the trailhead. Pull off on the north side of the road, where an information board reads CORRAL HOLLOW ORV ROUTE. From U.S. 395 take SR 89 (Monitor Pass Road) 18 miles to a junction with SR 4. Proceed 30 miles on SR 4 to the trailhead, 0.7 mile beyond Bear Valley Road.

Directions to Summit: Saunter up the initially level, forest-shaded jeep trail. In about 1.3 miles you reach a junction at the edge of a hillside meadow. Keep right and climb a steepening grade that tops out at a four-way saddle junction. Turn left (west) and follow a gently rising jeep trail ½ mile to a wire gate. Walk about 200 yards past the gate to a flat with several grey tree snags on the right side of the road. Leave the road at this point and tramp northward ¼ mile to the highest point on the open ridgetop, bordered by east-facing cliffs. The topmost rockpile holds a register. This tentative highpoint needs survey confirmation; two hills immediately to the south with 8160-foot contour lines look almost as high and deserve inspection.

The View: Mokelumne Peak and the Mokelumne Tetons rise dramatically in the north, across the deep Mokelumne River canyon. In the east, ski lifts on Bloods Ridge and Mount Reba catch the eye. In the south, high peaks in Carson-Iceberg Wilderness engrave the skyline. In the west, timbered ridges fall away toward the Central Valley.

The Environment: About 10 million years ago, volcanism reached its peak in this region. Vents spewed andesitic lava, ash, and detritus, and generated massive mudflows. These volcanic deposits created Corral Ridge. The deposits overlie metamorphic rock intruded by granitic masses bearing the gold-quartz veins sought by Mother Lode miners. Logging debris, off-road-vehicle tire ruts, and clanging cattle bells reflect the area's "multiple use" status. Yet much beauty remains. Steller jays and Clark nutcrackers glide among uncut pines and firs. Grassy openings parade wildflowers like golden stars, mariposa lilies, and cream cups, and the large hillside meadow displays a sea of yellow mule ears with butterflies fluttering from flower to flower.

Nearby Campgrounds: Forest Service campgrounds string along SR 4. Find pretty Lake Alpine and Silver Tip campgrounds about 2 miles up the road and several others in the vicinity of Ebbetts Pass. Big Meadows campground lies 5 miles southwest of the trailhead. Calaveras Big Trees State Park has a campground 22 miles down the road.

The County: The county takes its name from a river called *Calaveras*, "skulls" in Spanish. Early explorers gave the macabre name to the river because they found many Indian skulls along its banks. The county experienced feverish activity during Gold Rush days at mining camps like San Andreas and Angels Camp. Mark Twain immortalized Angels Camp in his short story, "The Celebrated Jumping Frog of Calaveras County," in which the favored frog won't jump after a rival feeds it buckshot. Today, the town's annual Jumping Frog Jubilee attracts more than 50,000 spectators and over 1000 entries. Frog jockeys stomp, blow, and yell to get their entries airborne. The current world champion, Rosie the Ribiter, jumped over 21 feet in 1986.

Additional Sources of Information/Recommended Reading:

Calaveras Ranger District
P.O. Box 500
Hathaway Pines, CA 95233
(209) 795-1381

Clark, W.B., and P.A. Lydon, *Mines and Mineral Resources of Calaveras County, California,* California Division of Mines and Geology, 1962.

Summit rocks on Corral Ridge

Calaveras

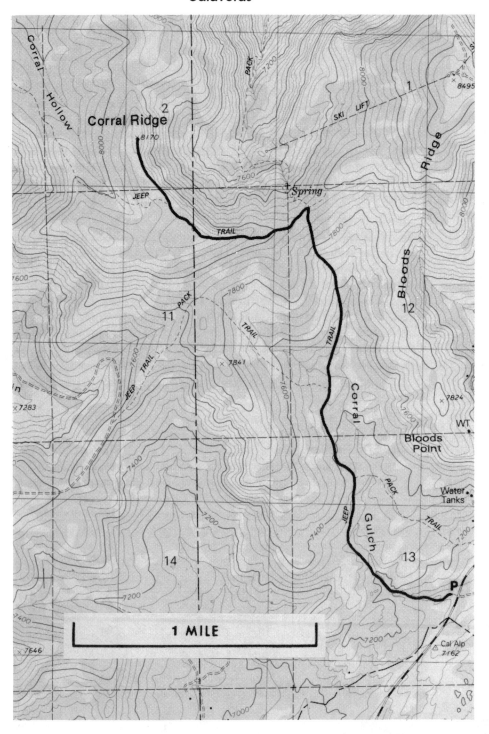

Colusa

Snow Mountain East   7040+′   **#28**

Location and Maps:	Northwest corner of the county
	USGS 7½ minute *St. John Mountain, Crockett Peak, Fouts Springs, Potato Hill;* USFS *Snow Mountain Wilderness*
Distance:	8 miles round trip/2000′ elevation gain
Grade:	Moderate/Class 1
Hiking Time:	4 hours
Season:	Late May through early October

Trailnotes: The highpoint caps Snow Mountain Wilderness, a lovely, little-known, and lightly used 37,000-acre wildland. Low visitation prompted the Forest Service to discontinue requiring a wilderness permit here, but please sign the visitor's register at the Summit Spring trailhead. Less than 4 hours from San Francisco or Sacramento, the journey includes a lengthy stretch of dirt-surfaced road suitable for passenger vehicles. The hike can be done as a dayhike, or a backpack. Bring water, since most of the springs and creeks are seasonal. A fortuitous boundary alignment lets county-summit seekers enjoy a "two-for-one" outing, because Snow Mountain East is the highest point in both Colusa and Lake counties. The mountain's relative closeness to the ocean assures plenty of moisture, and its height assures that much of the precipitation falls as snow, giving Snow Mountain its name. This white mantle may linger through June.

Approach: From I 5 take the SR 20 exit, approximately 60 miles north of Sacramento and 70 miles south of Red Bluff. Go 9 miles west on SR 20 and then, at an inconspicuous junction, turn right onto Leesville Road. Narrow, bumpy, and occasionally unpaved, Leesville Road winds 13 miles over pastoral foothills to an intersection with the Leesville-Lodoga Road. Turn right and proceed 9 miles to another junction, at Lodoga. Bear left and travel 8 miles to Market Street in Stonyford (passing the Stonyford Ranger Station just outside of town). Turn left on Market Street and after 0.2 mile steer left onto Fouts Springs Road, designated as Forest Road 18N01/M10. From here it's about 26 miles to the trailhead.

Follow 18N01/M10 as it meanders up into the mountains, passing signed spur roads, Fouts Springs Ranch, off-road vehicle crossing, and the Sanford Cabin Site turnoff (13 miles from Stonyford). The pavement ends here. At 1.6 miles beyond the Sanford Cabin spur, keep right where the Letts Lake turnoff branches left. After another 6.5 miles, bear right where a sign points to Bear Creek and Summit Spring. Two miles past this junction, turn right again onto Road 24N02 (a sign indicates Summit Spring). Drive 1.8 miles to a four-way junction at the Lake-Colusa county line. Go straight ahead and up steep Road 17N06, which heads north and then east along a ridge and, after 1.7 miles, drops down to a turnaround loop at the Summit

Spring trailhead. Drainage ruts may impede low-clearance vehicles about 0.3 mile before the trailhead; if so, park along the roadside and continue on foot.

From U.S. 101 at Hopland (about 104 miles north of San Francisco and 15 miles south of Ukiah), take the SR 175 exit. Go 18 miles east on SR 175 and then north 11 miles on SR 29 to an intersection with SR 20 at Upper Lake (north of Clear Lake). Turn right and go 0.5 mile to where a sign indicates Upper Lake Ranger Station and Lake Pillsbury. Turn left here onto Elk Mountain Road/County Road 301/Forest Road M1. Drive 15 miles and then turn right at dirt-surfaced Forest Road 18N01/M10. A sign points to Bear Creek and Snow Mountain. Follow this road for just over 7 miles, bearing left when Road 18N01/M10 branches south. Shortly after passing the Bear Creek Ranger Station, turn right onto Forest Road 17N16. Continue 5.5 miles to the four-way junction at the Lake-Colusa county line (described above), and proceed up steep Forest Road 17N06 for 1.7 miles to the Summit Spring trailhead.

Directions to Summit: The trail takes off to the right of the information board. A single switchback brings you above the trees to an immediate view of the surrounding mountains. In the foreground, blackened tree trunks project above the grass and brush. A lightning-caused fire swept through the area in 1987, charring thousands of acres. At about 1 mile, the trail steepens to ascend a southwest slope sprinkled with oak, pine, and fir. Here, a new trail segment on the left parallels the old trail on the right, deemed too steep and erosion-prone. Past the new segment, the path continues up to a forested flat and a trail junction. Signs point north toward SNOW SUMMIT and east toward FOUTS CAMP. Head north on the faint, tree-blazed trail, which shortly descends to a small meadow. Signs at the meadow's edge read SNOW SUMMIT 2, MILK RANCH 3, and CEDAR CAMP (good campsites, but no cedars are evident). Skirt the right (east) side of the meadow to where ducks guide you along the trail, signed as route 8W50.

The trail trends north, climbs gradually through the forest, makes a brief descent amid an understory of chaparral, and then ascends steeply to a ducked ridgetop. From here, the track dips again, and along this stretch of trail the rust-colored flanks of Snow Mountain East appear for the first time through trees on the right. You soon come to a signed junction. Stay left as your trail slips down into a bowl and up the other side, past a little creek and springs on your right. You top out on a dramatic summit-spanning ridge where a marker points in the direction of East and West peaks, each 0.5 mile away. Venture east along the faint ridge trail, keeping to the left as you surmount the final slope to reach a craggy summit plateau. Among the northern crags you'll find a register placed by the California Alpine Club. Walk about 20 yards south from the 7056-foot highest point (Lake County's summit) to cross the invisible Lake-Colusa boundary line and reach the slightly lower Colusa County highpoint (7040+').

The View: Looking north, Signal Peak on the left and St. John Mountain farther on the right, rise above the foreground valleys, backed by many peaks of the North

Coast Ranges. Mount Shasta appears as a tiny white triangle suspended on the far horizon, as does Lassen Peak in the northeast. In the east, deep canyons plunge toward the Sacramento Valley, with the Sutter Buttes and the distant High Sierra farther away. Beyond lookout-capped Goat Mountain to the south, Clear Lake, Mount Diablo, and Mount St. Helena are sometimes visible. Past the level summit of Snow Mountain West (just 18 feet lower than its sister summit), serried Coast Ranges extend to the Pacific Ocean.

The Environment: Snow Mountain's elevation, precipitation (averaging 60″ per year at the higher elevations), and temperature (averaging 18° in January and 64° in July) create a montane environment for an array of plants that spread no farther south than this "sky island." In fact, it's the southernmost subalpine environment in the entire Coast Range Province (and not found again in the western half of California until the higher Transverse Ranges, 400 miles to the south). Fully 25% of Snow Mountain's flora are at the southern limit of the species. A rapid decline in the elevation of mountains to the south and a corresponding loss of suitable habitats help explain this.

Vertical zonation is well developed: chaparral at lower elevations, grading into oaks and mixed conifers higher up. However, most of the plants that are at the limit of their range thrive not in the forests but among the forest openings, on the outcrops, and on the subalpine barrens. Species at their limit, such as rockcress, pearlwort, and wintergreen grow unnoticed—except by the knowing eyes of botanists who visit the area.

Nearby Campgrounds: Developed and undeveloped campsites are available in adjacent Mendocino National Forest, and you may camp outside designated sites. (Obtain a free fire permit from a ranger station.) A brochure map provided by the Forest Service delimits "concentrated ORV use zones" in the vicinity, which many hikers may wish to avoid. South of Snow Mountain, Letts Lake has 40 campsites, and to the west, large Lake Pillsbury has three campgrounds that together provide over 100 sites.

The County: Snow Mountain and the adjacent highlands occupy only the northwest part of Colusa County, named after the Colus Indians, who formerly inhabited the area. Most of the county stretches over the flat, fertile northern Central Valley, where agriculture reigns. Major crops include tomatoes, sugar beets, prunes, almonds, and rice. Colusa ranks as the leading rice-producing county in the United States. The heavy, water-retentive soils of the Sacramento River flood basins allowed the region to become a "rice bowl." The thousands of acres of green rice plants growing in immense diked paddies make an impressive sight. The flood basins also form part of the Pacific flyway for waterfowl. Three of the four Sacramento Valley National Wildlife Refuges are located in Colusa County. Each autumn, thousands of hunters and birders flock to the refuges. As many as three million migrating ducks and geese visit the refuges yearly, and nearly 200 species of birds have been recorded.

Additional Sources of Information/Recommended Reading:

Stonyford Ranger District
5080 Lodoga-Stonyford Road
Stonyford, CA 95979
(916) 963-3128

Adkison, Ron, *The Hiker's Guide to California,* revised ed., Falcon Press, 1990.

Bernstein, Art, *The Best Day Hikes of The California Northwest,* Mountain N'Air Books, 1991.

Colusa

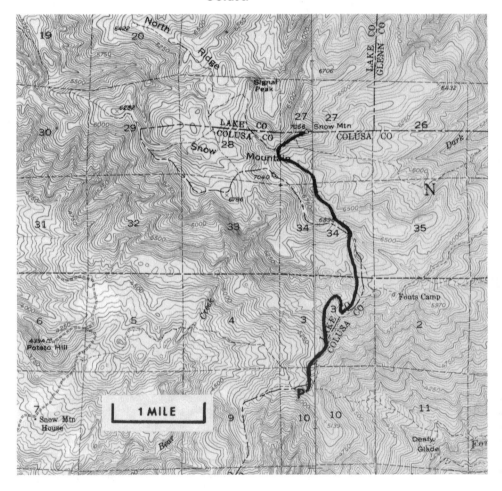

Contra Costa

Mount Diablo 3849′ **#43**

Location and Maps:	Center of the county
	USGS 7½ minute *Diablo, Clayton;* CDPR *Mount Diablo State Park;* Mount Diablo Interpretive Association, *Trail Map of Mount Diablo State Park and Adjacent Parklands*
Distance:	5.5 miles round trip/1700′ elevation gain
Grade:	Moderate/Class 1
Hiking Time:	3 hours
Season:	Year-round

Trailnotes: This East Bay landmark rises from the surrounding lowlands in solitary splendor and commands one of the world's finest views. Mount Diablo State Park protects nearly 18,000 acres of Contra Costa County's fast-disappearing natural landscape. A road and an excellent trail network provide many avenues to the summit, from a drive-up to a lengthy hike. The described route makes a moderate loop around the mountaintop to sample the scenery. The park opens at 8:00 A.M. and closes at sunset. The road to the summit comes within earshot of parts of the trail; start early, preferably on a weekday, for a quieter hike. Watch out for poison oak. No alcohol allowed, and no dogs on the trails. Rangers occasionally close the park during times of extreme fire hazard.

Several stories purport to account for the mountain's name. In 1806, according to one, Spanish soldiers and Indians clashed near the peak. During the battle, a bizarrely dressed medicine man appeared. The soldiers thought *El Diablo* ("The Devil" in Spanish) had sided with the Indians, so they fled, giving the Indians a rare victory and the mountain a name.

Approach: From I 680 in Danville, exit on Diablo Road. Drive east 3 miles and then turn left onto Mt. Diablo Scenic Boulevard, which becomes South Gate Road. Proceed 3.5 miles to the South Entrance kiosk and another 3 miles to Park Headquarters, at the junction of North Gate and South Gate roads. Park at Junction Picnic Area across the road (north) from Park Headquarters.

From I 680 in Walnut Creek, take the Ygnacio Valley Road offramp and go 2.2 miles to Walnut Avenue. Turn right on Walnut, which becomes North Gate Road, and wind up the mountain 9.6 miles to the Junction Picnic Area.

Directions to Summit: Begin at the east end of the Junction Picnic Area where a trailhead sign reads JUNIPER CAMP 1.6, SUMMIT 2.1. A moderately steep fireroad, canopied by oak and pine, climbs to a junction with the Summit Trail at 0.2 mile, and to a junction with the Deer Flat (Juniper) Trail at 1.1 miles. Follow this as it zigzags steeply at first, dips into a shady drainage cleft, and then contours around brushfields and grassy slopes to Juniper Camp. From a horse trough on the edge of Juniper Camp, walk southeast on a graded road to a trail marker placed just to the left of a LAUREL NOOK GROUP PICNIC AREA sign. The marker reads JUNIPER TRAIL TO SUMMIT TRAIL 0.9. Forge up a fairly steep path, past ugly communication towers, to an asphalt lot. Cross the lot and follow a trail that bisects the road loop to reach the top. A masonry rock tower and a lookout beacon crown the peak.

To continue the hike, walk around the summit on the view-filled 0.7-mile Fire Interpretive Trail. At the end of the Interpretive Trail, walk about 30 yards west to find a SUMMIT TRAIL marker on your left. Descend on the Summit Trail for a mile to the previously passed junction with the Deer Flat Trail and retrace the first leg of the hike back to the trailhead.

The View: Positioned above the adjacent Coast Ranges at the very edge of the Central Valley, Mount Diablo's viewshed sweeps over 40,000 square miles. Only the view from Africa's 19,000-foot Mount Kilimanjaro takes in a greater area. On a rare snapping-clear day you can see into 35 California counties! The Golden Gate Bridge and the skyscrapers in San Francisco shimmer in the west. Loma Prieta caps the Santa Cruz Mountains in the southwest, and Lick Observatory gleams atop Mount Hamilton in the south. Beyond the Central Valley, the Sierra Nevada lines the eastern horizon, with Half Dome in Yosemite visible through binoculars. Mount Tamalpais looms above San Francisco Bay in the northwest. Lassen Peak rises distantly in the northeast; directly north, a diminutive Mount Shasta appears as a refracted image, some 200 miles away. These far-ranging views prompted the USGS to use baselines and meridian lines passing through Mt. Diablo to survey two-thirds of California and parts of Nevada and Oregon beginning in 1851. To this day, surveyors describe land in relation to these lines.

Mt. Diablo from the east

The Environment: Mount Diablo rises high enough to produce occasional winter snowfall, a treat for Bay Area residents. The mountain attained its height around 100 million years ago. Colliding crustal plates forced a massive metamorphic plug to pierce through 6 miles of overlying sedimentary rock. The plug forms the summit, while tilted and overturned sedimentary beds gird the lower slopes. Within the beds lie fossilized mastodons and sabretooth cats. Contemporary wildlife includes fox squirrel, badger, bobcat, and the rare Alameda whipsnake. Oak woodland, grassland, and chaparral characterize the vegetation. Sycamore and alder thrive in moist canyon streambeds. Widespread Digger pine, scattered stands of knobcone and Coulter pine, and many seasonal wildflowers adorn the hillsides. In all, the park harbors over 400 species of plants.

Nearby Campgrounds: The park has three family campgrounds, Liveoak, Juniper, and Junction, as well as several group camps. You can reserve sites through MISTIX up to 8 weeks (family) or 12 weeks (group) in advance for stays from October 1 to May 31. At other times, the campgrounds operate on a first-come, first-served basis.

The County: *Contra Costa* means "opposite coast" in Spanish, a reference to the county's position opposite San Francisco. Steep rolling hills and various-sized valleys typify Contra Costa. Large regional parks such as Tilden, Wildcat Canyon, and Briones mantle the hills. Expanding towns like Concord, Walnut Creek, and Lafayette spread over the valleys. A 70-mile coastline extends from San Pablo Bay and Suisun Bay to the Sacramento-San Joaquin River delta. Industrial and shipping ports line the shore, including Richmond, Pittsburg, and Antioch. Martinez, the county seat, has oil refineries, new residential areas, and the John Muir National Historic Site. Here, visitors can walk through the Victorian home to ring a third-story rooftop bell, and to see the "Scribble Den" where Muir wrote many of his influential articles and books.

Additional Sources of Information/Recommended Reading:

Mount Diablo State Park/Mt. Diablo Interpretive Association
P.O. Box 250
Diablo, CA 94528
(510) 837-2525

Rogers, Tom, "The Geology and Origin of Mt. Diablo," handout, Mt. Diablo Interpretive Association, 1990.

Wayburn, Peggy, *Adventuring in the San Francisco Bay Area,* Sierra Club Books, 1987.

Contra Costa

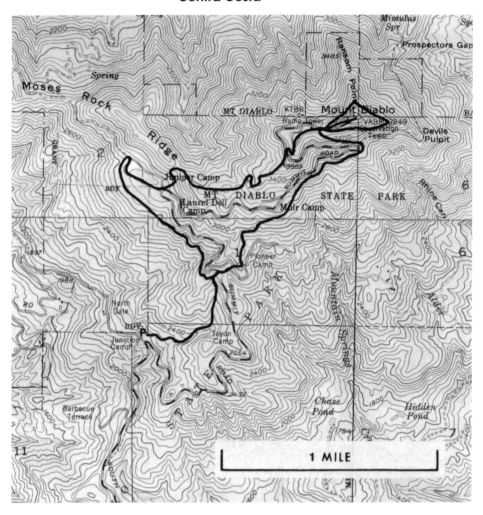

Del Norte

Bear Mountain	6400+′	#33

Location and Maps: Northeast corner of the county
USGS 7½-minute *Devils Punchbowl;* USGS 15 minute *Preston Peak;* USFS *Six Rivers National Forest*

Distance: 15 miles round trip/3300′ elevation gain
Grade: Strenuous/Class 2-3
Hiking Time: 9 hours
Season: Mid-June to mid-October

Trailnotes: An outstanding highpoint, located in the 153,000-acre Siskiyou Wilderness. This northernmost county summit offers lush woods, cascading creeks, unusual wildflowers, and striking nearby peaks. A steep trail reaches a lovely glacial-cirque lake, Devil's Punchbowl. The north face of Bear Mountain towers 1600 feet above the lake. A cross-country route, with a short class 2-3 talus pitch, takes you from the Punchbowl to the peak. It's a long dayhike or a backpack. No wilderness permit is required. Free campfire permits are available at the Gasquet Ranger Station. The road to the trailhead has a brief bumpy stretch near the end, negotiable by most automobiles; check with the ranger station for the latest conditions. Warm days and cold nights characterize the summer, with rain always a possibility. "Bear" Mountain refers to a commonly seen resident of Siskiyou Wilderness, *Ursus americanus,* the black, or cinnamon, bear.

Approach: From U.S. 199, 10 miles east of Gasquet, turn south onto signed Little Jones Creek Road (close by the Allen F. Lehman Memorial Bridge). At 1.3 miles a road forks left; keep to the right and follow the narrow paved road 8.3 more miles to a junction. Turn left at the junction onto Road 16N02, intermittently paved. Travel 2.7 miles to another junction. Keep left and drive briefly up and then down an increasingly rough dirt road for 1.5 miles to the Doe Flat trailhead.

Directions to Summit: The trail begins to the right of the parking area, marked by a sawed log and a SISKIYOU WILDERNESS sign. Walk down a gullied road that turns into a trail, dropping some 850 feet in 2.5 miles, to reach a signed junction for Devil's Punchbowl. Turn south, cross Doe Creek, and follow switchbacks sharply up a steep hillside. The uphill trudge ends in about a mile, as the trail contours along a ridge and drops down to a creek. An imposing peak juts to the south; Bear Mountain lies behind it. From the creek, climb an indistinct, ducked trail over a rocky bluff and down to a little lake. Walk around the south end of the lake to its west side, where a tall overhead snag marks the trail's continuation. Proceed southward up granite shelves to the Punchbowl, ¼ mile past the little lake.

Go clockwise around the east and south shores of the Punchbowl to reach the huge talus slope on the west side of the bowl. Keep to the shoreline rocks as much as possible to avoid brush and trees (heavy brush on the west side of the bowl merits this roundabout approach to the talus slope). Carefully ascend the talus and scree, which becomes quite steep near the ridgetop. After gaining the ridgeline, head southeast and thread through brush along the edge of the ridge. In ¼ mile, the ridge meets the western flank of Bear Mountain. Work your way to the right and climb a forested slope, littered with deadfall and brush. Near the top, an open rocky rise invites you to scramble up the backside of "The Bear" to the summit. A benchmark positioned on the first and highest of three summit crags reads 6436 feet, 25 feet higher than the topo-map elevation. (You cross the actual county highpoint just before reaching the peak; the county line lies about 50 yards southwest of the summit at a slightly lower elevation).

The View: At first the precipitous drop-off to the Punchbowl arrests you; then you see the gorgeous vistas. Preston Peak commands the northeast skyline, with Clear Creek Basin at its foot. A Klamath knot of ranges wraps around Bear Mountain. They include the Marbles to the southwest, the Siskiyous to the north and south, and Bear Basin Butte to the west. Lower crests stretch to the Pacific Ocean, seen as a watery blue line—or a foggy grey one. A sea of forest green, the Kalmiopsis Highlands, rises beyond the Oregon boundary; the border lies only 14 air miles away.

The Environment: Siskiyou Wilderness harbors a magnificent old-growth woodland, one of the finest coniferous forests in the world. Heavy precipitation, (up to 100 inches per year) sustains some 16 cone-bearing species including Alaskan cedar, Port Orford cedar, western hemlock, and the rare weeping spruce, all seen along the trail route. The botanic wonderland displays luxuriant vine maple, delicate five-finger fern, rose-flowered bitterroot, and a large concentration of lily species. Wildlife includes spotted owl, flying squirrel, wolverine, and allegedly, sasquatsch (a Salish Indian word for "wild-man-of-the-woods"). The wild recesses hereabouts generate more Bigfoot sightings than any other place in California.

Nearby Campgrounds: Three developed campgrounds afford ready access to the trailhead. They are adjacent to the Smith River on U.S. 199 between Gasquet and the Little Jones Creek Road turnoff. The drive from these campgrounds to the trailhead takes around an hour. Three other alternatives: roll out sleeping bags at the trailhead campsite, backpack a short distance to campsites along the first leg of the trail, or backpack a long distance to the Punchbowl. A few fair campsites nestle beside the Punchbowl's north, northeast, and southeast shorelines.

The County: The Spanish phrase *Del Norte* (locally pronounced "Del NORT"), means "of the north," referring to the county's geographic position. Mountainous terrain characterizes Del Norte, except for a small coastal plain that extends from the Smith River to Crescent City. This town, the only large community in the county, fronts a natural harbor used by the lumber and fishing industries. In the 1930s, hybrid Easter lilies first blossomed near the Smith River. Today Del Norte growers ship Easter lilies nationwide. The U.S. Government owns about 74% of the county, mostly in national-forest lands and in state parks. Jedediah Smith Redwoods State Park and Del Norte Coast Redwoods State Park protect some of California's finest redwood groves.

Additional Sources of Information/Recommended Reading:

Gasquet Ranger District
P.O. Box 228
Gasquet, CA 95543
(707) 457-3131

Six Rivers National Forest
1330 Bayshore Way
Eureka, CA 95501
(707) 442-1721.

Hart, John, *Hiking the Bigfoot Country,* Sierra Club Books, 1975.
Wallace, David Rains, *The Klamath Knot,* Sierra Club Books, 1983.

Devils Punchbowl from top of Bear Mountain

Del Norte

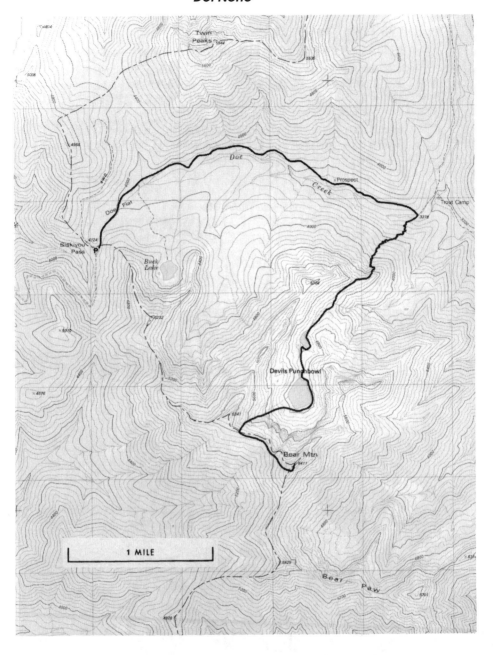

El Dorado

Freel Peak   10,881′   **#10**

Location and Maps:	Southeast corner of the county
	USGS 7½-minute *Freel Peak, South Lake Tahoe,*
	USFS Lake Tahoe Basin Management Unit Map
Distance:	11 miles round trip/3200′ elevation gain
Grade:	Strenuous/Class 2
Hiking Time:	7 hours
Season:	Mid-July to early October

Trailnotes: Mountains rim Lake Tahoe, and Freel Peak tops them all. The summit lies in Eldorado National Forest, a major sentinel rising above the lake's south shore. The Forest Service recommends the described Fountain Place route as the best approach to Freel Peak. You first hike established trails, including a segment of the new Tahoe Rim Trail (TRT), and then follow a use trail to the top. Expect to plod through snowbanks early in the season. Dayhike or backpack. In the late 1800s, Illinois native James Freel, a squatter, miner, and rancher, settled at the foot of the mountain that now bears his name.

Approach: From I 5 in Sacramento, drive 104 miles east on U.S. 50 to reach a junction with SR 89 at the south end of the Lake Tahoe basin in Tahoe Paradise/ Meyers. From the junction, proceed 0.8 mile northeast on U.S. 50/SR 89 and then turn right onto Pioneer Trail. Go 0.9 mile northeast on Pioneer Trail and bear right on Oneidas Street. Follow the central paved road 4.1 miles to the Forest Service gate displaying a private-property sign. Park here. The landowners allow hikers to cross their property.

Directions to Summit: From the gate walk south along the main dirt road, passing a right fork at 0.5 mile and a left fork at 0.7 mile. (The left fork links up with a gruelingly steep, sandy use trail to Freel Peak that climbs almost 2000 feet in 1.7 miles. This path parallels the northeast fork of Trout Creek, reaches a 9680-foot saddle, intersects the TRT, and joins the regular route.) The regular route passes the left fork and continues southeastward. Cross a boggy meadow, enter a lodgepole pine and aspen forest, and hop the southeast fork of Trout Creek. A good trail (18E09) climbs moderately for 1.8 miles to connect with the TRT at Armstrong Pass. Go left on the TRT. Contour above the canyon and ascend two big switchbacks to arrive at the 9680-foot saddle mentioned above.

From the saddle, 15 yards west of a SENSITIVE PLANT sign, a faint trace wends steeply southwest among boulders and whitebark pines up the northwest flank of the peak. The way is obvious, even though the path isn't. Keep on the right side of the ridge for about 0.4 mile, until a sloping bowl opens up to the east. Curve eastward, traverse across the bowl, and trek up a final steep, sand- and boulder-laden rise to the highpoint. You must share the summit shelf with a microwave station. A register rests among the topmost rocks.

The View: Beautiful. The Tahoe Sierra landmark, Mount Tallac, rises above Fallen Leaf Lake in the northwest. Prominent Pyramid Peak caps Desolation Wilderness in the west. Grassy Hope Valley stands out amid forested mountains in the south. White-quartz-veined Jobs Sister projects immediately to the east, backed by the Carson Range and desert ranges beyond. Mount Rose bulwarks the northeast end of the Lake Tahoe Basin. But the largest subalpine lake in North America steals the scene.

The Environment: Envision Lake Tahoe's genesis from your sky-high granite observation deck. Around 25 million years ago crustal forces uplifted the Carson Range to the east and the main Sierra crest to the west. Massive parallel faultlines later cleaved the upthrust blocks and a block between the faults sank, forming a graben, or trough. Volcanic flows plugged the trough's ancestral outlet, stream waters filled the basin, and the lake was born. Today, the cobalt jewel extends 22 miles long and 12 miles wide, with some 72 miles of shoreline. The average depth is about 1000 feet and the greatest depth plumbs 1645 feet. The lake holds 40 trillion gallons of water, enough to flood a flat area the size of California over 14 inches deep! Given its great depth, Lake Tahoe will probably remain a large water body long after many other lakes have filled with sediments. But the lake's fabled clarity has deteriorated in recent years due to shoreline urbanization, with consequent pollution and soil erosion. Conservationists continually work to protect this lake, one of California's greatest natural treasures.

Nearby Campgrounds: Public and private campgrounds ring South Lake Tahoe. Municipal El Dorado County Campground lies off U.S. 50 2.5 miles east of SR 89. Private Camp Richardson, the Forest Service's Fallen Leaf Lake, and the state's Emerald Bay and D.L. Bliss State Park campgrounds all lie near SR 89. The Forest Service takes reservations for some of its popular sites. The state parks require reservation through MISTIX. An early arrival time helps to secure an unreserved site during the crowded summer season.

The County: El Dorado, "The Gilded One," refers to a mythical South American Indian chief who covered himself with gold powder during religious rites. The name came to connote a place rich in gold. Following the discovery of gold at Sutter's Mill in 1848, miners flocked to sites along the American River and the Consumnes River, which form the county's north and south boundaries, creating an El Dorado of their own. Ghost towns echo the past in this mostly mountainous region. One settlement, called Hangtown (for its oak-tree justice) and later Placerville, lives on as a major town and county seat. Here, the only city-owned gold mine in America, the Gold Bug Mine, offers fascinating tours. Tourism, lumbering, and fruit farming drive the economy. El Dorado's main population center, South Lake Tahoe, swarms with summer recreationists and winter ski buffs, near the gambling glitz of Stateline, Nevada.

Additional Sources of Information/Recommended Reading:

USFS Lake Tahoe Basin
  Management Unit
870 Emerald Bay Road, Suite 1
South Lake Tahoe, CA 96150
(916) 573-2600

Forest Service Visitors Center
SR 89, just west of Fallen Leaf
  Lake Road
(916) 573-2674
Open from June to October,
  provides many free handouts on
  the Basin's natural history, and
  sells books and maps.

Schaffer, Jeffrey P., *The Tahoe Sierra,* 3rd ed., Wilderness Press, 1987.
Strong, Douglas H., *Tahoe: An Environmental History,* University of Nebraska Press, 1984.

El Dorado

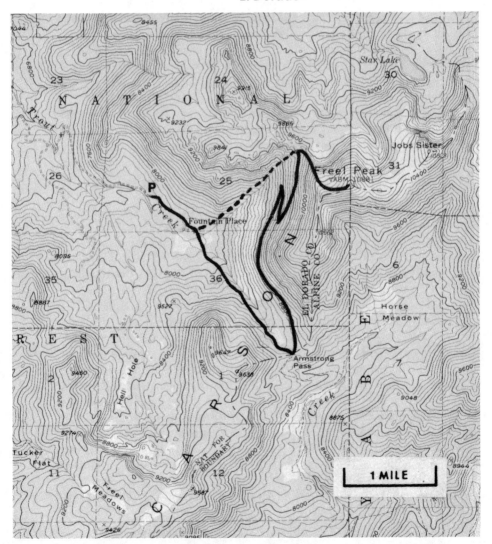

Fresno

North Palisade   14,242'   **#3**

Location and Maps:	East edge of the county
	USGS 7½-minute *North Palisade, Mt. Thompson;*
	USFS *John Muir Wilderness*
Distance:	19 miles round trip/7200' elevation gain
Grade:	Strenuous/Class 4
Hiking Time:	25 hours
Season:	Late July to late September

Trailnotes: A spectacular county summit. Many mountaineers consider North Palisade *the* classic High Sierra peak, distinguished by jagged pinnacles, precipitous ledges, and heart-stopping verticality. The 9-mile-long Palisade crest contains five of the eleven 14,000-foot mountaintops in the Sierra Nevada, and "North Pal" crowns the group, the highest point in Kings Canyon National Park as well as the highest point in Fresno County.

The least demanding route to the top has a Class 4 rating. This makes North Pal by far the most difficult county summit. To ascend the peak you should have basic rock-climbing experience. Know how to belay and rappel. Most climbers use a rope, a harness, and carabiners. Rockfall-prone chutes make a hard hat advisable. Early in the season and in years of heavy snowfall, an ice axe and crampons aid the traverse of snowfields and snow-laden chutes. Complex terrain and tricky route finding add to the challenge. Accredited guides lead parties to the summit, an expensive but possible option. Highpointers accustomed to easier treks may enjoy a dayhike or backpack to the vicinity of North Palisade; to experience such awesome alpine scenery makes the trip worthwhile.

Climbers generally take three or four days to do North Palisade. You follow an exceptionally scenic trail to Bishop Pass, go cross country to Palisade Basin, and camp beside upper Barrett Lake, approximately 8.5 miles from the trailhead. The actual climb begins at 11,600 feet, covers about a 2-mile round trip, gains 2650 feet, and takes a grueling 6 hours or more. Altitude, steepness, and technical climbing account for the time. Start early to lessen the risk of a thunderstorm—you need good weather, in addition to good conditioning and planning, to succeed.

Planning includes a wilderness permit. The White Mountain Ranger District's application procedures match those of the Mammoth Lakes Ranger District; see the Madera County entry for details. Pick up reserved permits from the Bishop Creek Entrance Station kiosk, 9 miles west of Bishop on State Route 168. Reservations unclaimed by 8:00 A.M. are canceled. Rangers dispense first-come, first-served permits at the Entrance Station beginning at 6:00 A.M. daily. Sunday through Wednesday are the best days to obtain a first-come, first-served permit.

The Whitney Survey of 1864 named the serrated crest "the Palisades" because they were "very grand and fantastic in shape." A party led by Joseph LeConte first scaled North Palisade on July 25, 1903. LeConte's route, described below, proved to be the "easiest" way to the top.

Approach: From U.S. 395 in Bishop, around 270 miles from Los Angeles and 320 miles from San Francisco, take SR 168 (West Line street) west 15½ miles to a fork (left) with South Lake Road. Go 7 more miles on South Lake Road to the trailhead parking lot. An overflow parking area lies 1.3 miles back down the road.

Directions to Summit: Climb gently for the first mile to a junction with the Treasure Lakes Trail. Bear left and in another mile pass a spur to Bull and Chocolate lakes. Then you cross and recross the South Fork of Bishop Creek, skirt Long Lake, and pass a side trail to Ruwau Lake. The moderately pitched trail goes by large Saddlerock Lake and Bishop Lake before steepening in a switchbacked pull up to the pass.

Two metal signs mark the apex of spacious Bishop Pass. One announces entry into Kings Canyon National Park; the other, 80 yards beyond the first, proscribes wood fires in Dusy Basin. Leave the trail anywhere between the signs and hike south, winding around the left side of a rise. From the rise, aim for clearly visible Thunderbolt Pass, the pronounced notch on the ridge directly below Thunderbolt Peak. Contour southeast above the level of Lake 11,400+ and below the faces of Mount Agassiz and Mount Winchell. Ledges and joints in the rock make for easy going until near the notch. Some tough maneuvering with backpacks over loose talus and piles of rock brings you to the pass (12,400′). Several campsites dot Thunderbolt Pass, and you may wish to camp here, if snowbanks provide water. Most parties descend 850 feet south over talus and small cliffs to upper Barrett Lake

North Palisade and Palisade Glacier

to a base camp near water. Thunderbolt Pass rates Class 2. For a longer but easier
Class 1 route, follow the Bishop Pass Trail to near the lowest lakes in Dusy Basin.
Then head southeast across open country to the noticeable gap just south of
Columbine Peak, Knapsack Pass (11,673'). From the pass, hike east beneath
Columbine Peak and then diagonal down to the north end of the largest Barrett Lake.

From upper Barrett Lake, look toward North Palisade to see three white, shield-
shaped cliffs at the lower right base of the peak, separated by two chutes. Climb
steep talus and enter the right-hand chute. The chute leads to the noticeable U-notch
on the crest. About halfway up, at 13,100 feet, the chute widens in an area covered
by large slabs. Just above the slabs, a rubble-laden outcrop begins to subtly divide
the chute into a larger passage on the right and a smaller passage on the left.
Advance to the left for about 100 feet and watch for a duck beside the sheer rock
wall along the north side of the chute. The duck signals a ledge directly above you,
the linchpin of the climb. A small waterfall often trickles just above the key ledge
threshold (early season chilly air freezes the falls in the morning). The ledge lies
very near level with the tops of the white-shield cliffs, a good landmark for
bearings. The ledge cannot be seen from below and remains invisible until you are
literally on it. This hard-to-find ledge crosses an otherwise untraversable vertical
face. The narrow, *descending* ledge winds into the next chute to the north. Gingerly
walk the shelf, in places only a foot or two wide, facing increased exposure as you
inch your way down the ledge and around the corner to easier ground.

With the ledge behind you, climb several hundred feet up the attained chute. At
13,500 feet, scramble to reach a narrow, steep gully on the right. This defile
contains two chockstones and often fills with snow. Loops of nylon webbing,
artificial handholds, and carabiners left by previous climbers sometimes hang on
the damp rock. Snow footholds aid Class 4 moves at this point. Above the defile,
a broad, steep talus slope leads northwest up to a phalanx of huge broken boulders
guarding the summit ridge. Ascend the talus slope, not difficult except for the
altitude, and then carefully work your way among the massive blocks to reach the
highest point. On a broad, gently sloping summit boulder you will find a benchmark and a weathered Sierra Club register.

The View: A thrilling aerie! The glistening Palisade Glacier sweeps downslope
below the northeast dropoff. In the east Mount Sill and Mount Gayley rise above
the glacier in the foreground, while the Whites, the Inyos, and endless desert ranges
crowd the background. Aretes, cirques, and couloirs sculpt the steepled Palisade
crest, extending northwest to Mount Agassiz and southeast to Split Mountain.
Lake-filled basins fall away from the divide—Big Pine and Bishop Creek to the
north, Dusy and Palisade to the west. To the southwest, the vast Middle Fork Kings
River drainage indents the backcountry of Kings Canyon National Park.

The Environment: About 5000 years ago a worldwide warming cycle reached
its peak and probably melted every Ice Age glacier in the Sierra, including those
that carved the Palisades' dark granite spires. About 2500 years ago, temperatures
declined and small glaciers began to form again. Some 60 glaciers remain in the

Sierra from this neoglacial period, most of them so small as to hardly show evidence of iceflow. The Palisade crest shelters some of them, as well as the largest ice sheet in the range. The Palisade Glacier covers over ½ square mile; North Palisade provides towering shade for it, favorably positioned to allow snow accumulation and later compaction to glacial ice. Hardy plants accent the glaciated terrain between Bishop Pass and Palisade Basin. Subalpine grasses grow in sandy pockets alongside white heather, yellow columbine, and blue sky pilot. Contorted whitebark pines cling to rocky shelves. Pounded by winds and pressed down by snowpacks, the indomitable trees somehow survive, their dark green foliage and reddish-brown bark adding life to the granite barrens.

Nearby Campgrounds: Several Forest Service campgrounds edge SR 168 and South Lake Road. They include Big Trees (9 sites), Bishop Park (22 sites), Four Jeffreys (106 sites), and Willows (7 sites), the latter located just 2 miles from the trailhead. North Lake campground at 9500 feet, offers the highest sites, good for acclimatization before your climb.

The County: *Fresno* means "ash tree" in Spanish, a reference to the native ash growing along the county's riverbanks. Fresno, the largest city in the San Joaquin Valley, is a cultural and marketing center for this agricultural heartland. Fresno County is the leading farm county in the nation, with annual farm revenues of over $2.5 billion. The county ranks first in the state for crops as varied as barley, onions, safflower, cantaloupes, boysenberries, nectarines, raisins, and wine grapes. Recently, smog from the populous Bay Area and the urbanizing Central Valley has reduced yields of sensitive crops like cotton, corn, and tomatoes. Horticulturists scramble to breed smog-resistant strains, and conservationists strive to implement regional air-quality standards to clear the skies.

Additional Sources of Information/Recommended Reading:

White Mountain Ranger District
798 N. Main Street
Bishop, CA 93514
(619) 873-2525

American Mountain Guides
  Association
P.O. Box 2128
Estes Park, CO 80517
(303) 586-0571

John Fischer, North Palisade Guide
P.O. Box 694
Bishop, CA 93515
(619) 873-5037
John Fischer, founder of the
  former Palisades School of
  Mountaineering, has climbed
  North Pal 70+ times.

Roper, Steve, *The Climber's Guide to the High Sierra,* Sierra Club Books, 1976.
Secor, R. J., *The High Sierra, Peaks, Passes, and Trails,* The Mountaineers, 1992.

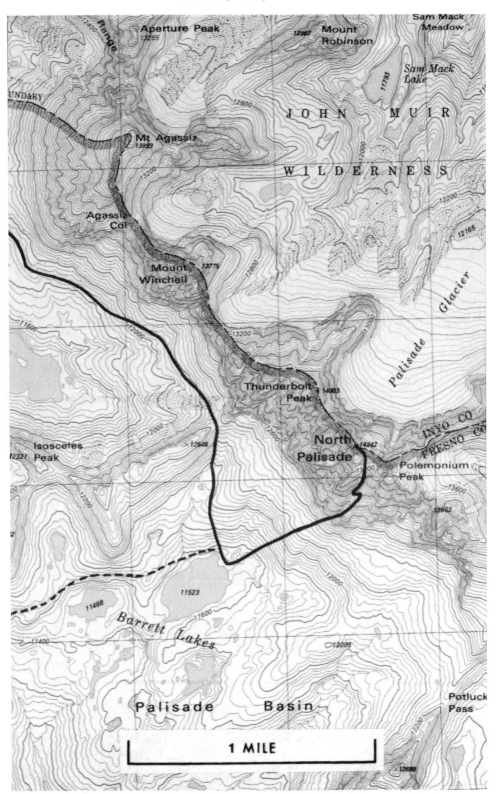

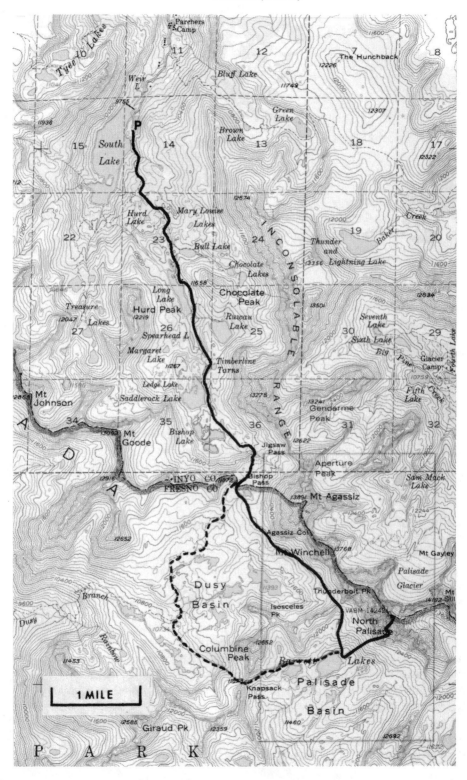

Glenn

Black Butte 7448' **#26**

Location and Maps:	Northwest corner of the county
	USGS 7½-minute *Plaskett Meadows, Plaskett*
	Ridge; USFS brochure map, *Meet the Mendocino*
	National Forest; USFS *Mendocino National Forest*
Distance:	2 miles round trip/550' elevation gain
Grade:	Easy/Class 1
Hiking Time:	50 minutes
Season:	Late May to October

Trailnotes: Black Butte hides in Mendocino National Forest, hard to see along the approach road until the last minute. A long drive for a short hike, done in tandem with neighboring Anthony Peak, the highpoint of Mendocino County. A jeep road and a footpath take you up the impressive crag. Dark volcanic rock inspired the name.

Approach: Please turn to the Mendocino County entry.

Directions to Summit: From the turnaround loop, head south on the jeep road to your left. The road shortly crosses a saddle, then slants upward into the forest, and ends by some fallen logs, 0.5 mile from the start. Walk to your right around the logs and follow a fairly steep trail that climbs the northeast shoulder of Black Butte. The trail zigs and zags 0.5 mile to emerge on a small rocky crest. On top, notice the slightly raised survey marker and the footing notches from a lookout tower dismantled about 30 years ago.

The View: Butte Creek drains the deep valleys to the west, backed by Etsel Ridge. Plaskett Ridge extends to the southwest, with Bald Mountain in the distance. Snow Mountain engraves the far southern horizon. Anthony Peak and the Yolla Bolly Mountains rise in the north. Mount Shasta seems suspended above the haze in the northeast, as does Lassen Peak to the east. At 7448 feet, standing atop Black Butte brings you closest to the average elevation of all the county highpoints, 7410 feet.

The Environment: Black Butte's volcanic origin stems not from molten surface lava, but from a block of volcanic rock lifted to the surface by crustal-plate movements. The block heaved high enough to spawn small glaciers during the Ice Age, unusual in the North Coast Ranges. Red fir predominates in the forest around Black Butte. The tree displays fragrant blue-green foliage and erect purplish-brown cones. Young trees have smooth, whitish trunks, mature trees rough-furrowed, reddish bark. Understory wildflowers include fairy lantern, woodland star, and pinedrops. A large black-tailed deer population inhabits the forest. So do wild hogs. Stout, quick, and stealthy, these European hogs were imported into northern California during the early 20th Century by hunters. Now the second most popular big-game animal in the state, the pigs have reached pest proportions in certain areas because they have no natural predators.

Nearby Campgrounds: The Plaskett Lake Recreation Area, 2 miles east of the Black Butte turnoff, has a 32-unit developed campground and two fishing lakes. See the Mendocino entry for additional sites.

The County: Black Butte tops the mountainous west side of Glenn County, while grassy, oak-strewn foothills grade to Sacramento Valley flatlands on the east side. Hugh J. Glenn (1824–1882), a Missouri dentist, came to California to mine gold and later turned to wheat farming. He became the state's largest grower, the "Wheat King," and Glenn County was named in his honor. In 1880 Glenn planted some 45,000 acres of wheat and barley. The feat required over 100 eight-mule teams and produced over 1 million bags of grain. Today, rice leads a list of crops that include corn, hay, sugar beets, and clover, as well as wheat. Orchards grow almonds, oranges, olives, peaches, and plums. Livestock ranching and dairying round out the economy. Tree-shaded parks in the main towns of Orland and Willows provide a welcome respite from the Sacramento Valley's summer heat.

Sources of Additional Information/Recommended Reading:

Listed under the Mendocino County entry.

Standing atop Black Butte

Glenn

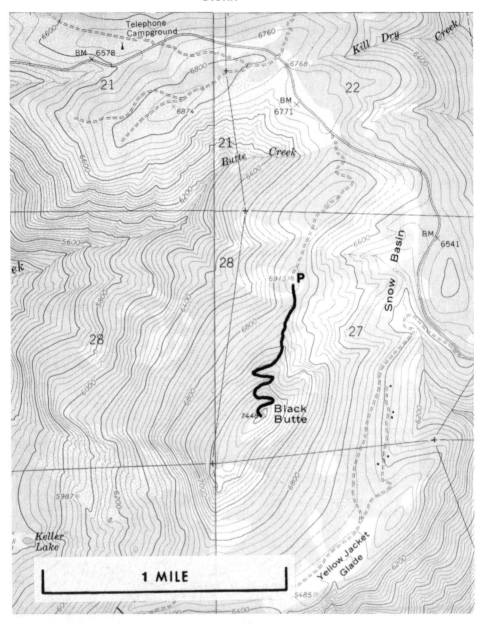

Humboldt

Salmon Mountain 6956′ #29

Location and Maps:	Northeast corner of the county
	USGS 7½-minute *Salmon Mtn.;* USFS *Trinity Alps Wilderness*
Distance:	7 miles round trip/1600′ elevation gain
Grade:	Moderate/Class 2
Hiking Time:	4 hours
Season:	Mid-June to mid-September

Trailnotes: An atmosphere of wild seclusion pervades Salmon Mountain. The massif sits at the northwest corner of half-million acre Trinity Alps Wilderness, California's most extensive wildland outside the Sierra Nevada. The remote western Trinity Alps receive few visitors, but the Forest Service still requires a wilderness permit, obtainable from the Orleans Ranger Station on your way to the highpoint. From the highway, a smooth, twisting, mostly paved road runs 18.5 miles to the trailhead. The outing makes a wonderful dayhike, or you can backpack for further exploration. You ramble along the Salmon Summit National Scenic Trail for most of the hike, and then scramble over boulders and brush to reach the view-filled crest. Salmon Mountain overlooks the Trinity, Salmon, and Klamath River basins, once famed for their bountiful salmon runs.

Approach: From I 5 in Redding take SR 299 west 102 miles to Willow Creek. From U.S. 101 in Eureka, take SR 299 east 51 miles to Willow Creek. From Willow Creek, go 38 miles north on SR 96 to Orleans. Stop at the ranger station on the left side of the road for a wilderness permit. From the ranger station continue down the road 0.3 mile, cross a Klamath River bridge, and immediately turn right onto Red Cap Road (FS 10N01). Set the odometer and follow this road to the trailhead. Pass through an intersection at 5.0 miles. Keep left when you reach junctions at 7.0 miles and 10.5 miles. Bear right on a fork at 15 miles, transferring from pavement to gravel. At 18.5 miles you arrive at the trailhead on the left side of the road.

Directions to Summit: Push through overgrown brush for 150 yards to pick up a good trail heading southeast through the forest. Contour gently up to a junction and Baylor Camp at 1.3 miles. Go right and presently reach a ridge, worthy of the "Scenic Trail" designation. Climb moderately to a saddle at Indian Rocks, a curious collection of mostly man-made cairn spires. Continue at a steeper pitch to a junction signed RED CAP LAKE, about 2.7 miles from the start. Keep left and proceed upward 0.6 mile to where the trail tops out at an opening in the forest. A steep, brushy slope capped with rock outcrops rises on your left. Look for a tall tree with a saguaro-cactuslike bend in its trunk. Leave the trail and scramble up the slope. Work around the right side of the rock outcrops to gain the summit plateau, topped by a substantial cairn over 7 feet high.

The View: Fantastic. To the southeast, the Salmon Mountains extend to the snow-streaked Trinity Alps highlands, crowned by 9002-foot Thompson Peak. Walk a short distance north along the summit plateau to see Indian Rocks, Whitey's Peak, and Orleans Mountain. Forested ridges file toward the ocean, only an occasional clearcut reflecting a human presence. The rounded Devils Backbone and Red Cap Creek Basin spread to the south. Immediately to the east, an escarpment drops away to the headwaters of Nordheimer Creek. Northern California's ever-present white beacon, Mount Shasta, shines in the distance.

The Environment: The Trinity Alps chain comes in three colors: the green, forest-cloaked western Salmon Mountains, underlain by greenstone and schist; the white central highlands, composed of light granite; and the red eastern peaks, rust-colored from the rocks' high iron content. Remnant glaciers dot the central highlands; adjacent Red Cap Lake formed in a miniature glacial cirque. Penny-royal, sulfur flower, scarlet gilia and many other wildflowers flourish in glades among Salmon Mountain's cedar, pine, and fir. Steelhead trout still run upstream in the nearby Klamath and Salmon rivers, but anglers no longer catch the mountain's namesake because fishery managers closed the salmon season year-round to give the endangered species a chance to recover. Salmon hatch in the rivers, travel to the sea, mature there, and return to spawn in their natal river. But overfishing, development, dams, drought, and sedimentation due to logging have drastically depleted their numbers.

Nearby Campgrounds: Three Forest Service campgrounds lie along SR 96 near Orleans. Find Perch Creek Campground just north of the Klamath River bridge. Adjoining Bluff Creek and Akens Creek campgrounds are about 8 miles south of the bridge. An informal campsite 30 yards north of the trailhead has no water.

The County: The county derives its name from Humboldt Bay, christened in 1850 to honor the great German naturalist and explorer Baron Alexander von Humboldt. Mountains separated by narrow valleys cover Humboldt County, except for alluvial lowlands around Arcata Bay and Humboldt Bay. Below Humboldt Bay, Cape Mendocino projects farther west than any other place in California. Eureka, the largest city on the North Coast, serves as a governmental, financial, and shipping center. Livestock ranching, dairying, and tourism generate income, but logging and forest products dominate the economy. Humboldt County contains most of the state's remaining unprotected old-growth redwood forests. Lumbermen seek to harvest the trees, while conservationists try to save them. Fortunately, parks preserve some of the finest groves, including one with the tallest known tree in the world. This remarkable redwood reaches a neck-craning 367.8 feet in the air.

Additional Sources of Information/Recommended Reading:

Orleans Ranger District,
P.O. Box B, Orleans Road
Orleans, CA 95556
(916) 627-3291

Bernstein, Art, *Best Hikes of the Trinity Alps,* Mountain N' Air, 1993.
Linkhart, Luther, *The Trinity Alps, A Hiking and Backpacking Guide,* 2nd
ed., Wilderness Press, 1986.

Humboldt

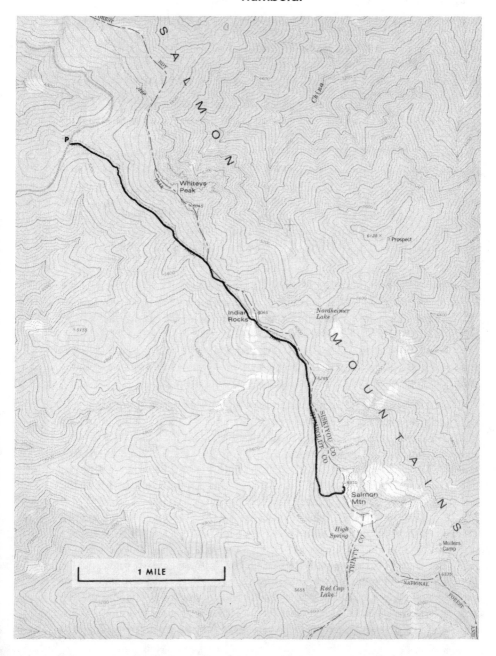

Imperial

Blue Angels Peak   4548'   **#39**

Location and Maps:	Southeast corner of the county
	USGS 7½-minute *In-ko-pah Gorge*
Distance:	5 miles round trip/1350' elevation gain
Grade:	Moderate/Class 2
Hiking Time:	3 hours
Season:	Year-round; best from November to May

Trailnotes: Blue Angels Peak lies on BLM land in the Jacumba Outstanding Natural Area, established in 1975 to protect the region's unique environment. Dry, rugged, high desert country. Often very windy. Carry plenty of water. The route follows a dirt road most of the way, with a cross-country stretch at the end. Watch for cactus ("jumping cholla") and rattlesnakes (seldom seen but present in the area). Off-road vehicles may be encountered along the road, but you will rise above them as you climb the peak. Blue Angels Peak derives its name from the famed Navy Flight Demonstration Squadron. A naval air facility in nearby El Centro has served as the Blue Angels' winter home, because of the excellent winter flying weather.

Approach: From San Diego, drive 78 miles east on I 8 (5 miles past the Jacumba exit and less than a mile beyond a brake-inspection area) to the In-ko-pah Park offramp. Turn right (east) at the stop sign, and right again at the intersection with Old Highway 80, toward Jacumba. Drive 0.2 mile southwest on Old Highway 80 and then turn left onto an unsigned dirt road. Follow the dirt road 0.5 mile and park at a pull-out on the left just before reaching overhead transmission lines. Additional pull-outs are located beneath and beyond the lines.

Directions to Summit: From the parking pull-out, walk south along the winding, steep-pitched, occasionally cemented road. In about 1.2 miles a BLM marker at a rise on the left reads WILDERNESS STUDY AREA BEHIND SIGN and a jeep road descends into a small valley to the east. Continue on the main road another 0.1 mile to a three-way road junction. Keep to the right, go 0.3 mile west to a fork just before an incongruous NOT A THRU STREET sign, and turn left (south). Bear to the left at road spurs. At 1.9 miles the road swings east, where a sign announces CLOSED ROUTE (closed to vehicles; four-wheel-drive rigs can be driven to this point). Proceed up the road until it deadends beyond a mining prospect on the left. Gaze southeast to see a mountain with a huge boulder perched on top looking ready to roll. Blue Angels Peak rises behind this mountain. Follow a faint use trail to a ridge dotted with pinyon pines, on the right side of the boulder-topped mountain. From the ridge scramble up to a saddle between the boulder-decked mountain and Blue Angels Peak, and then go southwest a short distance farther to the summit rocks, embedded with three benchmarks, the central one inscribed SMUGGLER. A register lies in a crevice just east of the benchmark.

The View: Upon reaching the benchmarks, don't be dismayed to see higher points close by and think you haven't quite made the top—these points are in Mexico. The international boundary lies just an eighth of a mile to the south, along a slightly northeast-trending line. (Blue Angels Peak is the highpoint closest to another country and the southernmost as well as the easternmost California county summit.) The mountains in Mexico are called the Sierra Juarez, Baja California's northernmost segment of the Peninsular Range province. Blue Angels Peak is structurally part of the Sierra Juarez, although U.S. cartographers label it as part of the Jacumba Mountains. The Jacumba and In-ko-pah ranges and flat-topped Table Mountain extend northward in the foreground, with the Palomar and Santa Rosa mountains in the distance. The Laguna Mountains, Cuyamaca Peak, and other peaks stand out in the west. The Sierra Juarez spreads southward, while to the east and northeast the Imperial Valley, the Salton Sea, and the distant Chocolate Mountains fill out the panorama.

From the peak look to the south to find a silvery obelisk, International Boundary Marker 231. A short walk and careful negotiation of a barbed-wire fence provide a closer look. (The fence demarks a 60-foot buffer zone before the actual boundary.) Consecutively numbered obelisks extend at intervals along the border from the Gulf of Mexico to the Pacific Ocean. It's tempting to "visit Mexico" here, but it's technically unlawful for U.S. citizens to cross the border except at legal entry points.

The Environment: Approximately 100 million years ago, what are now the peak's environs formed several miles beneath the surface as part of a vast, mostly granitic rock mass known as the southern California batholith. The overlying rocks gradually eroded away, and as the rock mass became closer to the surface, water seeped down into cracks and fissures, weakening the rock and cleaving blocks of varying dimensions. Once the granite was exposed at the surface, weathering and erosion further fractured and rounded it into the jumbled, boulder-strewn landscape seen today. Given sufficient rainfall, the rugged landscape becomes a rock garden of colorful spring wildflowers—yellow suncups, purple canterbury bells, crimson locoweed, and many others. Three plant communities intergrade here, producing a desert transitional melange: creosote scrub species such as yucca, mormon tea, and various cacti; chaparral shrubs like scrub oak, manzanita, and wild buckwheat; and pinyon-juniper woodland, with California juniper and both single- and four-needle pinyon pines. A continuous forest of pinyon pine grows in the Sierra Juarez to the south, but, stateside, past fires have swept through the area, eliminating most of the trees. Hoary trunk remnants of the once-extensive forest litter the ground around Blue Angels Peak.

Nearby Campgrounds: Camping and backpacking are permitted in the Jacumba Outstanding Natural Area. Obtain up-to-date information from the

BLM's El Centro Resource Area office. Adjacent 600,000-acre Anza Borrego Desert State Park offers a wealth of scenic, hiking, and camping adventures.

The County: The county takes its name from the Imperial Valley, in turn named for the Imperial Land Company, whose developers began reclaiming desert land at the turn of the century by diverting Colorado River water. Between 1905 and 1907, the river repeatedly overflowed irrigation canals and poured into the valley, creating the Salton Sea. Now 30 miles long and 8-14 miles wide, with an average depth of 20 feet, the sea is maintained by water drained from irrigated fields. It is now slightly more salty than the ocean, and the salinity increases yearly, jeopardizing a rich fishery and migratory bird habitat. Imperial County lies in the hottest part of the Unites States and ranks as one of the hottest places in the world, with a recorded high temperature of 130 degrees. Colorado River water has transformed a broad, alluvium-filled desert lowland into one of California's premier agricultural areas. The predominately Hispanic population (55 percent) resides in the small cities of Brawley, Calexico, and El Centro, the largest city below sea level in all of North and South America.

Additional Sources of Information/Recommended Reading:

Bureau of Land Management, El
Centro Resource Area
1661 S. 4th St.
El Centro, CA 92243
(619) 353-1060

Anza-Borrego Desert State Park
P.O. Box 299
Borrego Springs, CA 92004
(619) 767-5311

Lindsay, Diana and Lowell, *The Anza-Borrego Desert Region,* 3rd ed., Wilderness Press, 1991.
Schad, Jerry, *Afoot and Afield in San Diego County,* 2nd ed., Wilderness Press, 1992.

Hikers atop Blue Angels Peak

Imperial

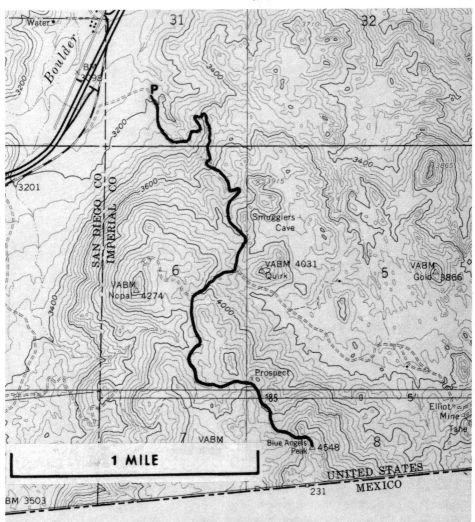

Inyo

Mount Whitney   14,491′   #1

Location and Maps:	Along the western border of the county
	USGS 7½-minute *Mt. Whitney, Mt. Langley;*
	USFS *John Muir Wilderness* (a three-map set);
	Wilderness Press *Mt. Whitney*
Distance:	22 miles round trip/6130′ elevation gain
Grade:	Strenuous/Class 1
Hiking Time:	13 hours
Season:	Mid-July to mid-October

Trailnotes: The preeminent county summit, and the most famous, most climbed peak in the High Sierra. The boundary line between Inyo County and Tulare County bisects the summit, so both counties lay claim to the highest point in the lower 48 states. An excellent trail leads to spectacular scenery in Inyo National Forest, John Muir Wilderness, and Sequoia National Park. Some 13,000 people a year hike on the trail and about half reach the top. Each year the Forest Service makes several major emergency rescues (using a helicopter) and dozens of minor first-aid assists with blisters, sprained ankles, altitude sickness, and exhaustion. Good conditioning and acclimatization forestall problems, so if possible, before the hike, spend overnight at a Whitney Portal campground for altitude adjustment. Backpackers take two or three days for the round trip; fit hikers do it in a day. Overnighters must apply in advance. Dayhikers don't need a permit. The Forest Service accepts wilderness-permit applications only by written request with postmarks dated March 1 through May 31. To increase your chances of getting a reservation, list several starting and ending dates on the form, obtained from the Mount Whitney Ranger District. A store near the trailhead provides information, food, supplies, and showers. Purify trailside water sources. Hikers swarm the trail in July and August. Lighter use prevails in September and October, and fewer people arrive on weekdays than weekends. *Early* (3 or 4 A.M.) departures and even moonlight ascents avoid the crowds as well as potentially dangerous afternoon thunderstorms.

Surveyor Clarence King named the peak for Josiah Whitney, chief of the State Geological Survey from 1860 to 1874.

Approach: From U.S. 395 in the center of Lone Pine, turn west on Whitney Portal Road. Drive up the road 13 miles to a parking area. If it's full, park along the shoulder of the road. The trail begins across the road from the overnight parking lot. A short, rock-lined stairway leads to a mileage sign and display boards.

Directions to Summit: Follow the beaten path. Hike up steep southeast-facing slopes—often hot by mid-morning—to reach Lone Pine Creek and a spur trail to Lone Pine Lake. A few more tacks bring you to Bighorn Park and Outpost Camp at 3.5 miles. Pass Mirror Lake and Trailside Meadow before reaching 12,000-foot Trail Camp at 6.0 miles. This main overnight stop for backpackers has many tent sites and the last reliable trailside water. Above Trail Camp, nearly 100 grinding switchbacks surmount a basin wall to top a narrow ridge at Trail Crest, 13,650 feet in elevation. Grand views open up in all directions. The path then drops slightly for 0.4 mile to a junction with the John Muir Trail. Keep right and resume climbing along a pinnacled ridge. Look through "windows" between the pinnacles for heart-pounding glimpses of tarns 2000 feet below. Finally, contour across a large talus-strewn bowl and scale a few more ill-defined switchbacks to the summit. A register sits against the wall of a stone structure, built in 1909 for astronomical study. A plaque affixed to a boulder proclaims Mount Whitney's elevation as 14,496 feet, which is reduced slightly to 14,491 feet on the latest USGS topographic map.

The View: A limitless, top-of-the-world panorama. Lone Pine Peak, Owens Valley, and a raft of desert ranges stretch out to the east. Third, Day, and Keeler needles, and Mount Muir pierce the sky immediately to the south, and massive avalanche, talus, and scree slopes fall away to turquoise lakes, granite valleys, and moraines far below. The craggy rust-red Kaweah Peaks rise in the west beyond yawning Upper Kern Basin. The glorious Sierra crest unfurls to the north, including Mount Tyndall and the distant Palisades. From almost 3 miles high, the atmosphere overhead displays an intensely deep blue cast, grading into lighter azure tints toward the horizon.

The Environment: Jeffrey pines and red firs shade the lower reaches of the Mount Whitney trail. Lodgepole and foxtail pines grow higher up, while contorted whitebark pines cling to the slopes at treeline. Higher still, alpine wildflowers like white phlox and blue sky pilot tinge the desolate, frost-shattered rock.

Mount Whitney is ensconced among granitic ramparts almost its equal. The sheer, glacier-quarried east face belies an astounding fact—the large, flat summit has no sign of glaciation. Geologists theorize that the present top was once part of an ancestral Sierra plateau, only about 2000 feet above sea level. Massive fault-block uplift over millions of years brought the mountain to its current height. During recent Ice Ages, glaciers girdled Mount Whitney but didn't quite gouge to the summit, leaving a remnant of the ancient plateau and a spacious place for leg-weary hikers to recline.

Nearby Campgrounds: First-come/first-served Forest Service campgrounds include Whitney Portal Trailhead, next to the overnight parking area, with 10 walk-in sites, and Whitney Portal, a mile down the road, with 44 units. Lone Pine campground, 7 miles down Whitney Portal Road, also has 44 units. All have piped water.

The County: "Inyo," a word of obscure origin, translates poetically as "dwelling place of the Great Spirit." The second largest California county boasts not only Mount Whitney's height but also Death Valley's depth: a sink dips to 282 feet below sea level, the lowest place in the Western Hemisphere, and just 80 air miles from Mount Whitney! Death Valley also holds the country's record high temperature, 134°. Inyo's small towns (Lone Pine, Independence, Big Pine), and large town (Bishop) string along U.S. 395 in Owens Valley, the nation's deepest valley. Tourism leads the economy, followed by livestock and mining operations. The county's largest taxpayer, the City of Los Angeles, acquired vast land holdings, secured water rights, and diverted the Owens River into aqueducts, built in 1913 and 1969, to supply the populous city. As a result, the valley lost much of its greenness and natural beauty.

Additional Sources of Information/Recommended Reading:

Mt. Whitney Ranger District
P.O. Box 8
Lone Pine, CA 93545
(619) 876-6200

Eastern Sierra InterAgency Visitor Center
Junction of SR 136 and U.S. 395
P.O. Box "R"
Lone Pine, CA 93545
(619) 876-4252

Hellweg, Paul, and Scott McDonald, *Mount Whitney Guide For Hikers and Climbers,* Canyon Publishing Company, 1991.

Wheelock, Walt, and Tom Condon, *Climbing Mount Whitney,* 5th ed., La Siesta Press, 1989.

Winnett, Thomas, *Mt. Whitney, High Sierra Hiking Guide #5,* 2nd ed., Wilderness Press, 1978.

Mt. Whitney (center) and adjacent 14,000′ peaks

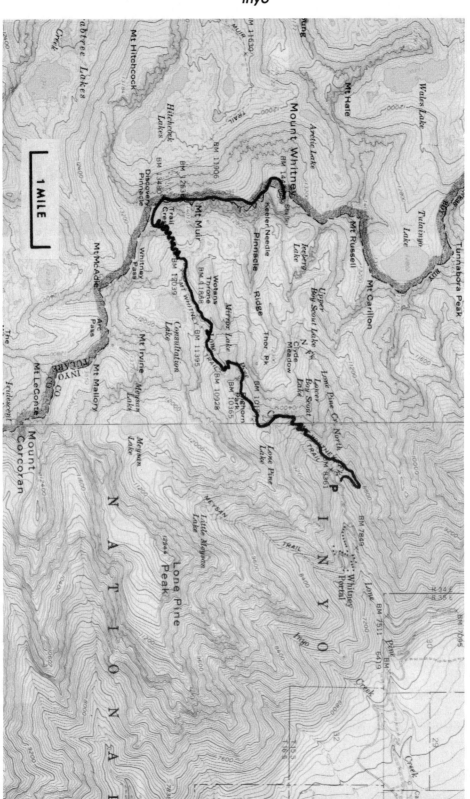

1 MILE

Kern

Sawmill Mountain   8818'   **#22**

Location and Maps:	Along the southwest border of the county USGS 7½-minute *Sawmill Mountain, Cuddy Valley;* USFS *Los Padres National Forest* (See Ventura County for this book's map.)
Distance:	3 miles round trip/800' elevation gain
Grade:	Moderate/Class 1–2
Hiking Time:	1.5 hours (done in combination with Mount Pinos; see explanation below)
Season:	April to November

Trailnotes: A handy trail leads to Sawmill Mountain from Mount Pinos, the highpoint of Ventura County. (See Ventura for all entries except the county.) The old topo map depicts a Kern County boundary line skirting the 8750-foot contour on Mount Pinos but intersecting the same contour on Sawmill Mountain, an indication of slightly higher ground. However, the new topo map, issued in 1991, shows the county boundary cutting across the 8800-foot contour on Mount Pinos, but just edging the same contour on Sawmill Mountain. The recent topo also lists a new spot elevation for Sawmill Mountain of 8818 feet. All this makes the Kern County highpoint a very close call. You should hike to Sawmill Mountain, but, for insurance, when on Mount Pinos, walk northwest from the summit about 300 feet to cross the invisible county boundary plane. One way or the other you will have topped Kern County. Sawmill Mountain's name reflects an old nearby logging enterprise.

The County: The county takes its name from the Kern River, named by General John Frémont to honor Edward Kern, a military colleague who nearly drowned in the river in 1845. The third largest county in California, bordered by mountain ranges, encompasses the south end of the great Central Valley and the west edge of the Mojave Desert. Although coniferous forests cover a quarter of the county (mostly in Sierra National Forest), the flat, arid San Joaquin Valley dominates the landscape. Thanks to irrigation, huge farms produce a cornucopia. Kern ranks first in the state for almonds, pistachios, navel oranges, carrots, and spring potatoes. Oil fields support the economy in Taft, Maricopa, and Bakersfield, the major city. Four of the ten largest fields in the United States lie under Kern County. The nation's biggest borax mine operates in the desert, near Boron. Also in the desert, a 38-square-mile natural area protects California's state reptile, the Desert Tortoise. The tortoise hibernates for half a year or more, emerges in early spring to feast upon desert herbs, and then retreats underground to sleep through the summer heat.

Kings

Table Mountain   3473′   **#48**

Location and Maps: Southwest corner of the county
USGS 7½-minute *The Dark Hole*

Private Highpoint Notes: Table Mountain lies at the south end of the Diablo Range. The benchmarked highpoint rests on a board-flat summit, flanked by steep downslopes. The summit plateau falls within public BLM land, but encircling private property hinders admittance and requests to gain access received no answer. Given access, Turkey Flat Road near Parkfield provides a jumping-off point to hike over hilly pastures and jeep roads to the Table's top. Views take in Cholame Valley in the west, the Temblor Range in the south, the San Joaquin Valley in the east, and mountains in the north, cut by deep recesses, one evocatively named the Dark Hole.

A horizontal mass of serpentinite forms the level surface of Table Mountain. The serpentinite contains chrysotile asbestos, as at San Benito Mountain, 40 miles to the north. Several old mining operations pock the landscape, including the King mercury mine northeast of the highpoint. Small oaks and Digger pines decorate the Table, along with a smattering of juniper, manzanita, yerba santa, and wild lilac. Oak-dotted grassy hills characterize the remote and peaceful grazing lands below the summit.

The County: The County's name comes from the Kings River, originally *Rio de Los Santos Reyes,* "river of the holy kings." The name refers to the three Biblical wise men. The San Joaquin Valley floor makes up over three quarters of the county's land area. Here, agriculture rules supreme—vegetable crops, field crops, fruit and nut orchards, dairying, poultry, and stock raising. The Kettleman Hills produce oil and natural gas. Population clusters around Hanford, the county seat and center of commerce. The southwest corner of the county has a potential for strong earthquakes. The USGS intensively studies a 20-mile segment of the San Andreas Fault near Table Mountain, known for regularly recurring temblors. Seismologists have installed more monitoring equipment here than along any other stretch of fault in the world, with an eye toward earthquake prediction. (Many big quakes have foreshocks that precede the most severe shaking by days, hours, or minutes.) Researchers hope to catch the longest, most active fault in the Northern Hemisphere in action.

Kings

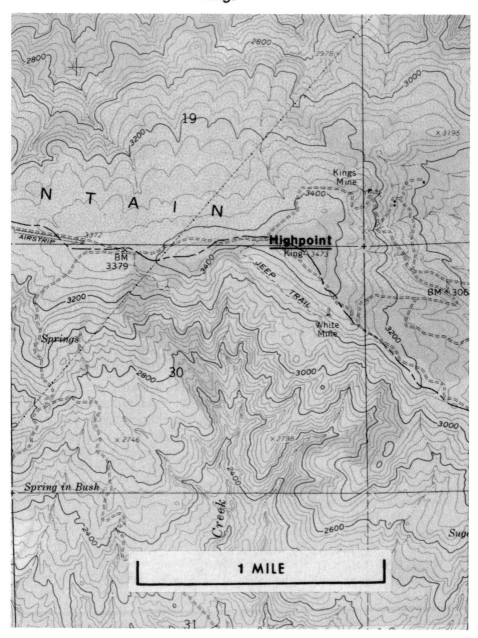

Lake

Snow Mountain East   7056′   **#28**

Location and Maps: Northeast corner of the county
Snow Mountain East is the highpoint of both
Lake County *and* Colusa County. Please turn to
Colusa County for all entries except the County.

The County: Lying within the North Coast Ranges, Lake County is largely mountainous terrain, higher and more rugged in the north, lower and gently rolling in the south, and creased by numerous small northwest-trending valleys. Agriculture, livestock ranching and tourism support the economy. The relatively sparse population has recently grown with an influx of migrants from the Bay Area, 100 miles to the south, attracted by the region's bucolic resorts and lakes.

The county's name stems from an outstanding geographic feature, Clear Lake. This natural freshwater body, the largest entirely within California, measures almost 20 miles long and up to 8 miles wide. It has 100 miles of shoreline, 70 square miles of surface, and an average depth of 27 feet. The shallow water warms to over 70° in the summer, augmenting algae blooms that cloud nearshore waters but do not appear to upset the lake's ecological balance. Clear Lake teems with black bass, crappie, catfish, and many species of waterfowl.

Snow Mountain East from Snow Mountain West

. . . .

Lassen

Hat Mountain   8737'   **#23**

Location and Maps:	Northeast corner of the county
	USGS 7½-minute *Snake Lake, Emerson Peak;*
	USFS *Modoc National Forest*
Distance:	5 miles round trip/2150' elevation gain
Grade:	Moderate/Class 2
Hiking Time:	4 hours
Season:	July to September

Trailnotes: Hat Mountain looks like a tremendous triangle or an abstract hat. The peak rises at the south end of the Warner Mountains within Modoc National Forest, in far northeastern California. Secluded and seldom visited, Hat Mountain gladdens hikers with a spring-fed creek, a limpid lake, and an invigorating cross-country climb over rugged terrain. You can overnight at a primitive trailhead campground or at a close-by developed campground. Paved and dirt roads, fine for passenger cars, lead to the starting point. Highpointers usually climb Hat Mountain in conjunction with Eagle Peak, the apex of Modoc County.

Approach: From U.S. 395 in Likely, turn east onto Jess Valley Road and go 9 miles to reach a junction. Turn right at the junction and set your odometer. The paved road, FS64, turns to gravel beyond a right-hand spur to Blue Lake Campground at 6.5 miles. Continue straight on FS64, through junctions at 9.1 and 11.2 miles, and past the Patterson Campground turnoff at 14.2 miles. Keep left at a junction at 14.3 miles and pass another junction sign at 17.1 miles. Watch for a sign CAMP ONE 2 MILES at 17.6 miles, and turn right (south) from FS64 here. Proceed down the roughening road. Keep left at forks at 18.8 miles and 19.0 miles. Hat Mountain looms ahead as you reach the edge of a sagebrush meadow at 19.4 miles. Park on either side of the road. This is the trailhead.

Directions to Summit: From Camp One amble down the jeep road, which dips slightly at first and then more steeply. After 0.4 mile, the road veers right (west). Leave the road at this point and proceed straight (south) along a sketchy path that parallels a creek. The path fades and reappears, drops steadily for about 600 feet, and breaks out of the trees near the shore of Lost Lake. Head left (southeast) along a shoreline use trail. Hop over logs and stones at the lake outlet and walk around the east side of the lake until you reach a jeep road.

From here walk along the road a very short way, then head southeast cross country into the forest and ascend the northwest slope of Hat Mountain. Clamber over rocks and deadfall. Sift through trees and brush. The trees thin as you surmount the "crown of the Hat," a tilted, rocky plateau. To shorten your cross-country jaunt, you can bushwhack directly toward the summit and scramble up the steep stair-step boulder field. To lengthen the jaunt and lessen the gradient, walk southwest along the road until it deadends, hike up a small creek bed (south of Skunk Cabbage Creek) to its headwaters, bend northeastward, and tramp to the highpoint. One way or another, you climb 1500 feet in more or less a mile. The table-topped summit culminates at an impressive overlook. A cairn near the overlook holds a register. A slightly higher rise to the south appears to mark the highest point.

The View: Splendid. Lost Lake shimmers below, the Camp One Meadow stands out beyond, and Mount Shasta spikes the northwest horizon. Directly north, Eagle Peak crowns the axis of the Warner Mountains. In the east, Surprise Valley fills the foreground and countless basin and ranges crowd the background. To the south, the brushy tableland of Hat Mountain merges with Red Rock Mountain. To the west, forested slopes grade into the Modoc Plateau.

The Environment: The rusty grey rock on Hat Mountain originates from Jurassic and Triassic metavolcanic formations. The volcanic material overlies older sedimentary beds subjected to fault-block uplift. Sagebrush and aspen predominate on the first leg of the hike, Jeffrey pine and white fir on the second. Lupine, larkspur, paintbrush, and corn lilies grow in profusion. Rainbow, brown, and brook trout ripple the waters of Lost Lake. Rocky Mountain mule deer, beaver, marten, porcupine, coyote, badger, weasel, and mountain lion all live in the area. Fourteen bighorn sheep, reintroduced in 1980, grew to be 50 by 1987. Disease wiped out the herd the following year, probably spread by domestic sheep, which graze throughout Modoc National Forest.

Nearby Campgrounds: Camp One consists of several primitive sites ensconced in a surrounding aspen grove. Lost Lake has primitive sites near the southeast shore. Developed campgrounds at Patterson (5 units) and Blue Lake (48 units) lie 5 and 15 miles, respectively, from the trailhead.

The County: Danish-born Peter Lassen (1800–1859) pioneered in the region. A peak, a college, a national forest, and a national park also honor his name, although historians dispute his fame, and his trail to California caused unnecessary hardship. The county's topography includes Cascade Range cinder cones and volcanoes in the west, Modoc Plateau volcanic uplands in the central area, and Basin and Range country in the east. The Diamond Mountains, west of Honey Lake, mark the northernmost extent of the Sierra Nevada. The Honey Lake Plain once held a major Ice Age lake. Today, the plain holds most of Lassen County's small population, centered in Susanville, the largest community in northeastern California. Lumbering and livestock raising generate income. Farmsteads and field crops dot the hinterland.

Sources of Additional Information/Recommended Reading:

Please refer to the Modoc County entry.

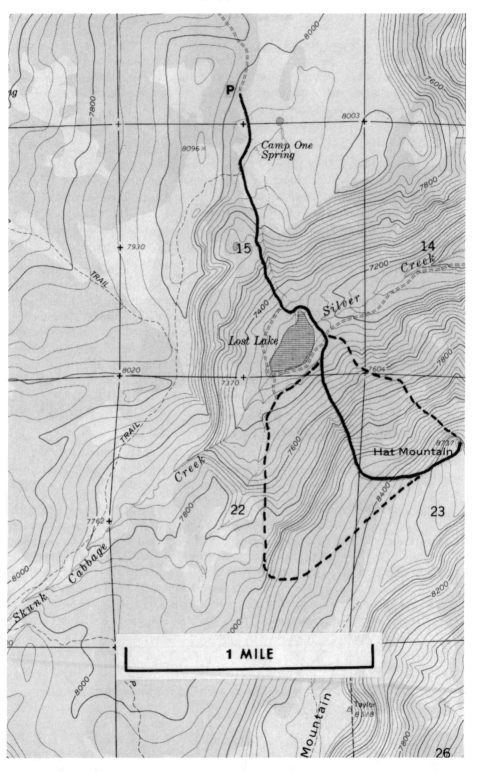

Los Angeles

Mount San Antonio   10,064′   **#13**

Location and Maps:	East edge of the county
	USGS 7½-minute *Mount San Antonio, Telegraph Peak;* USFS *Angeles National Forest*
Distance:	13 miles round trip/3900′ elevation gain
Grade:	Strenuous/Class 1
Hiking Time:	8 hours
Season:	May through October

Trailnotes: This massive peak tops the northeast rim of the Los Angeles Basin. Close to millions of Southlanders and easily accessible, San Antonio is probably climbed by more people than any other roadless mountain in western North America. Located in Angeles National Forest near a popular winter ski area. A ski lift near the trailhead operates on summer weekends and holidays from 9 A.M. to 4:30 P.M. The lift allows hikers to pare 3 miles and 1600 feet each way from the summit trek. A lodge at the top of the lift sells food and drinks. The described "Devil's Backbone" route is the most favored of several approaches to the peak. Early in the season be wary of ice along the dropoff parts of the trail. Dayhike or backpack. Bring garments to accommodate changeable weather. Pace yourself; the sudden shift from lowland to airy heights on this hike can take the wind out of you.

According to legend, padres from the Mission San Gabriel named the peak to honor Saint Anthony of Padua, Italy. Later settlers nicknamed the peak "Old Baldy" or "Mount Baldy" because the granite summit takes on a bare cast year-round, glistening silvery in summer, snow white in winter.

Approach: From I 10 in Claremont (35 miles east of downtown Los Angeles), take the Mountain Avenue/Mt. Baldy exit. Go north about 7 miles to a junction with Mt. Baldy Road. Follow it, steep and curvy, for 12 miles to a point just above Manker Flat Campground. Watch for a road on your left where a green and white street sign reads FALLS ROAD/BALDY ROAD. Park in the small dirt lot near the sign. If you choose to take the ski lift, continue 0.3 mile farther up Mt. Baldy Road to the facility's parking lot.

Directions to Summit: Walk around the vehicle barrier and up paved Falls Road to a viewpoint for seeing cascading San Antonio Falls. Here, the road makes a U-turn, becomes dirt, and then climbs at a moderate grade to the ski-lift lodge. (About ⅓ mile past the Falls, an unmarked path on the left leads to a Sierra Club ski hut, and from there continues as a rugged, unimproved trail to the summit, in about 4 arduous miles total.) From the lodge, go 200 yards on a broad dirt road to a desert overlook. Then turn left and head northwest up an ever-steepening chair-lift access road which ends at a trailhead with a sign-in register.

The trail begins by scaling a sharp ridge, the Devil's Backbone. Once harrowing before the Civilian Conservation Corps widened the tread and added hand rails in the 1930s (remnants remain), the dropoffs still raise adrenaline levels. Beyond the "Backbone," the trail curves gently around the south shoulder of Mount Harwood, dips slightly to a saddle, and then ascends a steep, rocky slope to the summit. An elevation plaque and several wind shelters deck the broad "bald" top—devoid of vegetation, except for diminutive alpine herbs and lichen.

The View: Great—air quality permitting. To the west, the San Gabriel Range melds with the Santa Monica Mountains, backed by a hazy blue band of ocean. The Mojave Desert sweeps to the north and northeast, along with the distant southern Sierra and Great Basin ranges. San Gorgonio Mountain stands out in the east, San Jacinto Peak in the southeast, and Santiago Peak in the southwest. Also in the southwest, the metropolis of Los Angeles blankets lowlands and foothills seemingly to no end.

The Environment: Positioned in the heart of the Transverse Range Province, the San Gabriel Mountains reach their climax at Mount San Antonio. The San Gabriels rise where crustal plates collide. The San Andreas Fault runs along the north and east base of the range, and many other fractures slice the mountains. Earthquake jolts result in slippage, compression, and uplift. These tectonic forces help sculpt the sheer slopes and squeeze the range upward an estimated tenth of an inch per year—mountain building in action. The mostly granitic range supports 12 species of conifers, including incense-cedar, Jeffrey pine, lodgepole pine, and limber pine seen along the trail. Some of these trees have weakened and died because air pollution inhibits photosynthesis. Prevailing winds push the lowland-generated smog pall right against the mountains on many days of the year.

Nearby Campgrounds: Manker Flat near the trailhead is the closest of more than 80 campgrounds in Angeles National Forest. The Forest Service allows backpackers to camp throughout the forest.

The County: California's most populous county. In the late 1700s, 44 Spanish pioneers founded the *Pueblo de Nuestra Senora la Reina de Los Angeles* (town of Our Lady the Queen of the Angels). Today, the largest and most populated city in the West (465 square miles and over 3,000,000 people) encompasses wall-to-wall communities connected by the most extensive freeway system in the world. In the last 20 years Los Angeles has become the nation's main "port of entry" for immigrants. The city thrives on diversified industries: oil, electronics, finance, tourism, and entertainment. Los Angeles filmmakers produce more than three fourths of all movies made in the United States.

Additional Sources of Information/Recommended Reading:

Angeles National Forest, Mt. Baldy District
110 N. Wabash Ave.
Glendora, CA 91740
(818) 335-1251

Mt. Baldy Information Station
(909) 982-2829.

Robinson, John W., *Trails of the Angeles,* 6th ed., Wilderness Press, 1990.
Schad, Jerry, *Afoot and Afield in Los Angeles County*, Wilderness Press, 1991.

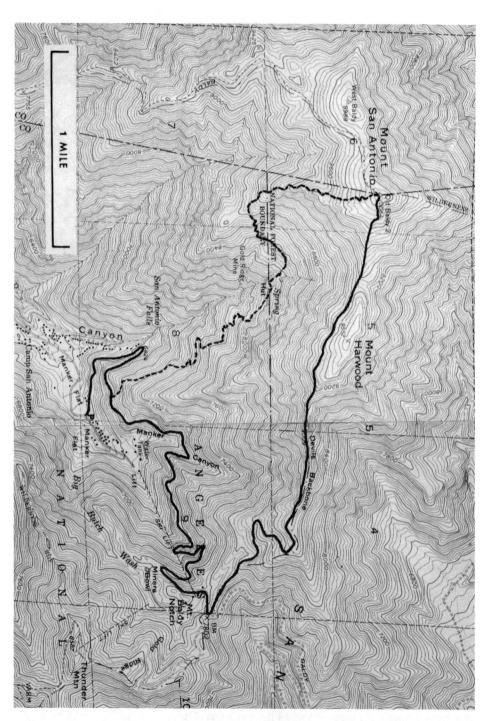

Los Angeles

Madera

Mount Ritter   13,143'   #5

Location and Maps:	East edge of the county
	USGS 7½-minute *Mt. Ritter, Mammoth*
	Mountain; USFS *Ansel Adams Wilderness*
Distance:	17 miles round trip/5300' elevation gain
Grade:	Strenuous/Class 3
Hiking Time:	14 hours
Season:	Mid-July to late September

Trailnotes: One of the grandest peaks in the High Sierra. Mount Ritter's steepness and size leave hikers agape. The mountain and its slightly lower twin, Banner Peak, tower above lovely Ediza Lake in the Ansel Adams (formerly Minarets) Wilderness. A delightful 6.2-mile trail from Agnew Meadows to Ediza Lake precedes a demanding cross-country trek to the peak. The cross-country leg gains 3800 feet in 2.3 miles. The described Southeast Glacier route proves the most accessible way to the summit and one of the least difficult. Two short Class 3 segments require you to climb a steep, bouldery slope and to scramble up a slanting chute strewn with loose rock. Climbers use an ice axe in the chute during times of heavy snow.

Well-conditioned hikers with a pre-dawn start can climb Mount Ritter as a long dayhike from Agnew Meadows. Backpackers stay overnight at Ediza Lake or at a site along the trail before the climb. Overnight trips require a wilderness permit. A quota system regulates trail use from the last Friday in June to September 15. The Mammoth Lakes Ranger Station apportions half the daily quota (around 15 permits) on a first-come, first-served basis, beginning at 6:00 A.M. on the day of entry. The Forest Service accepts permit reservations by mail, with postmarks between March 1 and May 31 only. You may pick up confirmed permits 24 hours in advance of the entry date. For convenience, rangers place next-day permits in a night box near the front door of the Mammoth Lakes Ranger Station. Outside the quota period, simply fill out a self-issue permit at the ranger station. A mandatory shuttle bus operates on the approach road during the summer months, from 7:30 A.M. to 5:30 P.M. Hikers who want to leave a vehicle at the trailhead must pass the Minaret Summit entrance kiosk before 7:30 A.M. or after 5:30 P.M. Wilderness permits do not entitle hikers to drive to the trailhead during the hours of shuttle operation.

The Whitney Survey named the mountain in 1864 to honor Karl Ritter (1779–1859), a noted German geographer, who helped define the modern science of geography. John Muir made the first ascent in a thrilling climb in 1872.

Approach: Take the Mammoth Lakes exit (SR 203) off U.S. 395, 37 miles north of Bishop and 25 miles south of Lee Vining. After 2.5 miles you come to Mammoth Lakes Ranger Station and Visitors Center. Continue on SR 203, which turns right at mile 4.0, passes the Minaret Summit entrance kiosk at mile 9.0, and arrives at a turnoff to Agnew Meadows Campground at mile 12.5. Bear right onto the dirt road and proceed to the large "overflow" parking lot, 0.3 mile from the turnoff.

Directions to Summit: The trail begins south of the Information Board, water faucet, and restrooms. Skirt the south side of Agnew Meadows and pass trail forks in a 350-foot descent to the Middle Fork San Joaquin River floor. Beyond Olaine Lake cross a bridge and switchback up the canyonside to Shadow Lake. Keep right at a John Muir Trail junction and bridge at the west end of the lake. Keep left at another junction about a mile farther up the trail. The trail parallels a creek and crosses a wobbly log-bridge before surmounting a rocky rise near the outlet of Ediza Lake.

Step on stones at the outlet and hop across the boulder field above the north shore of Ediza Lake. Follow a footpath past campsites beside the west lakeshore and then head west, up-canyon. A good use trail threads between a granite outcrop on the left and a creek on the right. The path crosses a creeklet, climbs through thinning trees, and tops grassy terraces to arrive at a rocky tarn basin, directly below Mount Ritter and Banner Peak.

In the tarn basin, cross the outlet and strike off to the southwest, up the very steep-sided rocky slope. Aim for the shelf beneath a prominent peaklet east of the largest glacier. (This glacier lies tucked in an amphitheater out of sight from below.) From the shelf, head west over easier slabs and rocks, skirting the foot of the glacier to reach a steeply inclined chute on the right. Early in the season, snow covers the scree-laden chute, making an ice axe necessary. Ascend the chute, which tops out at a saddle on the south flank of Mount Ritter. Scale talus blocks to the summit. The highpoint is on the left (west) end of the airy perch, where a register placed by the California Alpine Club can be found in the rocks.

The View: Staggering. The mountain falls off precipitously, leaving a deep ocean of air at your feet. A dozen lakes gleam below. To the northeast, Banner Peak hovers close by. Farther away lie San Joaquin Mountain, Carson Peak, Mono Lake, and the vapory desert. To the north, innumerable peaks line the horizon, with Mount Lyell, Mount Dana, Mount Gibbs, and Mount Lewis arrayed at mid-distance. In the west, upswelling ridges and domes fade into forested slopes that descend toward the San Joaquin Valley. In the south, peak beyond peak extends down the Sierra crest. And close in the southeast, the Minarets pierce the sky, backed by Mammoth Mountain, Owens Valley, and the White Mountains far away.

The Environment: In the vicinity of Mammoth, the Sierra Nevada's main crest sags to around 9000 feet, giving prominence to the Ritter subrange to the west. The principal peaks—Ritter, Banner, and the Minarets—stand out for miles around. Mount Ritter's dark, metamorphosed rock was the core of an ancient mountain formed over a hundred million years *before* the present Sierra Nevada evolved. The erosion-resistant rock contains vertical joint planes, and weathering of the joints creates almost vertical faces, needle-sharp ridges, and dangerous rockfalls. The region's alpine peaks and glaciers and the sparkling lakes and creeks draw visitors aplenty. During the backpack boom of the 1970s hundreds of people at a time camped tent-to-tent around Shadow Lake, degrading the environment. Overcrowding led the Forest Service to restrict camping there and to confine it to the west shore at Ediza Lake. These measures, and the wilderness-permit system, restored serenity to one of the Sierra's most beautiful settings.

Nearby Campgrounds: A handout available from the Mammoth Lakes Ranger Station lists the area's numerous campgrounds, open on a first-come, first-served basis. The campground at Agnew Meadows and several others farther down offer close trailhead access. Passes dispensed at the Minaret Summit kiosk let drive-in campers use the road, otherwise restricted to shuttlebus traffic in summer. A campground located behind the Mammoth Lakes Ranger Station accommodates backpackers arriving the night before their wilderness permit entry date.

The County: The geographic center of California lies in Madera County, about 35 miles northeast of Madera, the county seat and main town. *Madera* means "timber" in Spanish, the town so named when a lumber company built a flume to carry lumber to the settlement's railroad in 1876. Located in the flat Central Valley, Madera now serves as a processing center for surrounding agribusiness. Major products include cattle, poultry, grapes, figs, and pistachios. Recreational activities prevail in the mountainous eastern part of the county, as at Bass Lake and Devils Postpile National Monument. The monument preserves fascinating basalt lava columns along with Rainbow Falls, where water plunges over a 101-foot high volcanic cliff, creating iridescent mist.

Additional Sources of Information/Recommended Reading:

Mammoth Lakes Ranger District
P.O. Box 148
Mammoth Lakes, CA 93546
(619) 924-5500

Felzer, Ron, *Devils Postpile,* 5th ed., Wilderness Press, 1990.
Rinehart, Dean, Elden Vestal, and Bettie E. Willard, *Mammoth Lakes Sierra, A Handbook for Road and Trail,* 5th ed., Genny Smith Books, 1989.

Mt. Ritter, Banner Peak

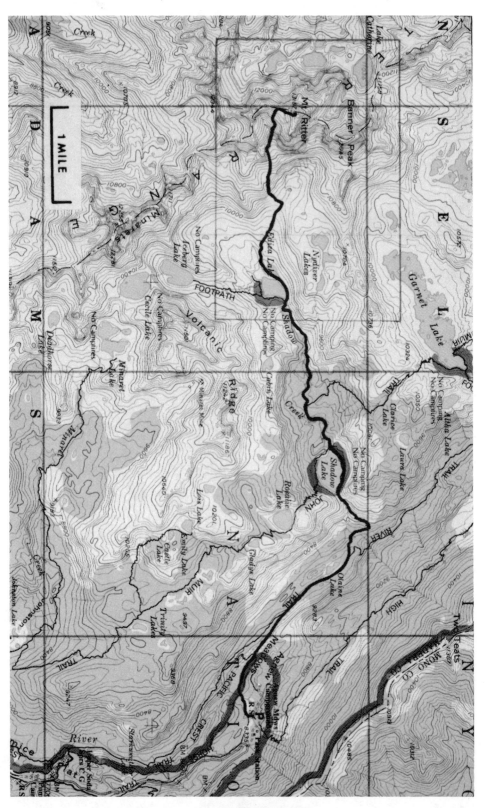

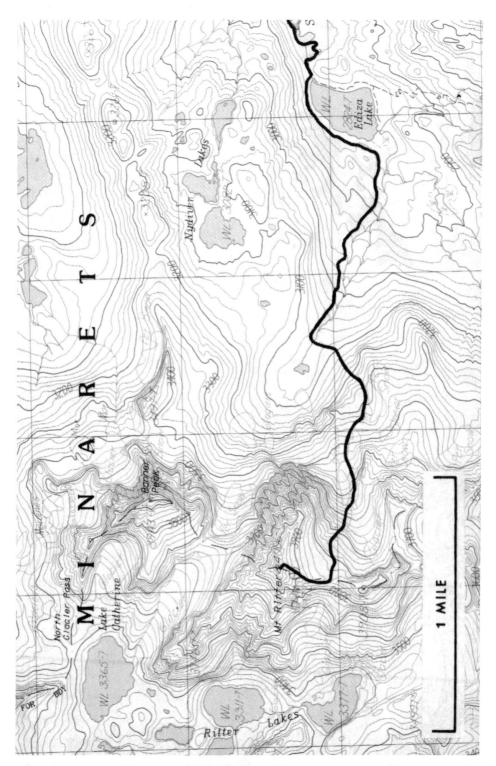

MINARETS

North
Glacier Pass

Lake
Catherine

Banner
Peak

Mt Ritter

WL 3365·7

WL
331·1

WL
337·1

Ritter   Lakes

Nydiver
Lakes

2321
Ediza
Lake

1 MILE

Madera (2 of 2)

Marin

Mount Tamalpais   2571′   **#53**

Location and Maps:	South-central part of the county
	USGS 7½-minute *San Rafael;* Mount Tamalpais State Park Brochure Map; Erickson *Mt. Tamalpais Trail Map;* Olmsted Bros. *Rambler's Guide to the Trails of Mt. Tamalpais and the Marin Headlands*
Distance:	3.8 miles round trip/1700′ elevation gain
Grade:	Moderate/Class 1
Hiking Time:	2 hours
Season:	Year-round, especially nice from January to June

Trailnotes: One of California's best-known and best-loved highpoints, renowned for its magnificent views, varied landscapes, diverse flora, and extensive trail network. Trails in Mount Tamalpais State Park and adjoining Muir Woods National Monument connect with paths in Marin Municipal Water District lands (open to the public) and the adjacent Golden Gate National Recreation Area to create a hiker's paradise. The described route to East Peak is one of many ways to gain the summit. Visitors can also drive to the top via the Panoramic Highway and Ridgecrest Boulevard. There is no day use fee but several parking lots have meters. Day use extends from ½ hour before sunrise to ½ hour after sunset. No pets allowed. The name "Tamalpais" is thought to come from the Miwok Indian language, perhaps influenced by Spanish, and has been variously interpreted to mean "country of the Tamal Indians," "coast mountain," and "bay country mountain." Indeed, it's the only major peak to overlook San Francisco Bay. Mount Tamalpais rises from sea level, practically without foothills, a landmark visible to literally millions of people throughout the region.

Approach: From Highway 101 take the Stinson Beach/Mill Valley Highway 1 exit, approximately 6 miles north of the Golden Gate Bridge and 6 miles south of San Rafael. Proceed on Highway 1 for a winding 3 miles to a junction with Panoramic Highway. Bear right and continue up Panoramic Highway 2.5 miles to Mountain Home Inn. Park in a lot on the left side of the road.

Directions to Summit: From the parking lot cross the Panoramic Highway and head north above Mountain Home (an expensive restaurant and hotel). Walk past a fire station, gate, and water tank along a fireroad flanked by chaparral. In about 0.3 mile you will see water tanks and signs pointing to the Matt Davis Trail and the Nora Trail, followed later by the Hoo-koo-e-koo Trail crossing, and then a junction with the Old Railroad Grade at 0.6 mile. Go left at the junction and continue for about 0.3 mile to the East Fork of Fern Creek. Watch for a marker announcing "Fern Creek to East Peak" and strike off to your right on the Fern Creek Trail. Now begins a 0.7-mile uphill trek. It's steep in places, but Fern Creek's lovely cascades and a shady overstory of bay, madrone, redwood, and Douglas-fir ease your exertion. (For a longer—by 2 miles—more gradual ascent, bypass the Fern Creek Trail and continue to follow the Old Railroad Grade, curving around the West Point Inn, where refreshments are available, and on up to the summit. Return by way of the Fern Creek Trail). After passing an old wooden water tank, the trail veers from the creek, cuts across slopes covered by sun-bright chaparral, and gains altitude rapidly until it tops out at a road and a parking lot below the summit. Amble northeast across the parking lot past a small visitors center (open on weekends), drinking fountain, and restrooms, and take the rocky-stepped Plankwalk Trail 0.3 mile to the highpoint. A benchmark inscribed EAST PEAK can be found among the boulders just northwest of the handsome Gardner lookout. The lookout has stonework walls and a rich brown wood observation deck.

The View: According to seasoned travelers, the view from "Mt. Tam" (as it is familiarly known) is one of the finest on earth. The peak often stands above fogs that obscure the lowlands and the lower slopes of the mountain. Hikers ascend through grey condensation to look down upon a celestial sea of bright white cloud tops. Piercing them are the Marin Headlands and the topmost parts of the Golden Gate Bridge, while the skyscrapers of San Francisco shine from across the bay. The City itself looks small against a backdrop of the distant Diablo Range, Mount Hamilton, and the Santa Cruz Mountains in the south. The Farallon Islands, 25 miles out to sea, appear as specks on the vast Pacific horizon. Bon Tempe and Lagunitas lakes nestle in the hills immediately below to the north, and beyond them stretches a procession of North Coast Ranges, accented by Mount St. Helena. To the east are arms of San Francisco Bay, the Oakland-Berkeley Hills, Mount Diablo, the Sacramento River delta, and finally the Sierra Nevada.

A cluster of radar installations, some looking like colossal white golf balls, mars West Peak, which once stood as the highest point at 2604 feet. During World War II and afterward, the military built facilities there and bulldozed the top of the peak in the process. Several contemporary maps still cite this obliterated "ghost" summit as the highpoint.

The Environment: From some Bay Area vantage points, Mount Tamalpais displays a conical profile that leads casual observers to think it's volcanic in origin. But geologists say the mountain was created from varied rocks and sediments that were mashed and metamorphosed over ages as the North American Plate overrode the Pacific Plate, and then were buckled, folded, faulted, uplifted and eroded to the present configuration. This jumble of rocks includes chert, sandstone, shale, serpentine, and (on East Peak) erosion-resistant quartz-tourmaline.

Mt. Tam rises high enough to squeeze extra moisture from incoming rain clouds, increasing precipitation on its west slopes and replenishing its many seasonal creeks, waterfalls, and springs. The mountain's height and bulk create a rain shadow on its east side, an area usually free of the sea fog that often shrouds the peak's west slopes. Varying precipitation, topography, and soils produce an array of plant communities—grassland, chaparral, oak and bay, and redwood–Douglas-fir, all brightened by seasonal wildflowers. The State Park lists an impressive 768 species of plants, 150 kinds of birds, as well as raccoons, squirrels, grey fox, bobcats, blacktail deer, and many other life forms. Muir Woods, tucked in a canyon on the south slope of the mountain, preserves the area's only stand of virgin coastal redwoods. Over one million visitors a year behold these awe-inspiring trees. This most accessible of California's redwood groves has been seen by more people than any other redwood grove in the world.

Nearby Campgrounds: Mount Tamalpais State Park has 16 walk-in campsites near the Pan Toll Ranger Station (first-come, first-served). Golden Gate National Recreation Area, termed "the grandest metropolitan parkland in the country," offers thousands of acres to explore and a number of backcountry campsites, as does Point Reyes National Seashore. Samuel P. Taylor State Park and China Camp State Park have family campgrounds.

The County: "It stands in Marin County, or rather, it is Marin County; for take away Tamalpais and what is left hardly fills a wheelbarrow." So wrote a journalist, with a snip of exaggeration. Although Mt. Tam crowns the county, an extensive maze of headlands, rolling hills, rugged low mountains, and steep canyons characterizes the Marin Peninsula, except along level coastal margins, where embayments scallop the shore. Marin may be named after a bay abbreviated from the 18th Century Spanish *Bahia del Nuestra Senora del Rosario La Marinera,* or it may be a corruption of *El Marinero* (the Mariner), the Christianized name of a local Indian and skilled navigator who ferried Spaniards across San Francisco Bay. The county's natural beauty and its proximity to San Francisco have long attracted affluent business and professional people to such exclusive residential communities as Fairfax, Ross, and Kentfield. Marin is the state's richest county in median family income. Thanks to the indefatigable efforts of Bay Area conservationists, over decades, more than 40% of the county stands protected in federal, state, city, and community parklands.

Additional Sources of Information/Recommended Reading:

Mount Tamalpais State Park
801 Panoramic Highway
Mill Valley, CA 94941

Pan Toll Ranger Station Headquarters
(415) 388-2070

Marin Parks
(415) 456-1286

Marin Municipal Water District
220 Nellen Avenue
Corte Madera, CA 94925
(415) 924-4600
For information on north-side
access to Mount Tamalpais

Hart, John, *San Francisco's Wilderness Next Door,* Presidio Press, 1979.
Martin, Don and Kay, *Mt. Tam: A Hiking, Running, and Nature Guide,* Martin Press, 1986.

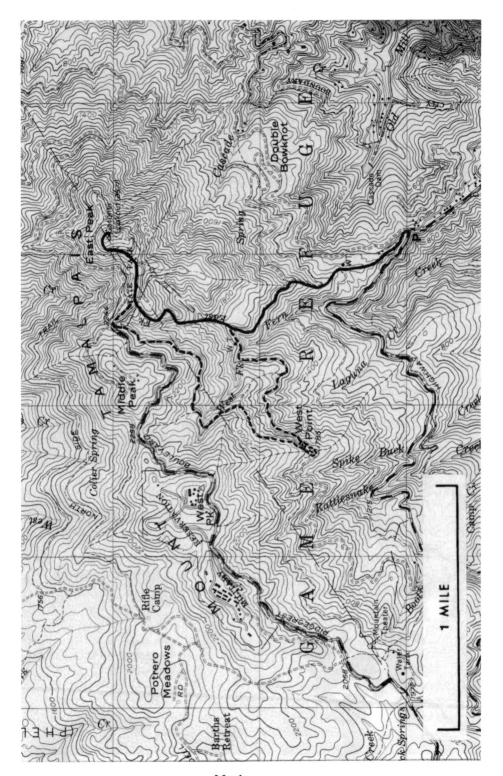

Marin

Mariposa

Parsons Peak Ridge   12,040+′   #7

Location and Maps: East edge of the county
USGS 7½-minute *Vogelsang Peak;* Wilderness
Press *Yosemite National Park and Vicinity*

Distance: 27 miles round trip/3500′ elevation gain

Grade: Strenuous/Class 2

Hiking Time: 16 hours

Season: Mid-July to late September

Trailnotes: Parsons Peak rises in the Cathedral Range of Yosemite National Park. The peak forms a hulking backdrop to Ireland Lake, a stark sheet of water on a grassy shelf 2000 feet above Tuolumne Meadows. You follow a good trail for about 11 miles to the lake and then climb cross-country 2.5 miles to the peak on your way to the county highpoint. A lengthy dayhike or a backpack. From a base camp in Lyell Canyon, you can access both Parsons Peak and Mount Lyell, the highest point in Tuolumne County. The summits lie just 3 air miles apart and share the same approach partway. Turn to Tuolumne County for all entries except those below.

Edward Taylor Parsons (1861–1914), an early director of the Sierra Club, worked closely with John Muir to protect the mountains they loved. His wife and fellow Club activist Marion Randall Parsons made the first ascent, sometime before 1931.

Directions to Summit: For the initial leg of the hike, read the first paragraph of Tuolumne County's **Directions to Summit**. From the trail fork 5.8 miles out, take the signed trail to Ireland Lake, 5.6 miles ahead. Climb on a moderately steep path shaded by lodgepole pines and serenaded by Ireland Creek. The trail curves away from the creek and the gradient lessens before you reach a junction signed IRELAND LAKE 3. A gently sloped path takes you past scattered whitebark pines and bunchgrass to an expansive meadow above timberline. From a rise overlooking Ireland Lake, leave the trail and cut southeast over spongy grasses to reach the lake's outlet. Step over stones at the outlet and head south, climbing boulders, slabs, and scree to the saddle just south of Parsons Peak. From the saddle scale the steep, boulder-strewn south slope of the peak to gain the summit. A small cairn fixes the highest point on Parsons Peak, but not the Mariposa County highpoint. From the apex, walk northwest down the gently sloping ridgeline. Go about 300 yards, crossing an invisible, indefinite county boundary line to reach the uppermost point in Mariposa County. At times, county-summit seekers must live with imprecision!

The View: Splendorous. Looking west, Yosemite Valley, Half Dome, and the

adjacent uplands appear in a unique aerial perspective. Vogelsang High Sierra
Camp, Vogelsang Peak, and many lakes lie directly below you. Mount Florence
rises prominently in the south. Mount Lyell and Mount Maclure peek above
Simmons Peak in the southeast. Amelia Earhart Peak lies directly east of Ireland
Lake. Lyell Canyon curves into Tuolumne Meadows in the north. Farther north, a
host of high peaks pack the skyline in nearby Hoover Wilderness.

The County: Mariposa County takes its name from Mariposa Creek, so named
by Spanish explorers because they found butterflies (*las mariposas*) flitting
everywhere along the stream. The county originally extended from the Coast
Ranges to Nevada, covering one fifth of the state. Later, politicians whittled away
at Mariposa to form 10 additional counties. Today Mariposa takes in a cross section
of the Sierra Nevada—foothills to the west, high peaks to the east, and one of the
world's most spectacular valleys, Yosemite. Lumbering, livestock raising, and
tourism anchor the economy. Mountain towns contain most of the small population, led by Coulterville and Mariposa. Mariposa has the state's oldest courthouse,
in continuous use since 1854, and also the California State Mineral and Mining
Museum. The museum displays a fortune in precious metals and gems, including
diamonds from Butte County, jade from Monterey County, and glimmering
nuggets of gold from the Mother Lode.

Parsons Peak from trail to Ireland Lake

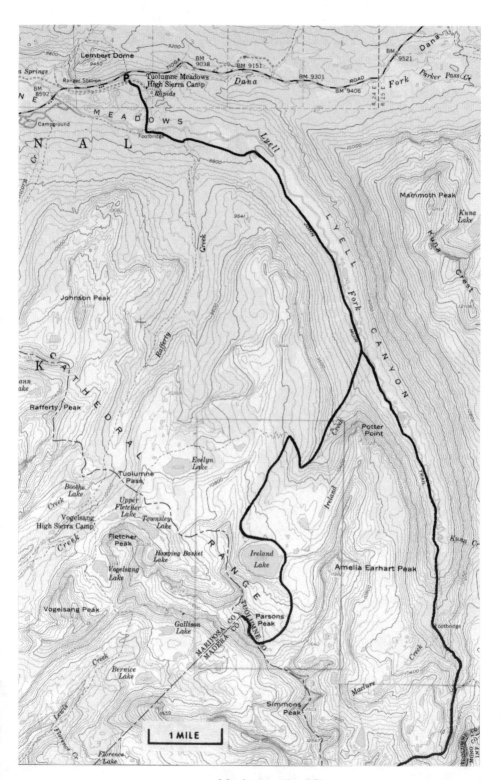

Mariposa (1 of 2)

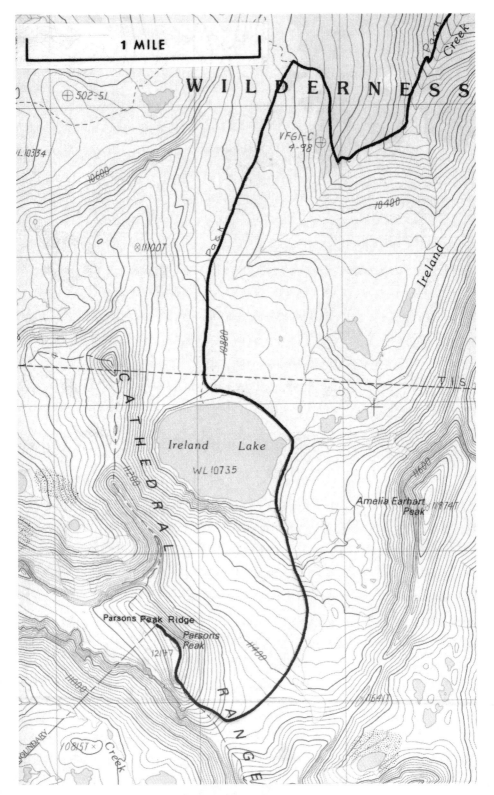

1 MILE

WILDERNESS

Rock Creek

502-51

VFGI-C
4-98

VL 10334

10600

10400

Ireland

110007

10800

C A T H E D R A L

T. 1. S.

Ireland Lake

WL 10735

11400

Amelia Earhart Peak   110747

11600

Parsons Peak Ridge
Parsons Peak
12147

R A N G E

11400

11400

10641

BOUNDARY

10815T ×   Creek

Mariposa (2 of 2)

Mendocino

Anthony Peak   6954′   **#30**

Location and Maps:	Northeast corner of the county
	USGS 7½-minute *Mendocino Pass;* USFS Brochure Map *Meet the Mendocino National Forest;* USFS *Mendocino National Forest*
Distance:	2.5 miles round trip/620′ elevation gain
Grade:	Easy/Class 1
Hiking Time:	1 hour
Season:	Late May to October

Trailnotes: Removed yet readily accessible, Anthony Peak lies in the northern part of Mendocino National Forest, close by Black Butte, the apex of Glenn County. The trip entails a long drive over dusty but well-maintained dirt and gravel roads that close in winter. A Forest Service campground near Anthony Peak makes a convenient overnight stop. Hikers walk up a dirt road (open to vehicles) to a summit lookout. In the 1880s, the Anthony brothers (James, Jess, and George) bought a homestead in the vicinity and grazed sheep on a broad ridge west of the peak.

Approach: From I 5 take the SR 162 exit, approximately 95 miles north of Sacramento and 45 miles south of Red Bluff. Go 21 miles west on SR 162 to a junction with Road 306 (0.5 mile north of Elk Creek). Turn right and continue 3.5 miles, then turn left on Alder Springs Road (FH 7). The pavement ends after 15 miles. Roll up your windows to avoid the dust of oncoming vehicles. Watch for ruts, cattle, and logging trucks. Continue on FH 7, passing the turnoff to Black Butte on your left just after milepost 16, 32 miles from SR 162. (For Black Butte turn left where a sign reads BLACK BUTTE SUMMIT TRAIL SCENIC VIEW. Follow the dirt/asphalt road 0.9 mile to a turn-around loop, and park). From the Black Butte turnoff, continue another 6.5 miles to Mendocino Pass. From the pass drive north on road M4 about 3 miles to the Wells Cabin Campground. Park alongside the road near the entrance to the campground.

From U.S. 101, take SR 162 at the Longvale turnoff, about 90 miles north of Santa Rosa and 120 miles south of Eureka. This scenic road meanders alongside the Eel River and then drops down into Round Valley and the little town of Covelo, 28 miles from Longvale. Proceed through Covelo, and after 1.5 miles turn right at Mendocino Pass Road (FH 7), and climb a steepening grade to Mendocino Pass, 24 miles away (the pavement ends 13 miles outside of Covelo). At the pass turn left (north) onto Road M4 and progress to Wells Cabin Campground. (For Black Butte, bear right at the pass, and proceed 6.5 miles to the aforementioned Black Butte turnoff.)

Directions to Summit: From the campground area walk up the signed lookout road. This moderately inclined road trends north and then west through scattered conifers and chaparral, doubles back, and shortly reaches the level summit. Pass a solitary wooden outhouse, a solar antenna unit, and a sign announcing ANTHONY PEAK ELEVATION 6954 on your way to the weathered, whitewashed lookout. A benchmark lies fixed in a cement slab at the south foot on the structure.

The View: In the west Anthony Ridge slopes gently down toward Round Valley, the largest piece of flat land in Mendocino County. Beyond Round Valley, a succession of densely forested North Coast Ranges reaches to the sea. On very clear days the Pacific Ocean can be seen. The West Fork of the Eel River flows through a deep canyon in the northwest. In the north, mountains in the Yolla Bolly Wilderness top 8000 feet, and you may see Mount Shasta in the distance. In the east, the Sacramento Valley, Lassen Peak, and the Sierra Nevada compose the horizon, and Black Butte rises in the southeast. Anthony Peak has had a fire lookout on its summit since the early 1930s; budget permitting, Forest Service personnel are in the tower from June through mid-October.

The Environment: Anthony Peak stands higher than many surrounding North Coast Range summits. Pacific storms blow in from the ocean just 45 miles away, strike the mountain barrier, and relinquish 40–70 inches of precipitation per year. Anthony Peak perches on the crest of the range so its west-side runoff enters the Middle Fork Eel drainage and ends up in the ocean near Eureka, while its east-side runoff flows down the Sacramento River to San Francisco Bay. Frequent winter snowfall makes snowmobiling popular around the peak and Mendocino Pass. Ample moisture supports healthy stands of Douglas-fir, red fir, and various species of pine, as well as oak woodlands at lower elevations, and chaparral on exposed slopes. Brewer oak, the dominant shrub in the brush field on Anthony Peak, is a dwarf variety of Oregon white oak. Lupine, sulfur flower, pussy paws, and many other wildflowers embellish the mountain in early summer. Small glaciers sculpted the region's highest peaks as in the North Yolla Bolly Mountains. The range is composed of Franciscan-formation rocks like schist, chert, and serpentine. Graywacke predominates around Anthony Peak. This sandstone rock contains quartz and feldspar particles in a clay matrix and often has a salt-and-pepper-like appearance.

Nearby Campgrounds: Below Anthony Peak the Wells Cabin Campground provides 25 campsites. Other nearby campgrounds include Eel River, with 16 sites west of Mendocino Pass, and Plaskett Lake, with 32 sites east of the pass. These campgrounds and several smaller ones are available on a first-come, first-served basis. Dispersed camping is permitted in most parts of Mendocino National Forest. The neighboring Yolla Bolly-Middle Eel Wilderness contains 175,000 acres of rugged mountains, verdant forests, brushlands, meadows, and seasonal creeks. Trails are faint and solitude plentiful in these remote wildlands.

The County: Rocky promontories, sand dunes, and marine terraces give way to a mountainous interior etched by small valleys and drained by countless creeks. Larger watercourses, such as the Eel and Russian rivers, are subject to periodic flooding. Forests of redwood and Douglas-fir cloak the coastal mountains. Oak woodlands and mixed coniferous forests prevail farther inland. Cape Mendocino, presumably named for a Spanish viceroy called Mendoza, gave Mendocino County its name, although the cape is located north of the present county boundary. When founded in 1850, the county had a population of 55 people. Settlers began pouring in when the Gold Rush and a construction boom in San Francisco triggered a "lumber rush" in the county. By 1900 lumber mills dotted most every river and navigable cove. Today the lumber and wood-products industry still employs almost a quarter of the county's work force. Commercial and sport fishing, the second major industry, centers in Fort Bragg. Agricultural crops including oats, pears, and wine grapes bolster the economy, as does tourism. The coastal villages of Mendocino, Albion, and Point Arena, and towns along U.S. Highway 101 like Ukiah, Hopland, and Willits possess historical and scenic appeal.

Additional Sources of Information/Recommended Reading:

Mendocino National Forest
420 E. Laurel Street
Willows, CA 95988
(916) 934-3316

Covelo Ranger District
78150 Covelo Road
Covelo, CA 95428
(707) 983-6118

For a 24-hour recorded message
covering road conditions,
recreation, and fire information
dial (916) 934-2350

Lorentzen, Bob, *The Hiker's Hip Pocket Guide to the Mendocino Highlands,* Bored Feet Publications, 1992.
Newcombe, Jack, *Northern California, A History and Guide,* Random House, 1986.

At the summit

Mendocino

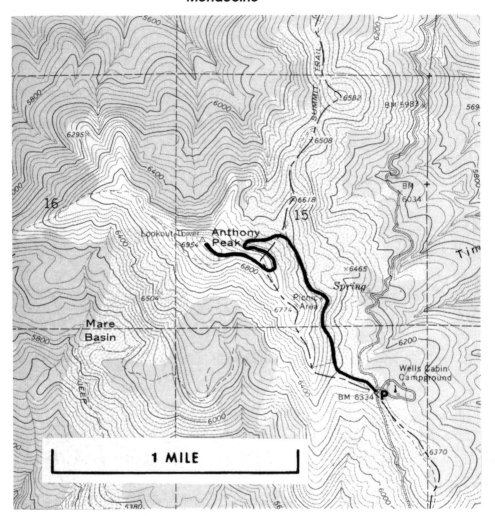

Merced

Laveaga Peak   3801′   **#46**

Location and Maps: West edge of the county
USGS 7½-minute *Mariposa Peak, Quien Sabe Valley*

Private Highpoint Notes: Look west from I 5 near the SR 152 exit to see
Laveaga Peak, the highest point on the distant rugged ridgeline. Located in the
heart of the Diablo Range, isolated and little known Laveaga Peak exhibits striking
volcanic terrain and a relatively pristine character. But few eyes can behold the
beauty close up. Well-fenced cattle ranches surround the peak, and requests to
cross private property en route to the peak almost always meet with refusal.

On the east side of the peak, unpaved Billy Wright Road allows closer views
until a gate blocks progress. On the west side of the peak, two paved county arteries,
Lone Pine Road and Quien Sabe Road, come to within 5 air miles of the highpoint
before gates bar the way. (Foreground mountains obstruct views of the peak from
the west.) If hiking were allowed, the route would follow ranch roads to the flanks
of the peak, and then traverse cross-country to the ridgecrest.

Geologists describe volcanic flows, dikes, plugs, and agglomerates in the area.
Vertical columns of erosion-resistant igneous rock overtop gentler mountain slopes
of weathering sedimentary strata. Laveaga's summit overlooks the magnificent,
secluded Quien Sabe Valley. Jose Vincente de Laveaga emigrated from Spain and
bought the Quien Sabe Ranch in the 1870s. His descendants built a 35-room
ranchhouse with 20-foot-high ceilings, 6 bedrooms, recreation rooms, a chapel, a
banquet room, a gun room, an indoor swimming pool, and a tiled belltower. In 1977
the family sold the ranch for $7 million. The new owner purchased adjacent smaller
ranches to amass a 110,000-acre spread, one of the largest in California, which is
laced with more fencing and cross fencing than any other ranch in the state. Over
the years, the San Benito Cattle Company property has become increasingly private.
According to Marjorie Pierce, in her regional work *East of the Gavilans,* even
requests from motion-picture companies to film western scenes on the ranch have
been denied. Perhaps someday a more hospitable policy will prevail. *¿Quién sabe?*

The County: The county's name derives from the Merced River, *El Rio de
Nuestra Senora de la Merced* (river of our lady of mercy), so called by Spanish
explorer Gabriel Moraga in 1806. The county stretches across the San Joaquin
Valley, bordered by the Diablo Range on the west and the Sierra Nevada foothills
on the east. Numerous irrigation canals crisscross the area, bringing water from the
San Joaquin and other rivers to dairies, livestock ranches, and farms. Major crops
include alfalfa, almonds, tomatoes, and sweet potatoes. Merced, the county's
major town, serves as a gateway to Yosemite. Boaters and fishermen enjoy sizable
San Luis Reservoir, located beside scenic Pacheco Pass. The reservoir is a key
storage facility of the California Water Plan, a giant dam-and-aqueduct system
built to carry "surplus" Northern California water to points south.

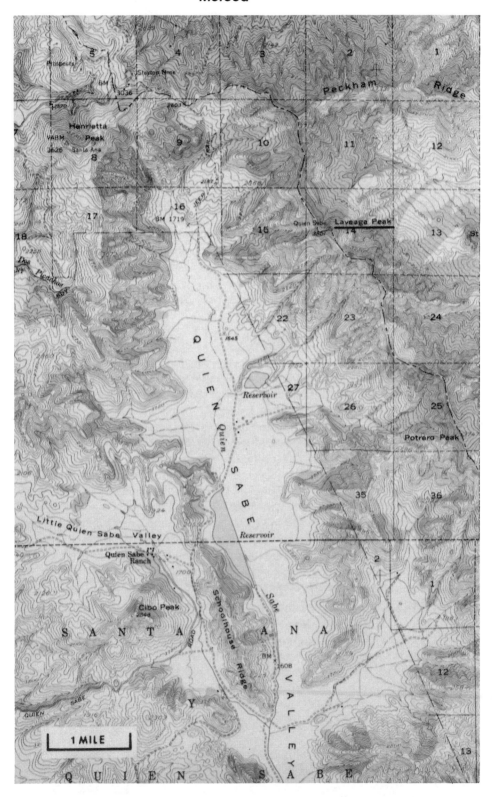

Modoc

Eagle Peak   9892′   **#14**

Location and Maps:	Southeast corner of the county
	USGS 7½-minute *Eagle Peak, Soup Creek;* USFS *South Warner Wilderness;* USFS *Modoc National Forest*
Distance:	16 miles round trip/4200′ elevation gain
Grade:	Strenuous/Class 2
Hiking Time:	9 hours
Season:	July to September

Trailnotes: A remote highpoint, located in South Warner Wilderness, the "Hidden Treasure" of California wildernesses. Snowcapped peaks, mountain meadows, aspen groves, and real solitude prevail. Highpointers usually spend two or more days in the area to climb both Eagle Peak and nearby Hat Mountain, the Lassen County summit. No wilderness permit required. Secure campfire permits in advance by mail from the ranger station. Dayhike or backpack. The described route, one of several approaches to the peak, offers the only paved-road access to the wilderness boundary. At road's end are a nice developed campground and an adjacent falls and lake. You follow a good trail for three quarters of the hike, and then go cross-country to the summit. Expect warm days and cool nights in July and August; rain or snow can fall during any month of the year. Bald eagles rarely visit the area, but golden eagles regularly wheel in the sky and probably inspired the peak's name.

Approach: From U.S. 395 in Likely (19 miles south of Alturas, 162 miles north of Reno, and 161 miles east of I 5 in Redding) turn east onto Jess Valley Road. Drive 9 miles down it to a junction. Turn left, go 3 miles, and then turn right at an intersection and proceed another 1.7 miles to the Mill Creek Falls Campground. The trail begins at the far (east) end of the campground.

Directions to Summit: Take the Poison Flat Trail, which begins to the left of an information board. The forest-canopied trail shortly passes a spur on the left to Mill Creek Falls, a two-minute jaunt to a tumbling cascade. In 0.5 mile you merge with a Clear Lake loop trail and skirt the south shore of Clear Lake (great for a dip on your return). About 1.0 mile from the start, your trail veers right (south) from the Clear Lake loop and switchbacks up a hillside. Atop the hillside, a leisurely stretch breaks out onto a meadow and a junction with the Mill Creek Trail, 2.6 miles from the trailhead. Proceed straight ahead (east) across the meadow and past a burned area and aspen groves to an intersection with the East Creek Trail. Go left (north) and climb for a mile at a moderate grade, through an open forest decked with sagebrush and mule ears, to reach the Summit Trail junction, on the southwest flank of Eagle Peak.

You may leave the trail at this junction and bushwack straight ahead (north) up moderately steep slopes. The brush thins out as you ascend. Follow the ridgeline as it bends northeast and wend your way through a whitebark-pine forest to the top. Alternatively, you may continue east on the Summit Trail 0.5 mile to where the trail crosses a creekbed. Walk up the stream channel for about 0.3 mile and choose your route up ever-steepening slopes to the ridgetop. Go northwest to tramp through brush, grass, and scattered clumps of trees. Go north or northeast to encounter less brush, but be prepared for very steep, gravely slopes. All routes end up on an elongated summit shelf, a little under 2 miles from the Summit Trail junction. A small cairn holds several register containers, including a big pickle jar with matches and pennies.

The View: Immediately east of the summit platform, a rocky palisade and slanting slopes decline toward irrigated fields and alkali lake beds in Surprise Valley, over 5000 feet below. The Black Rock Desert in Nevada sprawls in the distance. Triangular Hat Mountain stands out in the south. Lassen Peak dwells behind lakes and valleys in the southwest. The Modoc Plateau spreads in the west, Mount Shasta rises in the northwest, and the backbone of the Warner Range extends to the north, topped by 9710-foot Warren Peak.

The Environment: The Warner Mountains form a tilted fault block some 90 miles long and 15 miles wide. Sedimentary beds, about 35 million years old, outcrop along the steep east escarpment. Younger volcanic lava and ashflows overlie the sedimentary rock. This double composition leads geologists to label the Warners both a Great Basin Range and a spur of the Cascade Range. Small glacial lakes and cirques fleck the high country. The 70,385-acre wilderness has an unusual vegetation mix. Sagebrush flourishes from the foothills to the highest peaks. Pinyon and juniper grow on lower slopes, replaced by aspen and white fir, as well as Jeffrey, ponderosa, lodgepole, and whitebark pine at higher elevations. Abundant wildflowers like lupine, owls clover, paintbrush, and salsify adorn the meadows. Prairie falcon, goshawk, northern harrier, osprey, and many other species share the sky with Eagle Peak's namesake.

Nearby Campgrounds: In addition to the trailhead campground at Mill Creek Falls, alternative trail routes to Eagle Peak depart from Patterson Campground and Emerson Campground. Dirt roads access Patterson along the south boundary of the Wilderness, and Emerson along the east boundary. Emerson has no drinking water. Creeks and springs in the Wilderness give backpackers many good choices for campsites.

The County: The word "Modoc" derives from a local Indian tribe who fought in California's largest Indian war. Ill-treated Modocs entrenched themselves in a lava-rock fortress—now part of Lava Beds National Monument—where 71 warriors stood off an army of about 1000 U.S. soldiers and volunteers for six months. Basaltic lava flows and cinder cones spread over the western two thirds of the county, the Modoc Plateau. The plateau comprises the largest volcanic-rock expanse in California. Livestock ranching, forestry, farming, and tourism support the economy. Fishermen enjoy the many lakes and trout streams. Hunters set their sights on plentiful mule deer and the largest pronghorn-antelope herd in the state. The county's extreme northeastern location leads to cultural as well as physical isolation from the rest of California; many residents shop in Lakeview and Klamath Falls, Oregon.

Additional Sources of Information/Recommended Reading:

Warner Mountain Ranger District
P.O. Box 220
Cedarville, CA 96104
(916) 279-6116

Adkison, Ron, *Hiker's Guide to California,* revised ed., Falcon Press, 1991.
U.S. Forest Service pamphlets provide exceptionally detailed accounts of natural history, trails, and management policies in South Warner Wilderness and surrounding Modoc National Forest.

Eagle Peak from the south

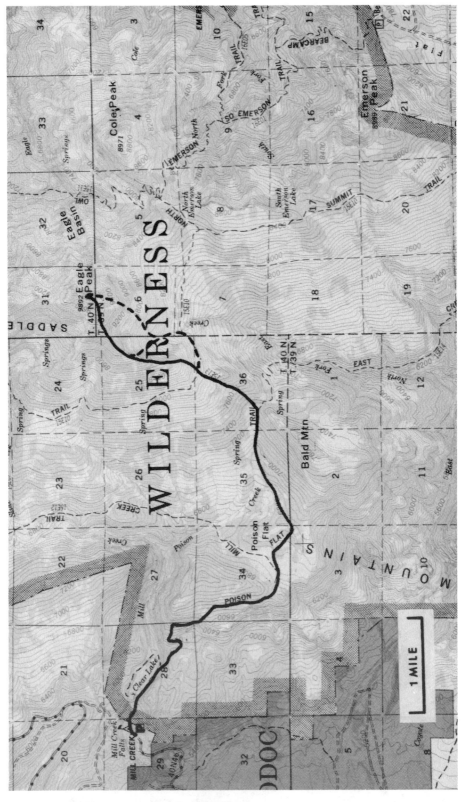

Modoc

Mono

White Mountain Peak   14,246′   **#2**

Location and Maps: At the south end of the county
USGS 15-minute *White Mtn. Peak, Mt. Barcroft;*
USGS 7½-minute *White Mtn. Peak, Mt. Barcroft,
Juniper Mtn, Chalfant Valley;* USFS *Inyo National Forest*

Distance: 15 miles round trip/2700′ elevation gain
Grade: Strenuous/Class 1
Hiking Time: 8 hours
Season: June to October

Trailnotes: An incomparable, surreal highpoint. The loftiest peak in the Great Basin and the third highest peak in California (only 245 feet lower than Mount Whitney). White Mountain Peak lies within Inyo National Forest near a famous bristlecone-pine forest. An old roadbed serves as the trail. The entire hike takes place above treeline amid a desolate, moonlike landscape. The *trailhead* elevation (11,650′) exceeds the height of 50 of the county summits! A rib-rattling dirt road, passable by most passenger cars, leads to the starting point. Many hikers spend a night at Grandview Campground to acclimatize before the climb. No water available. Dress for changeable weather; the peak can be cold and windy, even in midsummer. The White Mountains may take their name from the seasonally snow-covered crest.

Approach: Take SR 168 east from U.S. 395, 0.5 mile north of Big Pine and 14 miles south of Bishop. Drive 13 miles and then turn left (north) onto White Mountain Road. Pass the Schulman Grove of bristlecone pines in 10 miles. Here the pavement ends and the washboard begins. Proceed up the dirt road 11 more miles to reach a turnoff to the Patriarch Grove. Keep left and go another 4.6 miles to a locked gate, about 26 miles from SR 168. Park along the roadside.

Directions to Summit: Walk around the gate and up the moderately inclined road. After 2 miles you reach the University of California Barcroft Laboratory, where botanists, physiologists, and others carry on high-altitude studies. Beyond the buildings, a rough jeep road winds above the laboratory and past a rusty astronomy tower. Now your objective comes into full view. The road undulates across gentle terrain for about 3 miles and then climbs to a spacious flat. From the flat you turn northwest, drop down to a saddle, and switchback up taxing talus slopes to the top. A locked stone research hut is on the summit. A large green metal register lies cached in a wind shelter southeast of the hut.

The View: Phenomenal. The entire High Sierra sweeps panoramically across the western horizon, with Owens Valley below. The White Mountains extend to the north, from Pellisier Flats to Boundary Peak, the highest point in Nevada. To the south, Mount Barcroft heads a procession of peaks that connect with the Inyo Mountains down-range. To the east, dry desert basins and ranges stretch for miles before melding with the skyline.

The Environment: "The Whites" rise as a faulted granitic block overlaid by older metamorphic and sedimentary rocks, some over 600,000,000 years old. Due to the Sierra Nevada rain shadow, the range receives only about 15 inches of moisture per year, 80% falling as snow. Above treeline, low-growing tundra herbs and grasses survive on the scant moisture. Below treeline, some of the world's oldest living trees make their stand. One specimen, called Methuselah, dates back 4700 years! Bristlecone pines grow atop many Great Basin ranges, but the higher, harsher environment of the White Mountains paradoxically helps the trees live longer. These trees grow more slowly, producing a denser, more resinous wood that is better able to withstand insects, disease, and the elements. The Forest Service protects the bristlecones in a 58,000-acre preserve. Self-guided nature trails at Schulman Grove and Patriarch Grove let you see the gnarled and weather-beaten trees up close.

Nearby Campgrounds: Grandview Campground, 5 miles up White Mountain Road from SR168, serves as a convenient stopover. The Forest Service also allows camping outside the Bristlecone Pine Forest boundary, with a campfire permit. You may stay overnight at the trailhead, but no campfires or stoves are allowed.

The County: An Indian tribe called "Monanchie," or "fly people," gave Mono Lake the name that was later extended to the county. The Indians used the pupae of flies blown across the lake for food and trade. Early mining settlements like

Hiking toward the summit of White Mountain

Monoville and Bodie drew people to Mono County in the 1850s. Bodie still does, as a ghost-town historic park kept in a state of "arrested decay." Tourism provides major income to the county. High Sierra scenery, a ski resort at Mammoth Mountain, and lakes like Crowley, June, and Silver attract thousands yearly. Mono Lake, a shimmering blue gem set in an arid desert basin, supports millions of migratory shorebirds and gulls. Beginning in 1941 water diversions by Los Angeles drastically reduced the lake's level and threatened the million-year-old ecosystem. Fortunately, recent court cases require more water to reach the lake.

Additional Sources of Information/Recommended Reading:

White Mountain Ranger Station
798 N. Main Street
Bishop, CA 93514
(619) 873-2525

Hall, Clarence A., Jr., Ed. *Natural History of the White-Inyo Range,* University of California Press, 1991.
Hart, John, *Hiking the Great Basin,* revised and updated, Sierra Club Books, 1991.

On top of White Mountain

Mono

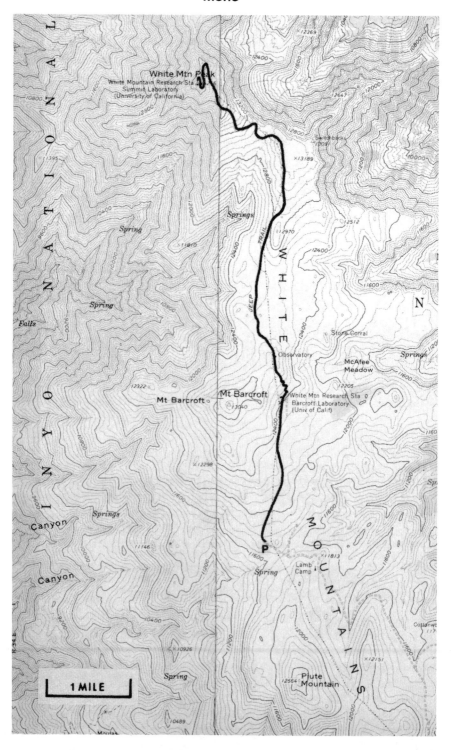

Monterey

Junipero Serra Peak   5862'   **#34**

Location and Maps:	Central part of the county
	USGS 7½-minute *Junipero Serra Peak, Cone Peak;* USFS *Ventana Wilderness*
Distance:	12 miles round trip/3900' elevation gain
Grade:	Strenuous/Class 1
Hiking Time:	8 hours
Season:	Year-round, best from November through April

Trailnotes: This premier county summit rises over a mile above sea level, with the sea itself in view just 17 miles to the west. Junipero Serra Peak edges Ventana Wilderness in Los Padres National Forest. The peak marks the loftiest point not only in the 167,323-acre wilderness, but in the sprawling Santa Lucia Coast Range as well. A paved access road goes to the trailhead and a signed trail winds to the summit. The route requires energetic hiking and provides far-reaching views. Seasonal creeks flow at the mountain's base, but no water is available higher up. In summer, begin the dayhike by 6 or 7 A.M. to avoid hot sun exposure along the steep mid-part of the trail. In winter, snow occasionally falls on the crest and impedes travel over the north-shaded upper part of the route.

Originally called Santa Lucia Peak, the mountain was later renamed to honor padre Junipero Serra (1713–1784) who founded nine California missions. Serra supervised the missions from a headquarters at Carmel Mission near Monterey, and he lies buried there.

Approach: From U.S. 101, 1 mile north of King City and 105 miles south of San Jose, take the Jolon Road exit (G14). Proceed 16.8 miles on Jolon Road to Mission Road. From the south on U.S. 101, 1.3 miles north of Bradley, follow in order G18 (Jolon Road), and G14 for 22 miles to Mission Road. Turn onto Mission Road, pass a Hunter Liggett Military Reservation checkpoint, and proceed 5 miles to an intersection with Del Ventura Road, signed SANTA LUCIA MEMORIAL PARK. Turn left onto Del Ventura Road, which later becomes Milpitas Road. A sign warns that the road may be closed in wet weather. You see why as you cross a creek after 0.3 mile and ford another 7 miles later. From the second stream crossing continue north 10 more miles to reach the trailhead, marked by a SANTA LUCIA TRAIL sign on the right side of the road, adjacent to a 10 MILE-PER-HOUR sign. Turn right and proceed on a short dirt road to a large parking lot.

Directions to Summit: Walk through a gate and head up an old jeep road. Shortly cross a creekbed and see a sign indicating PIMKOLAM PEAK 6 MILES. (Pimkolam is an Indian name for the peak.) The peak stands dauntingly high above you to the east. The trail gently ascends and descends before dropping down into a shady canyon bottom. You pass strangely eroded sandstone outcrops in a flowery meadow and a rusty abandoned tractor in a black oak grove. Dip in and out of washes as the trail becomes faint among grasses and berry vines and occasional poison oak. As you emerge from the riparian canopy a sign announces LUCIA LOOKOUT 4 MILES, and, after you switchback up a steep-walled canyon to a saddle at 4170 feet, another sign points to the lookout, 2 miles ahead. Zigzag steadily northeast up a ridge, threading through high chaparral to reach a saddle at 5440 feet.

From the saddle, the trail curves east and enters a forest of oak and pine. In 1993 downed tree limbs, debris, and encroaching brush made a 0.2-mile segment of the path hard to follow, until the trail swings south and up into an open forest on the northwest side of the crest. The trail tops out at the foot of an abandoned lookout tower. Two benchmarks are set in the rocks just south of the lookout (within a 5860' contour line). However, the highest point appears to lie at a rock pile surrounded by prostrate manzanita, about 0.1 mile east of the lookout. A curious cinderblock structure flanked by benchmarked boulders caps the summit.

The View: Oceanic. The blue Pacific (or sometimes a blanket of stratus clouds) spreads expansively behind Cone Peak and lesser prominences in the west. The Arroyo Seco and Tassajara Creek drainages display yawning canyons in the northwest. The Nacimiento and San Antonio river valleys extend to the south, backed by a conglomeration of mountains in the southern Santa Lucia Range. The Salinas Valley in the east lies mostly hidden by trees and foreground ridges. The Diablo Range, topped by San Benito Mountain, appears in the background. On the clearest days, you can detect the Sierra Nevada on the distant eastern horizon.

The Environment: Astronomers first blazed a trail to the summit in 1880 to observe a solar eclipse, and to this day scientists journey to the mountaintop for astronomical study. The trail displays four vegetation zones. Oak woodland, riparian woodland, and chaparral occur throughout Ventana Wilderness, but the coniferous forest of sugar and Coulter pines grows only on the highest mountain slopes, such as Junipero Serra Peak. Sugar-pine cones, the *longest* of all the pines, hang pendant from branches like Christmas tree decorations. Coulter pine cones, the *heaviest* of all the pines, mature as large as footballs and weight up to 10 pounds! These coniferous "scraps," far removed from their counterparts in the Sierra Nevada, form the remnant of a widespread forest that grew in moister times. Today's drier climate restricts the pines to the highest peaks, where adequate moisture allows their survival.

Nearby Campgrounds: An 8-unit developed Forest Service campground, Memorial Park, is conveniently located 0.1 mile north of the trailhead. Escondido Campground, another developed site, lies about 3 miles farther up the road.

The County: The county takes its name from Monterey Bay, christened in 1602 by Spanish explorer Sebastian Vizcaino for the Conde de Monterey, then viceroy of Mexico. North-south trending mountains fill the west and east parts of the county, separated by the broad, 130-mile-long Salinas Valley. The valley's rich soil and long growing season produce bountiful harvests. Monterey leads the nation in growing artichokes, broccoli, cauliflower, lettuce, mushrooms, and strawberries. The county possesses some of the finest scenery in California, from plunging promontories at Big Sur to cypress-topped coastal bluffs on the Monterey Peninsula. The famed 17-mile drive between Carmel and Pacific Grove highlights trees massed with millions of migrating black-and-orange monarch butterflies. The Monterey Bay Aquarium on Cannery Row exhibits more than 6500 marine animals and features a 3-story kelp forest display, the tallest aquarium tank in the world.

Additional Sources of Information/Recommended Reading:

Monterey Ranger District
406 S. Mildred Ave.
King City, CA 93930
(408) 385-5434

Henson, Paul, and Donald J. Usner, *The Natural History of Big Sur*, University of California Press, 1993.
Schaffer, Jeffrey P., *Hiking the Big Sur Country, The Ventana Wilderness*, Wilderness Press, 1988.
Ventana Chapter, Sierra Club, *Trail Guide to Los Padres National Forest, Monterey Division*, 4th ed., Angel Press, 1985.

Junipero Serra Peak from the east

Monterey

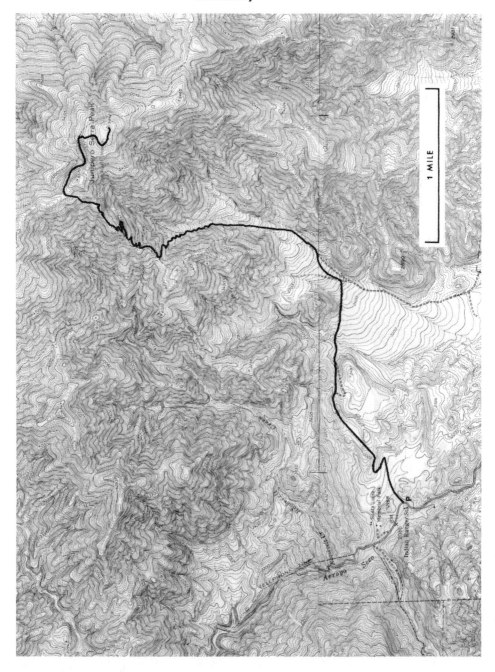

Napa

Mount Saint Helena East 4200+′ **#42**

Location and Maps: Northwest edge of the county
USGS 7½-minute *Mt. St. Helena, Detert Reservoir*
Distance: 9.6 miles round trip/1900′ elevation gain
Grade: Moderate/Class 1
Hiking Time: 6 hours
Season: Year round

Trailnotes: Eye-appealing Mount Saint Helena rises high above the vineyards of Napa and Sonoma counties. The Napa County highpoint lies on the upper eastern flank of the mountain at a triple boundary with Sonoma and Lake counties. Robert Louis Stevenson State Park provides access; its 3592 acres take in Mount Saint Helena's eastern slopes and wrap around the peak. The undeveloped park currently has no fee, no water or restroom facilities, and limited parking. Open to day use only. The route begins as a trail, which after a scant mile leads onto a fireroad/transmitter access road for the rest of the ascent. According to legend, Helena Rotcheva, princess and wife of the last commandant of Fort Ross, scaled the mountain with a party of Russian explorers in 1841. The Russians later named the height in honor of the princess's patron saint.

Approach: From San Francisco drive north on U.S. 101 approximately 20 miles and then follow a series of state highways: turn east on SR 37, north on 121, east on 12/121, and finally north on 29. Pass Yountville, St. Helena, and Calistoga. In Calistoga, turn right with SR 29 and continue 8 miles as the road snakes up to Robert Louis Stevenson State Park. Watch for roadside mileage marker 45.41, and park in a turnout on either side of the road.

Coming south on U.S. 101, take SR 128 from Geyserville for 24 miles to Tubbs Lane in the outskirts of Calistoga. Turn left onto Tubbs Lane and after a mile turn left onto SR 29, which leads up to the park.

From the East Bay, drive north on I 80 over the Carquinez Bridge, and then follow SR 29 through Napa and points north as described above. From the Central Valley, head west on I 80, 5 miles south of Fairfield take SR 12 west 9 miles to SR 29, and proceed as above.

Directions to Summit: Begin near a pole gate on the west side of the highway. Walk up stair steps and pass several picnic tables on your right before reaching the trail sign. Switchback for about a mile up a tree-shaded slope to the Stevenson Monument (a stone pedestal topped by an "open book" of polished granite). From the monument, an eroded segment of the trail shortly zigzags up to a fireroad. Follow the fireroad toward the summit signed North Peak. Chaparral, scattered groves of trees and intriguing volcanic formations border the road. You may also see vehicles; the California Department of Forestry, communications companies, and owners of inholdings have easements to use the road. Vistas expand as you wind up a moderate grade, eventually reaching a flat saddle junction where signs point to South Peak and North Peak. Over the next mile you walk beneath utility lines and past an optional, steep road-loop cutoff before coming to a sharp bend in the road. Here, your direction shifts from north to west. Also at this bend, a spur road forks south, climbing gently for 0.2 mile to the Napa County highpoint. Walk up the spur road. The road deadends on a knoll containing some stubby knobcone pines, some manzanita, and a small transmitting facility.

When you return to the main fireroad, continue on for another ½ mile to reach the rounded, antenna-clad crest of Mount Saint Helena at 4343 feet, some 140 feet higher than the Napa County summit. On top, you will find a plaque commemorating the establishment of Fort Ross and the 1841 Russian ascent of the peak ingloriously situated next to a shed behind the fire lookout.

The View: The view from the top of Napa County parallels the one from Mount Saint Helena proper except to the northeast, where the taller crest limits eyereach. Calistoga nestles in the upper end of the Napa Valley in the south, with Sugarloaf Ridge, Sonoma Valley, and the larger Santa Rosa Valley in the southwest. Farther south, distant views of the Bay Area, Mount Tamalpais, and even the skyscrapers of San Francisco may be seen. Looking southeast, the scraggly, volcanic Palisades fill the foreground, and far beyond, Mount Diablo appears on the horizon, as does the Sierra Nevada to the east. Steam billows from The Geysers in the northwest, with Snow Mountain in the background. Sweeping views of the Pacific Ocean extend to the west. On the clearest days observers see surf pounding on the beach at Point Reyes National Seashore.

On your way back, you may wish to explore the Stevenson Monument site (a use trail southwest of the stone pedestal leads up a steep tailings slope to a mineshaft). The noted Scottish writer, for whom the park is named, honeymooned here in an old prospector's shack. The shack's long gone, but Stevenson's experiences in the region vividly come to life in his book *The Silverado Squatters.* Stevenson relished "the Mount Blanc of the Coast Ranges." Its rocky outcrops may have inspired the Spyglass Hill locale for his classic, *Treasure Island.*

The Environment: In the throes of volcanism about 10 million years ago, Mount Saint Helena arose as multiple layers of lava poured over older Franciscan sediments. Later folding and faulting intergraded the volcanic and sedimentary strata. Serpentine, a metamorphic rock formed as hot igneous material extruded through apertures in sedimentary formations, contains many mineral elements, including the gold and silver mined on the slopes of Mount Saint Helena. The minerals also infuse nearby springs with trace elements to create "therapeutic mineral baths" and a popular source of bottled mineral water.

The mountain supports an abundant flora. Chinquapin, redberry, yerba santa, and many other chaparral species cover the hillsides. Some north-facing slopes and the wooded canyons contain Douglas-fir, madrone, California nutmeg, and several species of oak. Knobcone pines and a few sugar pines appear on the higher slopes. Mount Saint Helena remains one of the few places in California where the rare and endangered peregrine falcon may be seen year-round. The mountain's open, rugged topography and ample prey (mostly other birds) suit the falcon, easily identified by its distinctive black-helmet head marking and long, pointed wings, bent back at the wrist (like a scimitar). Among the fastest birds in the world, peregrines overtake prey in midair with blindingly swift "power dives" of 100 to 275 miles per hour.

Nearby Campgrounds: Bothe-Napa Valley State Park provides camping facilities about 15 miles south of Mount Saint Helena, as does Sugarloaf Ridge State Park east of Santa Rosa.

The County: "Napa," an obscure Indian word, has been variously translated to mean "house," "fish," "grizzly bear," "abundant," and "motherland." Today "Napa" usually brings to mind another four-letter word, "wine." Napa Valley, only 30 miles long and 1 to 5 miles wide, forms the heart of the county and stands out as the most acclaimed wine-producing region in the United States.

Dozens of wineries dot the valley, drawn by ideal grape-growing conditions. Mount Saint Helena to the north and lower ranges to the east and west shelter the valley. Warm summers, mild winters, and the consequent long growing season combine with varied soils and intervalley microclimates to support many kinds of grapes. Over two million sightseers a year visit Napa Valley. They sample the vintners' offerings and enjoy one of the most attractive rural landscapes in the state. Many local residents strive to protect their "Agricultural Yosemite" from growing commercialization, as evinced by the controversy over the Wine Train. The train brings passengers past 27 wineries between the towns of Napa and St. Helena, but the train also brings noise, pollution, traffic disruption, and a carnival atmosphere to the valley.

Additional Sources of Information/Recommended Reading:

Robert Louis Stevenson State Park and Bothe-Napa Valley State Park
3801 St. Helena Highway North
Calistoga, CA 94515
(707) 942-4575

Fish, Timothy, *The Napa and Sonoma Book*, Berkshire House, 1992.
Whitnah, Dorothy L., *An Outdoor Guide to the San Francisco Bay Area,* 5th ed., Wilderness Press, 1989.

Napa

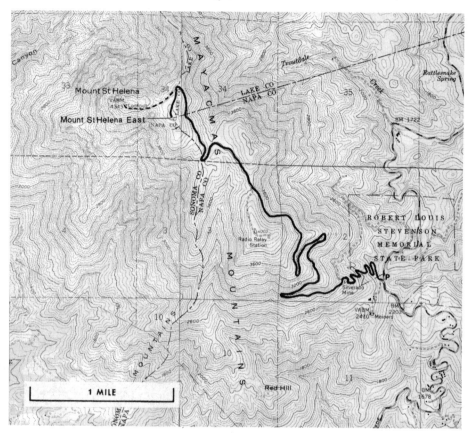

Nevada

Mount Lola   9148′   **#17**

Location and Maps:	Northeast edge of the county
	USGS 7½-minute *Independence Lake, Webber Peak;* USFS *Tahoe National Forest*
Distance:	10 miles round trip/2600′ elevation gain
Grade:	Moderate/Class 1
Hiking Time:	6 hours
Season:	Mid-June to October

Trailnotes: Mount Lola rises higher than any other peak between Lake Tahoe's Mount Rose and the Cascades' Lassen Peak. A 3-mile dirt road, fine for passenger cars, extends to the trailhead. A good Forest Service trail runs to the peak, located in Tahoe National Forest. Tumbling creek music and beaver ponds highlight the enjoyable trail, marred in a few places by logging. From the top of Mount Lola, a 1.2-mile cross-country ramble conveniently brings you to a sister summit, the highpoint of Sierra County.

Mount Lola commemorates Lola Montez (1818–1861), the legendary actress and dancer. In her famous "Spider Dance," she wore flesh-colored tights and a short skirt decked with loosely attached toy spiders. As Ms. Montez whirled about, simulating horror as an imaginary web entangled her, the spiders gradually fell to the floor, whereupon she indelicately stomped on them, to peals of laughter and applause.

Approach: From SR 89, 17 miles north of Truckee and 8 miles south of Sierraville, turn west onto FS 07, signed WEBBER LAKE/INDEPENDENCE LAKE. Proceed 6 miles on FS 07 and then bear left onto Road 19N10, where a sign indicates PERAZZO MEADOW. Set odometer. Proceed on the rough dirt road 0.7 mile to a four-way intersection. Turn left after the cattle guard onto Road S301. Cross a bridge at 1.1 miles and another at 2.7 miles before turning right into the trailhead parking area at 3.0 miles. A trailhead sign and information board stand a short distance west of the parking area, 100 feet beyond a dirt mound.

Directions to Summit: The trail leads south into a shady forest and climbs moderately along a canyonside, with Cold Stream cascading below. The tread flattens before you break onto a road and a bridge to cross Cold Stream, about 2 miles from the start. Presently, you skirt a big, beautiful meadow, brimming with wildflowers and dotted with beaver ponds, then re-enter the forest to climb Cold Stream's headwaters slopes. The trail zigzags up to an open ridge and veers west to ascend the east shoulder of Mount Lola. The pitch steepens amid thinning trees before you reach the summit, topped by benchmarks, wind shelters, and three intriguing red brick pillars.

Mt. Lola from the south

On Mt. Lola

The pillars supported a heliograph used by Geodetic Survey crews between 1863 and 1877 to aid their mapping efforts. The heliograph housed a huge mirror in a tripod tower to flash messages by reflected sunlight to Mount Diablo, over 130 miles away.

The View: Grand! The Sierra Nevada sweeps to its terminus in the north. Perazzo Canyon lies at the northwest foot of Mount Lola, backed by Webber Peak and the distant Sierra Buttes. The sizable Sierra Valley spreads to the northeast. Elongated Independence Lake sparkles in the east. Rounded Basin Peak and triple-pinnacled Castle Peak reach skyward in the south. White Rock Lake sits directly below in the southwest, and English Mountain rises above the meadowlands in the west.

The Environment: Mount Lola is the remains of an old volcano. Pliocene pyroclastic rock underlies the summit, and similar-aged basalt rock caps Mount Lola North. Glaciers flowed down Perazzo Canyon to merge with a broad river of ice that filled the valley you traveled through to get to the trailhead. The checkerboard pattern of public and private land in Tahoe National Forest resulted from federal giveaways to commercial interests in the late 1800s to encourage development in the West. Conservationists seek to reacquire acreage in scenic areas to prevent incompatible activities such as logging and large hotels. (Disney Enterprises tried briefly to develop a year-round resort at Independence Lake after their defeat at Mineral King.) A recent acquisition encompassed Mount Lola, to protect the viewshed along the Pacific Crest Trail, which passes beneath the peak.

Nearby Campgrounds: Upper and Lower Little Truckee campgrounds lie near the junction of SR 89 and FS 07. Spurs off FS 07 access campgrounds at Independence Lake and Webber Lake. The Forest Service allows dispersed camping throughout the area.

The County: Mountainous Nevada County stretches from the east edge of the Sacramento Valley to the Nevada state line. *Nevada* means "snowy" or "snow-covered," and in winter snow indeed blankets the county. Boca, a mountain hamlet, has recorded California's coldest temperature, 45° below zero. The county's growth rate has spiraled as ex-urbanites have migrated to attractive rural communities like Nevada City and Grass Valley. Tourism and logging mainstay an economy formerly based on gold mining. Empire Mine State Park in Grass Valley contains the largest, deepest, and richest hardrock gold mine in California. Active from 1850 to 1957, the mine's tunnels burrow over 360 miles, some to a depth of over a mile beneath the surface.

Additional Sources of Information/Recommended Reading:

Sierraville Ranger District
P.O. Box 95
Sierraville, CA 96126
(916) 994-3401

Schaffer, Jeffrey P., *The Tahoe Sierra,* 3rd ed., Wilderness Press, 1987.

Nevada

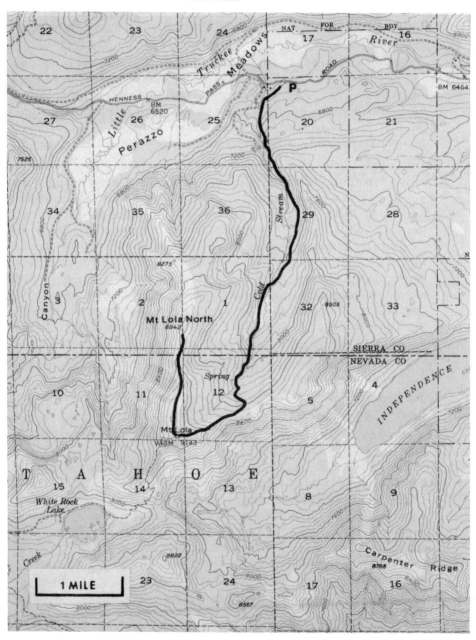

Orange

<table>
<tr><td>**Santiago Peak**</td><td>5687′</td><td>**#35**</td></tr>
</table>

Location and Maps:	Southeast edge of the county
	USGS 7½-minute *Santiago Peak;* USFS
	Cleveland National Forest
Distance:	16 miles round trip/4000′ elevation gain
Grade:	Strenuous/Class 1
Hiking Time:	9 hours
Season:	Year-round, best November through May

Trailnotes: Santiago Peak rises high above the coastal plain, just 20 miles from the sea, providing one of the grandest mountaintop views of the Pacific Ocean to be had in California. A bone-jarring dirt road, passable by most passenger cars, leads to the trailhead. Start early, and carry ample water. Your route follows a footpath and a fireroad within the northern part of Cleveland National Forest. You may come upon vehicles; several truck trails provide public motor access to the summit. The Forest Service usually closes the gates to these roads during the rainy season, a boon to foot travelers. Call the Trabuco Ranger District for information about truck trails and possible fire-season closures (rare).

Santiago is a contraction of "Saint James." The name derives from an adjacent creek and canyon, so named by early Spanish explorers to honor the patron saint of Spain. Santiago Peak, and slightly lower Modjeska Peak to the north, form a pronounced saddle when viewed from certain angles; hence, local residents familiarly call the mountain Old Saddleback.

Approach: Take the El Toro Road exit off Interstate 5, approximately 30 miles south of Los Angeles and 80 miles north of San Diego. Proceed east on El Toro Road (S18) 7.3 miles to an intersection with Live Oak Canyon Road (S19). Turn right and follow Live Oak Canyon Road 4.3 miles, passing O'Neill Regional Park on your right and Trabuco Oaks Drive and Rose Canyon Road on your left. Just beyond a point where the road crosses Arroyo Trabuco Wash, watch for unsigned, unpaved Trabuco Canyon Road on your left. Ease your way up this rut-riven road for 4.7 miles. Eventually you reach a volunteer-fire-department building and, 100 yards farther, a dirt flat on your left. Park here.

Directions to Summit: Amble up Holy Jim Road (6S14). Pass cabins with fancy rockwork on your way to a locked gate, ½ mile up the road. From the gate, a path continues up the canyon beneath a canopy of oak, alder, and sycamore. You repeatedly cross Holy Jim Creek. Watch for poison oak. Notice fig plants and small fish dams, a legacy of early settlers. (A profane settler named "Cussin Jim" Smith gave the creek and canyon their name, but prim mapmakers later changed the sobriquet "Cussin" to "Holy.") About a mile past the gate, the main trail abruptly doubles back to ascend the west slope of the canyon, while a fainter tread continues upstream ¼ mile to Holy Jim Falls; this small but inviting cascade merits a side trip on the way back.

The main trail switchbacks steeply at first, and then contours at a moderate grade around the canyonside. You hike for a good 3 miles amid sundrenched chaparral and then drop briefly into a shady grove before reaching a dirt road, the Main Divide Truck Trail. A nearby cement tank marks Bear Spring (no water available). From here, follow the sinuous uphill road 3 more miles to the summit.

On top, a horde of antennas, microwave dishes, and related structures crowds the scene. The mile-high peak, ideally positioned to beam signals to an enormous population from San Diego to Ventura County, rates as one of the most important electronic sites in America. Over 200 permittees and hundreds of additional sub-leasers utilize the transmitters—pager services, cab dispatchers, telephone companies, radio and television stations, public utilities, government agencies, and many more. An unused lookout tower adds to the clutter. The Forest Service abandoned the tower because frequent heavy smog impaired visibility and because forest visitors and overflying pilots reported fires efficiently. A benchmark sits near the southwest corner of a green wire fence surrounding the lookout. A road spur next to the benchmark leads to a fine ocean overlook. Walk around the perimeter of the facilities to gain unobstructed views in all directions.

The View: Monumental urban sprawl spreads across the Los Angeles Basin. Distant skyscrapers in downtown L.A. and adjacent city centers accent the paved-over landscape. On the far side of the basin, a purple wall of mountains etches the skyline; from left to right, the Santa Monica, San Gabriel, and San Bernardino ranges. In the east Lake Matthews stands out in the foreground and the San Jacinto Mountains rise in the background. In the south a jumble of Peninsular Ranges extends toward the border, with distinctive Table Mountain visible in Baja California. An enthralling ocean panorama takes in over 150 miles of coastline, from Point Loma in San Diego to Point Dume near Malibu Beach. Santa Catalina Island and San Clemente Island lie offshore. The limitless Pacific horizon gives you almost an astronaut's feel for the curvature of the globe.

The Environment: Santiago Peak caps the Santa Ana Mountains, a compact fault-block range, roughly 35 miles long and 10 miles wide. High ridges, plunging ravines, and deep canyons carved by intermittent streams characterize the topography. The "cloud catching" upper reaches of the range snare up to 30 inches of precipitation per year, enough to sustain small groves of Coulter pine, big-cone Douglas spruce, and live oak. Riparian woodland fills the canyon bottoms and intermittent stream channels. But coastal sage scrub and chaparral dominate in the Santa Anas. Chamise, toyon, and dozens of other drought-tolerant species blanket the slopes. These plants are combustible, especially when whipped by Santa Ana winds, which commonly gust through South Coast canyons in fall and early winter. (Santa Ana Canyon, on the north slope of the Santa Ana Mountains, gave the winds their name.) Air flowing from a high-pressure zone over interior deserts to a low-pressure zone offshore generates the phenomenon. Heated during descent, the winds may exceed 100° by the time they reach sea level. The Santa Anas lower humidity and disperse smog, creating crystal clear skies for several days, until air pressures equalize and the winds die down.

Nearby Campgrounds: O'Neill Regional Park, located about 5 miles from the trailhead, offers the closest camping facilities. Forest Service campgrounds and hiking trails along Ortega Highway (State Route 74), and San Mateo Canyon Wilderness in the southern section of the Trabuco Ranger District invite exploration.

The County: This smallest of Southern California counties contains just 786 square miles (as compared to San Bernardino's 20,000+ square miles). Broad sandy beaches, tidal flats, and a gently sloping coastal plain in the north give way to a narrow coastal strip, high terraces, and rolling hills in the south, backed by the Santa Ana Mountains. Prevalent shell mounds along the coast reveal a long-term Indian presence before the arrival of Spanish conquistadores in 1769. Periods of ranching and agriculture preceded the explosive urbanization of recent decades. Despite its small area, Orange now ranks as the second most populous county in California, chock-a-block with aerospace, pharmaceutical, and computer industries, shopping centers, and residential suburbs. Development has drastically reduced the orange groves that inspired the county's name. Ironically, not a single grove remained in the town of Orange until the city planted an acre of Valencia orange trees in a park.

Additional Sources of Information/Recommended Reading:

Cleveland National Forest, Trabuco
  Ranger District
1147 E. Sixth Street
Corona, CA 91719
(909) 736-1811

O'Neill Regional Park
P.O. Box 372
Trabuco Canyon, CA 92678
(714) 858-9366

Croker, Kenneth S., *Santa Ana Mountains Trail Guide,* 4th ed., Whale and Eagle Publishing Co., 1991.
McPherson, Alan, *Nature Walks in Orange County,* Bear Flag Books, 1990.
Schad, Jerry, *Afoot and Afield in Orange County,* Wilderness Press, 1988.

Benchmark on Santiago Peak

Orange

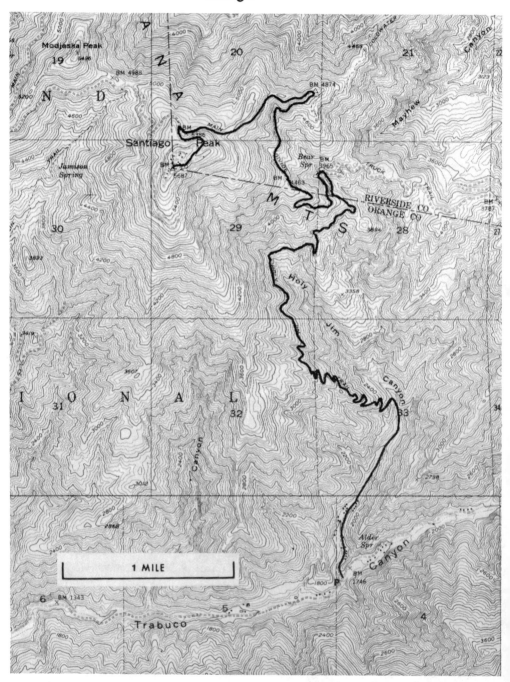

Placer

Granite Chief 9006′ **#19**

Location and Maps:	East corner of the county
	USGS 7½-minute *Granite Chief, Tahoe City;*
	USFS *Tahoe National Forest*
Distance:	11.2 miles round trip/3000′ elevation gain
Grade:	Strenuous/Class 1
Hiking Time:	7 hours
Season:	Mid-July to early October

Trailnotes: Granite Chief stands tall, if somewhat tarnished, behind the northwest rim of the Lake Tahoe Basin. The peak overlooks 25,680-acre Granite Chief Wilderness *and* one of the largest ski facilities in North America. Squaw Valley's 27 ski lifts spread over the countryside, and one reaches right up to the Chief's chin. An aerial tramway, open throughout the summer, can lop off nearly 2000 feet of elevation and 7 miles in distance from the hike. But the trail proves more rewarding. A maintained route leads to the Chief's southeast shoulder, and an unmaintained path extends on to the top. Neither dayhike nor backpack requires a wilderness permit. Start early to avoid sunny exposures on the first leg of your hike. The name, Granite Chief, underscores its light rock composition, which contrasts noticeably with the region's predominant dark volcanic rock.

Approach: From Truckee, take SR 89 south 8.5 miles to Squaw Valley Road. From Tahoe City, go 5.2 miles northwest on SR 89 to the turnoff. Follow Squaw Valley Road 2.3 miles to a Fire Station sign on your right. Park in the small lot beyond the sign. If full, park in the immense lot to the south. The trail begins at the far (west) end of the small parking area.

Directions to Summit: Walk up the trail 120 yards to reach a fire station. Just downslope, an information board and map announce the Granite Chief Trail. Proceed along the gently sloping path, which soon rises above the resort complexes and comes within earshot of Squaw Creek. A half mile from the start, watch for a USFS boundary sign. A shortcut takes off to the right of the boundary sign and later intersects the main trail. The main trail continues for 70 yards and then forks. Take the right fork (the left fork goes to Shirley Lake). Now a good, moderately pitched trail climbs the north canyonside above Squaw Creek. Wildflowers embellish sun-bright openings in the woods. Faint orange-painted lines guide you across a stretch of bare granite slabs before you enter a shady forest posted as a University of California Ecology Study area. Gentle switchbacks bring you to a junction with the Pacific Crest Trail, where signs indicate SQUAW VALLEY 4, GRANITE CHIEF 1.5. Head south on the PCT. The undulating trail drops down to a subalpine meadow below the east face of Granite Chief, and then zigzags up (and under an obtrusive ski lift) to a broad, windswept saddle.

At the saddle, trails branch off left and right from the PCT before it begins a descent into Granite Chief Wilderness. Follow the trail to the right, which quickly fades to a trace. Head northwest (west of a ski-lift fence), up through scattered trees and boulders to reach the open south slope of Granite Chief. On the slope you pick up a good footpath and ascend steeply 0.3 mile to the top. Find a benchmark and two register canisters placed on the Chief's "headbonnet," a wide bench sprinkled with rounded boulders, low brush, and straggly trees.

Back at the saddle, the trail to Watson Monument curves southeast, gently dipping and then rising to reach the monument at Emigrant Pass in about 0.3 mile. Tram users climb west from tram's end on ski-facility dirt roads and trails, bearing right at junctions to arrive at the monument. Then follow the aforementioned trail to the saddle and onward to the summit.

The View: Exhilarating. Needle Peak threads the sky a mile to the west, backed by Lyon Peak and Royal Gorge, a 4000 deep canyon cut by the North Fork of the American River. In the north Tinker Knob projects in the foreground and a welter of northern Sierra peaks rise in the background. In the east lies developed Squaw Valley, azure Lake Tahoe, and the Carson Range in Nevada, topped by Mount Rose. In the south, Squaw Peak stands out across from Emigrant Pass. On the horizon, Freel Peak caps the south end of the Tahoe Basin, and the snow-flecked Crystal Range sparkles in distant Desolation Wilderness.

The Environment: Over the last 30 million years, lava flows repeatedly covered the region, but Granite Chief avoided the inundations. Glaciers later eroded some of the adjacent volcanic deposits, exposing older metamorphic and granitic rocks. You find all three rock types along the trail, as well as a rich assemblage of trees and plants. Trees include cottonwood, alder, incense-cedar, western juniper, red and white fir, and Jeffrey, mountain white, and lodgepole pines. Snow bush, manzanita, and huckleberry oak blanket dry hillsides. Mule ears, purple aster, and red-flowered bee plant join an array of wildflowers. The unusual insectivorous sundew plant once grew around a Squaw Valley bog, until construction obliterated it. For decades the valley remained a quiet hay ranch and dairy farm. Then, in the late 1940s, entrepreneurs opened the first modest ski lodge. In 1955, to the surprise of almost everyone the International Olympic Committee chose Squaw Valley to host the 1960 Winter Olympic Games. Development snowballed from then on.

Nearby Campgrounds: Three Forest Service campgrounds border the Truckee River along SR 89—Silver Creek, Goose Meadow, and Granite Flat. The Forest Service also has campgrounds around the north and west shores of Lake Tahoe at Tahoe City, Kaspian, and William Kent. State park campgrounds, with reservations required, include Sugar Pine Point, D.L. Bliss, and Emerald Bay, all located along SR 89, and Donner Memorial, off I 80 just south of Truckee.

The County: Placer County's topography ranges from the flat Sacramento Valley upward through rolling foothills and steepening mountains to the 9006-foot summit of Granite Chief. *Placer* means "shoal" in Spanish, a mining term for sand

and gravel washed (typically from a riverside shoal) to extract particles of gold. Auburn, the county seat, sits at a transportation crossroads and served as a gateway to the northern mining camps. It contains an Old Town with buildings from the 1850s, and a county museum displaying Gold Rush memorabilia. Hinterland farms specialize in cattle, fruits, nuts, and grain crops. Tourism stokes the economy in the mountainous part of the county. Many urbanites who visited Placer County's attractive Sierra foothills and Lake Tahoe locales decided to stay. Between 1980 and 1990 the county's population jumped by 46 percent, among the fastest growth rates in the state.

Additional Sources of Information/Recommended Reading:

Truckee Ranger District
10342 Hwy 89N
Truckee, CA 96161
(916) 587-3558

Squaw Valley USA/Aerial Tramway Information
Squaw Valley, CA 95730
(916) 583-6985

Evans, Lisa Gollin, *Lake Tahoe, A Family Guide,* The Mountaineers, 1993.
Schaffer, Jeffrey P., *The Tahoe Sierra,* 3rd ed., Wilderness Press, 1987.

Placer

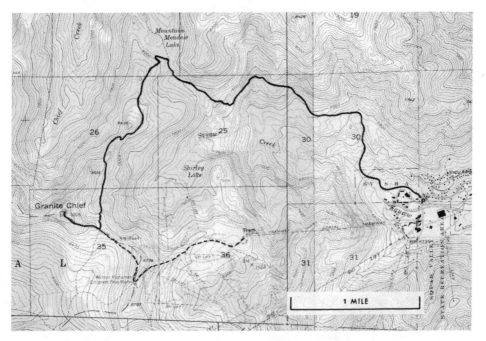

1 MILE

Plumas

Mount Ingalls   8372′   **#24**

Location and Maps: Central east side of the country
USGS 7½-minute *Mt. Ingalls, Grizzly Valley;*
USFS *Plumas National Forest*
Distance: 2 miles round trip/540′ elevation gain
Grade: Easy/Class 1
Hiking Time: 50 minutes
Season: Mid-June to October

Trailnotes: An unsung northern Sierra mountaintop tucked in the far-off recesses of Plumas National Forest. Logging roads crisscross the area and lead close to the summit. Passenger cars can handle the circuitous, dusty dirt roads, but keep an eye out for logging trucks. Mount Ingalls, named after a noted local pioneer, receives few callers. Your visit entails an easygoing amble up a four-wheel-drive lookout road. A riddle: How can the Mount Ingalls' lookout stand 4940 feet *below* the highpoint?

Approach: From I 80 near Truckee, take SR 89 north 49 miles to Blairsden. From Marysville, take SR 70 130 miles northeast to Blairsden. Continue east from Blairsden on SR 70 for 9.4 miles to the outskirts of Portola and turn left on West Street (signed DAVIS LAKE). Set your odometer. At 5.3 miles stay right on the main road. At 7.6 miles turn left onto Beckwourth-Greenville Road. At 11.6 miles the pavement ends. At 12.7 miles pass a spur named Clover Valley Road. At 13.7 miles turn right onto FS 25N10. At 15.9 miles pass through a junction. At 19.1 miles you reach a four-way junction; keep left and continue straight ahead on FS 25N10, following signs for 3.1 miles to a four-way junction announcing MOUNT INGALLS 1 MILE. Park along the roadside.

Directions to Summit: Walk up the jeep road. A steady upgrade, a couple of switchbacks, and *voilà!* you're there. Angular rocks litter the rounded, open summit. A small cairn sits beside a cement platform. In answer to the riddle above, the platform supported a lookout constructed in 1935 by the Civilian Conservation Corps. In 1986 a sky crane lifted the lookout onto a flatbed truck. The truck hauled the structure to the Plumas County Fairgrounds (elevation 3432), where it remains on display throughout the year. Forest Service employees open the tower during the annual fair to answer questions about lookout operations and fire prevention.

The View: Plentiful mountain scenery encircles you. In the south Grizzly Ridge occupies the foreground and the jagged Sierra Buttes jut up in the background. In the west Argentine Rock, Tower Rock, Grizzly Peak, and Mount Jura extend from left to right. Lassen Peak, Lake Almanor, and Mountain Meadows Reservoir appear in the northwest, with Genesee Valley directly below. The

Diamond Mountains wall the northeast horizon. Squaw Valley Peak rises behind Squaw Valley in the east. Dixie Mountain, Plumas County's second highest point, looms large to the southeast, with Davis Lake off to the right and the expansive Sierra Valley in the background.

The Environment: Dark Pliocene volcanic basalt caps Mount Ingalls. Yellow sunflowers and sulfur flowers brighten the scene. Sparse, wind-sheared, snow-bent summit trees grade into lush forests downslope. Sugar, ponderosa, and Jeffrey pine, along with red, white, and Douglas fir thrive in one of the best timber-growing regions in the West. Much of the 1,154,000-acre forest has been logged through the years. In the late 1980s loggers cut enough trees each year to build almost 20,000 three-bedroom houses, and Plumas supplied nearly a third of California's white fir Christmas trees. But timber harvesting has declined recently due to court-ordered restrictions designed to reverse overcutting and to protect spotted owls.

Nearby Campgrounds: Three developed lakeshore campgrounds hug the shoreline of Davis Lake along the Beckwourth-Greenville Road—Grizzly, Grass-hopper Flat, Lightning Tree.

The County: A Spanish explorer observed brightly plumed waterfowl along a river and called it *El Rio de Las Plumas*, "River of the Feathers." The county took the name, appropriately, since the river's headwaters and three major forks course through the mountainous region. The Feather River is the largest river in the Sierra Nevada. Several wild stretches remain, but dams and power plants harness most of the flow. The county's economy relies mainly on lumbering and tourism. Quincy, the largest town, hosts a celebrated county fair and displays pioneer relics in a distinguished county museum. East of Quincy lies the historic mining town of Johnsville. Plumas Eureka State Park completely surrounds Johnsville. The 6749-acre park, called the most picturesque in the state-park system, contains glacier-carved mountains, clear-water lakes, and many babbling creeks.

Additional Sources of Information/Recommended Reading:

Greenville Ranger District
P.O. Box 329
Greenville, CA 95947
(916) 284-7126

Plumas County Historical Society
P.O. Box 677
Quincy, CA 95971

Durrell, Cordell, *Geologic History of the Feather River Country, California,* University of California Press, 1988.

Plumas

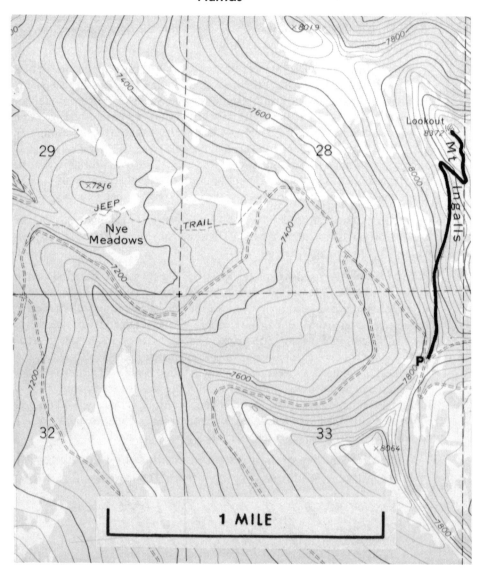

1 MILE

Riverside

San Jacinto Peak   10,804'   #11

Location and Maps:	Upper central part of the county
	USGS 7½-minute *San Jacinto Peak;* CDPR
	Mount San Jacinto State Wilderness
Distance:	16.2 miles round trip/4500' elevation gain
Grade:	Strenuous/Class 1
Hiking Time:	10 hours
Season:	June to October

Trailnotes: San Jacinto Peak climaxes a spectacular escarpment that rises over 9000 feet in less than 6 miles—one of the most abrupt mountain faces on Earth. The massif stands as the highest point in the Peninsular Ranges and the second highest point in Southern California. The peak lies within Mount San Jacinto State Park and Wilderness, bordered north and south by San Bernardino National Forest wilderness.

You must obtain a wilderness permit from either the State Park or the Forest Service before your dayhike or backpack trip. Secure a permit by mail or in person up to 56 days in advance through the State Park, and up to 90 days through the Forest Service. No phone reservations accepted. Both agencies have a self-issue system outside their offices in Idyllwild; both dispense day-use permits freely throughout the week. However, *only* the Forest Service issues day-use permits on weekends and holidays from Memorial Day to Labor Day for the Devils Slide Trail. During these times, the Forest Service releases 5 permits per day in advance, and places 20 permits in the self-issue station outside the office at 8:00 A.M. Both the State Park and the Forest Service limit overnight camping to specific campsites and zones demarked on maps available from their offices.

The primary route approaches the peak from the west side of the range on the popular Devils Slide Trail. A shorter approach, from the east side, uses the Palm Springs Aerial Tramway. The Long Valley Ranger Station at tram's end provides wilderness permits for the 12-mile round trip, with a 2300-foot elevation gain. Both routes take you through some of the most beautiful mountain scenery in Southern California.

The peak's name traces back to land grants from the 1840s named "San Jacinto," to honor Saint Hyacinth (1185–1257). That Silesian Dominican priest preached widely throughout Eastern Europe.

Approach: From I 10 in Banning, take SR 243 south 25 miles to Idyllwild. From I 215, 2 miles north of Sun City, take SR 74 east 31 miles to a junction with SR 243. Turn left onto SR 243 and continue 4.5 miles to Idyllwild. (For a day-use permit, stop at the Forest Service office near the corner of SR 243 and Pine Crest Road, one block north of North Circle Drive.) In central Idyllwild, follow the signs to Humber Park: Go 0.8 mile northeast on North Circle Drive, turn right on South Circle Drive for 0.1 mile, and then left on Fern Valley Road 1.8 mile to the parking lot. The trail begins at the upper right (northeast) corner of the lot.

For the eastern approach, drive on I 10 for 12 miles past Banning to SR 111. Take SR 111 for 9 miles to Tramway Road, turn right, and proceed 4 miles to Desert Station.

Directions to Summit: Ascend the east slope of Strawberry Canyon on an excellent trail, moderately inclined today but formerly steep-pitched, hence the name "Devils Slide." In 2.5 miles you top out at five-way Saddle Junction. Take the left trail, signed ROUND VALLEY/SAN JACINTO PEAK. Climb gradually at first and then more steeply through an open forest. Pass a junction at 1.9 miles, cross into the posted State Park Wilderness, and traverse lush Wellmans Cienaga (a Spanish word for marsh or marshy meadow). You break onto drier slopes to reach a saddle junction at Wellmans Divide. From here the right fork leads to the tram. (From the Mountain Station terminal, step down a cement walkway, which turns into a trail and shortly passes the Long Valley Ranger Station—get a permit here. Beyond the ranger station, follow a gently graded trail through an open forest 2.1 miles to Round Valley. A signed junction in Round Valley points to WELLMAN DIVIDE—1. Go left at this junction to reach the Divide.) From Wellmans Divide, wind upslope over a progressively rockier tread for 2.4 miles to another junction. From the junction take a 0.3-mile spur to the mountaintop. Pass a fine stone structure built by the Civilian Conservation Corps in the 1930s to shelter weather-stranded hikers. The trail fades out among the summit boulders, so pick your path and scramble up. Two benchmarked rocks lie just below the highest boulder, and a sign announces the elevation.

The View: "The most sublime spectacle to be found anywhere on this earth," exclaimed John Muir. Noted landscape architect F.L. Olmsted, slightly less laudatory, declared the view "unmatched in its impressiveness elsewhere in the United States." Palm Springs and the Coachella Valley's irrigated checkerboard lie directly below. The azure Salton Sea and the Imperial Valley extend to the southeast. Lesser San Jacinto Range peaks and interlying valleys sweep to the south. The Santa Ana Mountains rise behind the Inland Empire corridor in the west, while the San Bernardino Mountains soar above San Gorgonio Pass in the north.

The Environment: Light granite rock and subalpine forests give San Jacinto Peak the look and the feel of the Sierra Nevada. Indeed, both ranges are massive tilted granite fault blocks, and both exhibit gentle western slopes, alongside sheer eastern escarpments. Six life zones, from arid to alpine, band the escarpment. Nowhere else in California do such extremes in natural vegetation grow so closely together, within 5 horizontal miles. Between the extremes lie verdant timbered areas with incense-cedar, white fir, and Coulter, Jeffrey, ponderosa, sugar, lodgepole and limber pines. Dominant shrubs include manzanita, ceanothus, and chinquapin. Scarlet gilia, orange columbine, yellow monkey flower, and many other species splash trailside color. The varied habitats support abundant wildlife, from roadrunner to raccoon.

Nearby Campgrounds: Eight campgrounds line SR 243 in the Idyllwild vicinity. State-operated Idyllwild and Stone Creek reserve through MISTIX. Forest Service sites at Marion Mountain, Dark Canyon, Boulder Basin, and Fern Basin run on a first-come, first-served basis. Two county campgrounds, Idyllwild and Hurkey Grove, take reservations at (800) 283-CAMP, or (909) 659-2117 for information.

The County: The county's name traces back to the City of Riverside, so-named for its proximity to the Santa Ana River. The county stretches 184 miles across Southern California, from the Colorado River to within 10 miles of the Pacific Ocean. The San Jacinto Range separates the thinly populated eastern, desert side of the county from the bustling western hills and valleys. During the 1980s Riverside grew by 76 percent, the fastest growing county in California. The well-balanced economy includes construction, retail, and service sectors, as well as manufacturing and agriculture. Riverside played an early role in California's multimillion-dollar citrus industry. In 1873 a resident planted two mutant "navel" oranges sent from Brazil. The trees flourished and bud cuttings from the trees expanded to a 20,000-acre orchard by 1895. One of the original trees, protected by a high fence and surrounded by commercial buildings, still produces oranges.

Additional Sources of Information/Recommended Reading:

Mount San Jacinto State Wilderness
25905 Highway 243
P.O. Box 308
Idyllwild, CA 92549
(909) 659-2607

San Jacinto Ranger District
54270 Pine Crest Road
P.O. Box 518
Idyllwild, CA 92349
(909) 659-2117

Palm Springs Aerial Tramway,
  prices and schedules
(619) 325-1391

Robinson, John W., *San Bernardino Mountain Trails,* 4th ed., Wilderness
  Press, 1986.

**San Jacinto Peak
summit block**

Riverside

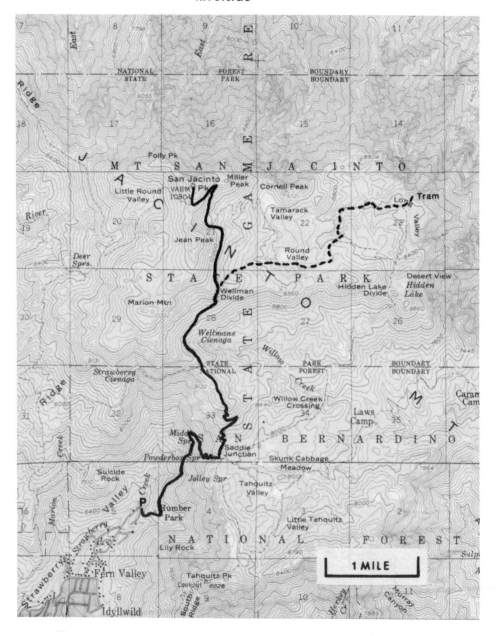

Sacramento

Carpenter Hill   828′   **#56**

Location and Maps: Northeast corner of the county
USGS 7½-minute *Clarkesville, Folsom*

Private Highpoint Notes: The mighty Sierra Nevada rises from humble beginnings like Carpenter Hill, a leading edge of the foothills that culminate in airy peaks 60 miles to the east. Antennas top the rounded hill, easily visible from U.S. 50. The busy highway cuts across a saddle between Carpenter Hill to the north and a slightly lower knoll to the south, less than 700 yards from the highpoint. Although esthetically unremarkable, Carpenter Hill holds a special distinction as the lowest highpoint among the 58 California counties*. Damé Construction Company of San Ramon owns much of the highpoint acreage, and the company formerly allowed highpoint seekers to visit the site. The Scott Road/East Bidwell exit off Highway 50, 22 miles east of Sacramento, goes north to Clarksville Road. A mile down Clarksville Road, hikers parked, hopped a fence, and walked up an asphalt road that serves the antenna facilities. Unfortunately, according to company spokesman M.W. Rupprecht, pending construction activity now precludes entry onto the property without specific written consent.

An easy 1.5-mile round-trip walk gained 270 feet to reach a benchmark embedded in a diagonal boulder among a rock pile near an antenna-facility fence. Carpenter Hill takes its name from the benchmark inscription, perhaps the surname of a local landowner at the time of the geodetic survey. The view is surprisingly expansive. The Sacramento Valley unfurls to the west. Grassy foothills spread to the south and steepen to the east. The Sutter Buttes rise above subdivisions and farmlands in the northwest. On clear days, the Capitol dome glistens from afar, and Mount Diablo marks the southwestern horizon, some 75 miles away. Dark Jurassic-Triassic metavolcanic rocks are scattered over the surrounding pastureland, accented by a few stately blue oaks. A community plan called for Carpenter Hill to be dedicated open space, but development holds a higher priority.

The County: Sacramento County takes its name from the Sacramento River. In 1808 explorer Gabriel Moraga named a tributary *Sacramento,* Spanish for "Holy Sacrament," and in time the main stream took the name. The state's largest river carries one third of California's annual runoff. The watercourse begins as a small lake outlet near Mount Eddy (Trinity County's highpoint), flows to a confluence with the American River at Sacramento, and later empties into San Francisco Bay, a 400-mile-long course. The river provides a great port; it allowed Sacramento to burgeon as a trade and supply center for gold miners and later for agriculture.

---

*Two highpoints (Mount Whitney and Snow Mountain East) are each shared by two counties (Inyo/Tulare and Colusa/Lake), making a total of 56, not 58, highpoints.

Sacramento became a terminus for the Pony Express, a depot for the state's first railroad, and a site for the state capital. Modeled after the nation's capitol, the neoclassic state capitol building shows off Roman Corinthian columns, a 210-foot-high dome, and a gilded cupola. Nearby, the California State Indian Museum chronicles native American culture, Sutter's Fort displays the first non-native settlement in Sacramento, and the California State Railroad Museum warehouses 21 locomotives and cars, the largest museum of its kind in the world.

Sacramento

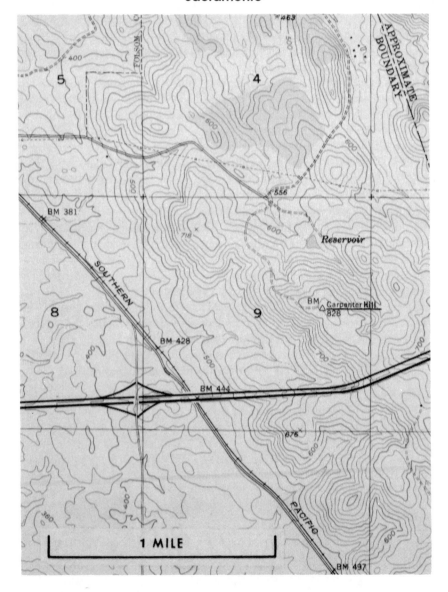

San Benito

San Benito Mountain   5241′   **#36**

Location and Maps:	Southeast corner of the county
	USGS 7½-minute *San Benito Mtn., Idria;* BLM
	Clear Creek Management Area
Distance:	2.2 miles round trip/600′ elevation gain
Grade:	Moderate/Class 1
Hiking Time:	1 hour
Season:	November to April

Trailnotes: The lofty Diablo Range stretches for almost 200 miles along the west side of the Central Valley; San Benito Mountain tops the range, and its high ridgeline entices mountain lovers as they drive along a monotonous section of I 5. The peak lies on BLM land within the 50,000-acre Clear Creek Management Area. However, the BLM issues this warning: "Air, soils, and water in the Clear Creek area contain asbestos which has been determined to be hazardous to your health." Despite the naturally occurring serpentine asbestos, around 42,000 people a year visit the locality, mostly off-road vehicle users, hunters, and rockhounds. Studies by the University of California concluded that people who have used the area over the past few years probably suffer no ill effects. Serpentine soils expert Arthur Kruckeberg maintains there should be no problem during the wet season, when dampness from rain and occasionally from snow avert airborn asbestos fibers. The BLM also recommends winter-to-spring visitation, using a respirator approved for asbestos, and washing your vehicle and attire after the trip. A maintained dirt road comes to within a mile of the summit, and a steeper jeep trail—used for the hike— leads to the top. Try to time your outing a week or two after a storm, because the dirt road becomes impassable to conventional cars and two-wheel-drive trucks when muddy. The mountain and the county's name trace back to a river named by Spanish explorer Juan Crespi in 1772, to honor San Benedicto (contracted as San Benito or Saint Benedict), the patron saint of the married, and founder of the Benedictine Order.

Approach: From I 5, 60 miles north of Kettleman City and 30 miles south of Santa Nella, take the Shields Avenue-Little Panoche Road offramp. Go 20 miles west on County Road J1 to the intersection of Panoche and Little Panoche roads. Or, from SR 25, 13 miles south of Hollister, take County Road J1 for 29 miles to the intersection of Panoche and Little Panoche roads. From the intersection, continue 3 miles south on Panoche Road, turn right onto New Idria Road and drive 22 miles to New Idria, an old mining town. (One of the deepest, most productive quicksilver mines in the world ceased operation here in 1973.) From New Idria the road becomes dirt and winds upward 3.5 miles to a signed junction with Clear Creek Road. Proceed straight ahead and after 1 mile pass a sign announcing SAN BENITO MOUNTAIN NATURAL AREA. Continue just over 3 miles beyond the sign and then watch for a sawed-off stump on the right side of the road. If you come to a fork in the road before seeing the stump, backtrack a short distance. Park along the roadside by the stump. Near the stump an unsigned spur road heads west up the mountain.

Directions to Summit: Hike up the moderately steep jeep road to the top, just over 1 mile. Several communication towers smudge the summit. Oak, pine, ceanothus, and manzanita surround the highpoint. A benchmark sits just northeast of the highest rockpile.

The View: Walk around the summit shelf to gain marvelous views. San Carlos Peak pokes up in the north, backed by ongoing links of the Diablo chain. Descending ridges fall away toward the Central Valley in the east. Antenna-topped Santa Rita Peak stands out in the south, while the Santa Lucia Range, capped by Junipero Serra Peak, silhouettes the western horizon.

The Environment: An enormous serpentine mass intruded into the overlying sedimentary formations during the Jurassic Period, about 150 million years ago. Serpentine soils tend to be stony, shallow, deficient in plant nutrients like nitrogen and phosphorous, and high in toxic metals like magnesium and iron. Unusual flora result, reflected in barren slopes, endemics, and odd plant associations. San Benito Mountain Natural Area protects the endemic rayless layia, talus fritillary, and San Benito evening primose. Only about 20 shrubs grow on the serpentine, notably leather oak, chamise, and bigberry manzanita. The thin forest includes Jeffrey, Coulter, and Digger pines. These three species grow together nowhere else on earth. The highly mineralized serpentine has been extensively mined for asbestos, mercury, and other minerals. Benitoite, the rare, fiery-blue state gemstone, draws rockhounds to the Clear Creek area.

Nearby Campgrounds: None currently. The BLM plans to develop sites outside the asbestos area at the entrance to Clear Creek and in the Jade Mill area.

The County: Mountainous terrain punctuated by isolated valleys character-izes San Benito's topography. Fremont Peak State Park typifies the uplands, clothed in chaparral, grass, and oak. Pinnacles National Monument features ancient volcanic spires and crags. Agriculture and population cluster around Hollister, the county's one sizeable flatland, an extension of the Santa Clara Valley. Hollister serves as a fruit and vegetable packing center and a supply point for the surrounding ranches. Several active fault lines cross the community, known as "the earthquake capital of California." In the Hollister Hills, 9 miles south, the San Andreas Geophysical Observatory utilizes some of the world's most sophis-ticated equipment to monitor the temblors.

Additional Sources of Information/Recommended Reading:

Bureau of Land Management
20 Hamilton Ct.
Hollister, CA 95023
(408) 637-8183

Kruckeberg, Arthur R., *California Serpentines: Flora, Vegetation, Geology, Soils, and Management Problems,* University of California Press, 1984.

Hiker on the summit block

San Benito

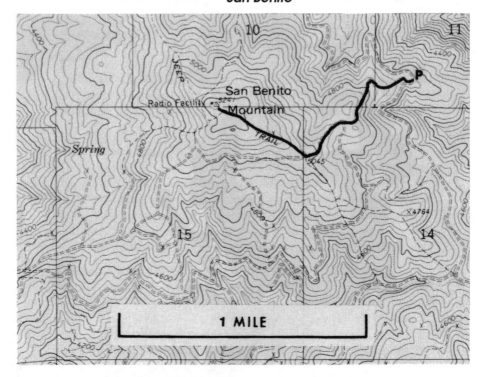

San Bernardino

San Gorgonio Mountain   11,502′   #8

Location and Maps:	Southwest-central edge of the county
	USGS 7½-minute *Forest Falls, San Gorgonio Mtn.;* USFS *San Gorgonio Wilderness;* USFS *San Bernardino National Forest*
Distance:	16.8 miles round trip/5500′ elevation gain
Grade:	Strenuous/Class 1
Hiking Time:	10 hours
Season:	June through October

Trailnotes: The highest point in Southern California. Towering 2 miles above the smog-shrouded lowlands, this matchless mountain thrills visitors with crisp air, blue skies, snow-fed creeks, and gleaming granite evocative of the High Sierra. The peak crowns San Gorgonio Wilderness, a 58,969-acre wildland within San Bernardino National Forest. Heavy visitation necessitates wilderness permits for both overnight camping and day use. Obtain camping permits up to 90 days in advance; pick up self-issue day-use permits at the Mill Creek Ranger Station on the day of your outing. It's a hefty dayhike or an overnight backpack. Bring water or purify trailside water sources. Start *early* (at least by 8:00 A.M.) for the dayhike. Several trails lead to the summit; your described route follows the Vivian Creek Trail. It's steep in places, exceptionally scenic, and the shortest path to the top.

The mountain's name traces back to a local 19th Century mission cattle farm called Rancho San Gorgonio, in honor of the obscure Third Century martyr Saint Gorgonius. From a distance the bare granite hogbacked summit appeared to the Indians as "grey-head." Similarly, early European settlers dubbed it "greyback," a nickname used to this day.

Approach: From I 10 in Redlands (60 miles east of Los Angeles), take the SR 38/Orange Street turnoff. Follow the SR 38 signs, going north 0.5 mile on Orange Street and then east on Lugonia Avenue through the town of Mentone. About 8 miles from I 10, watch for the Mill Creek Ranger Station on your right (to get a self-issue day-use permit), and in another 5 miles reach a junction with Valley of the Falls Boulevard. Turn right onto the boulevard and continue 4.5 miles to the Falls Picnic Area. Pull into the trailhead parking lot above the picnic area.

Directions to Summit: Stride eastward, past the *right* side of a Vivian Creek Trail sign, to connect with an asphalt/dirt road. (The initial vague path to the left of the trail sign often leads hikers to continue mistakenly up Mill Creek Canyon beyond the point where the trail crosses the wash.) Pass a small wooden water tank and several cabins on your way to the roadend, about 0.4 mile from the picnic grounds. At the roadend, a sign directs you across a broad, boulder-strewn wash.

A stiff, switchbacked ascent up a canyonside covered by chaparral, oak, and big-cone spruce brings you to a babbling stream and a shady glade amid tall conifers at Vivian Creek Trail Camp, the first of four possible backpack stops along the route. Continue straight ahead (east) on the main trail, avoiding paths that branch off left and right to campsites. Shortly, the trail crosses the creek and then parallels its north bank for just over a mile before recrossing it near a junction near Halfway Camp. From here you wind upward around steep-sided canyons, and then make a brief descent to lodgepole-pine-scented High Creek Camp, located at 9200 feet and 4.8 miles from the trailhead.

Above the camp you cross High Creek and head up a series of long switchbacks. The route then swings northward, climbs a steep ridge, and reaches a saddle near treeline, where the massive western flanks of San Gorgonio Mountain loom to the right. A moderately pitched, northeast-trending traverse takes you to an 11,050 intersection with the San Bernardino Peak Divide Trail. Bear right (east), and soon pass a trail link to Mineshaft Saddle on your right. A final easy incline brings you to the boulder-jumbled highpoint. The stacked-rock wind shelters of Summit Camp dot the scene. A recently affixed county survey benchmark confirms the elevation (three feet higher than the topo map's designation), while a signature-packed registry box cemented into a rock cleft confirms the peak's popularity; the Forest Service estimates that some 9000 persons a year reach the top.

The View: An unsurpassable wrap-around vantage from the zenith of Southern California. Tall peaks bulk to the north, counterbalanced by meadowlands of the upper Santa Ana River drainage. The San Gabriel Range, topped by Mount San Antonio, appears in the northwest above the often-smog-obscured Los Angeles Basin. On clear days the metropolis, the Pacific Ocean and even Santa Catalina Island are in view. The Santa Ana Mountains rise beyond the lowlands to the southwest. Directly south, the San Jacinto Mountains loft grandly above San Gorgonio Pass, alongside Palm Springs and the Coachella Valley. A Mojave Desert vista extends to the east, as far as the Colorado River and mountains in Arizona.

The Environment: Southern California's east-west trending Transverse Ranges crest in the San Bernardino Mountains, a massive upthrust fault block 60 miles long and 30 miles wide. Snow usually covers the peaks throughout winter and spring. In fact, more snow falls here than anywhere else in Southern California (winter resorts outside the wilderness area attract throngs of skiers). During the Pleistocene Epoch heavier snowfall compacted to form several small glaciers. The glaciers later melted but left behind cirques and moraines, the southernmost evidence of glacial activity in North America.

The airy heights sustain the largest subalpine life zone in California south of the Sierra, where delicate boreal wildflowers grow alongside gnarled limber pines, some over 2000 years old. Descending vegetation zones include lodgepole pine; Jeffrey and sugar pine; ponderosa pine and black oak; streamside alder, willow, and cottonwood; and chaparral. Sagebrush, juniper, and pinyon pine cloak lower desert-facing slopes. Many rare and endangered plants exist in the San Bernardino Range, as do botanical oddities—the world's largest lodgepole pine, the world's biggest Joshua tree, and California's southernmost grove of aspen.

Nearby Campgrounds: U.S. Forest Service campgrounds named Barton Flats, San Gorgonio, and South Fork, located along SR 38, provide car-camping closest to San Gorgonio Mountain. A scenic "Rim of the World Drive" on SR 18 passes ski areas and mountain resorts at Lake Arrowhead and Big Bear Lake, the largest mountain lake in Southern California. The availability of activities such as water skiing and snow skiing close to millions of Southlanders makes San Bernardino National Forest the most heavily visited national forest in America.

The County: San Bernardino County spreads over 20,160 square miles, making it by far the largest county in California and also the largest county in the contiguous 48 states. A valley basin in the southwest corner of the county contains most of the population. The imposing San Bernardino Mountains form a backdrop to the valley, and in the rain shadow north and east of the mountains lies the vast Mojave Desert. Desert ranges, basins, washes, dry lakes, lava flows, and sand dunes cover four fifths of the county.

In 1810 priests dedicated a branch mission on the feast day of Saint Bernardine, linking the saint's name to the area. The city of San Bernardino began in 1851 as a Mormon settlement modeled after Salt Lake City. Today, the city serves as a hub of the booming "Inland Empire" of western San Bernardino and western Riverside counties, one of the fastest growing regions in the nation. Proximity to business centers in Los Angeles and comparatively low land prices spurred the conversion of rural land to subdivisions in towns like Montclair, Rialto, and Rancho Cucamonga. Surrounding agricultural lands still support thriving citrus, poultry, and dairy industries.

Additional Sources of Information/Recommended Reading:

Mill Creek Station, USDA Forest Service
34701 Mill Creek Road
Mentone, CA 92359
(909) 794-1123

Robinson, John W., *San Bernardino Mountain Trails,* 4th ed., Wilderness Press, 1986.
Robinson, John W., *San Gorgonio, A Wilderness Preserved,* San Gorgonio Volunteer Association, 1991.

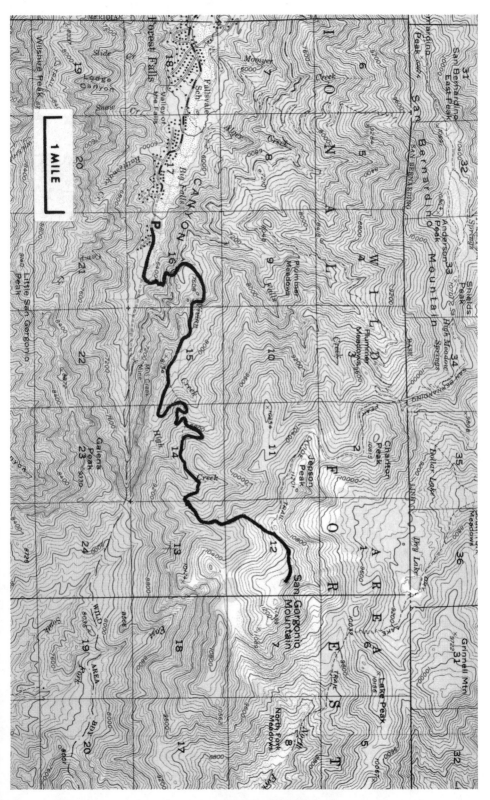

San Bernardino

. . . .

San Diego

Hot Springs Mountain   6533′   **#32**

Location and Maps:	Northeast part of the county
	USGS 7½-minute *Hot Springs Mtn.;* USGS 15-minute *Warner Springs:* Los Coyotes Indian Reservation Brochure-Map
Distance:	5.6 miles round trip/1200′ elevation gain
Grade:	Moderate/Class 2
Hiking Time:	3 hours
Season:	Year-round

PLEASE NOTE: Tribal leaders unexpectedly closed the reservation to visitors after this book was written. Los Coyotes spokesman Banning Taylor expects the reservation to reopen in the spring of 1994. Call the reservation for the latest information (number below).

Trailnotes: San Diego County contains more Indian reservations (18) than any other county in California, and perched atop its largest reservation sits Hot Springs Mountain. The 25,000-acre reservation, mountainous and sparsely populated, is home to the Los Coyotes Band of Indians. They welcome visitors on weekends and holidays. Obtain a day-use or a camping permit at the entrance-gate kiosk, normally open 8 A.M. to 4 P.M. Call or write ahead to arrange a weekday trip. Most passenger cars can handle the reservation's unpaved roads, except during periods of heavy winter rain or occasional snow. Dirt roads access the summit, making a "drive-up" possible. Or you may opt for a robust 14-mile hike on the signed Lookout Road, which begins 0.1 mile beyond the entrance gate. The described route takes a middle path between these two extremes. A brief boulder scramble at the top gives a Class-2 rating to an otherwise-Class-1 hike. Warner Springs, located at the base of the peak, and lesser hot springs said to have once flowed nearby gave the mountain its name.

Approach: From I 15 just south of Temecula, take SR 79 to Warner Springs, approximately 38 miles past the freeway turnoff. From I 8 in San Diego, drive east to El Cajon, and then take SR 67 to Ramona, SR 78 to Santa Ysabel, and SR 79 to Warner Springs, about 70 miles from San Diego. In Warner Springs, turn east onto Camino San Ignacio where a sign alongside SR 79 reads LOS COYOTES RESERVA-TION. Go 0.6 mile, turn right on Los Tules Road, and proceed about 5 miles to the reservation gate. After checking in, continue on the paved road, which soon becomes a dirt road, for 6.1 miles to a prominent junction. Bear left (west) at the junction and go 2.3 miles farther to a campsite (with tables, fire rings, and pit toilets) located on the left side of the road. Park here.

Directions to Summit: Strike off to the west beside a little creek along a rut-riven jeep trail. Shortly, the trail veers south and heads upslope steeply for about 1.2 miles to an intersection with the main Lookout road. Turn right (west) and follow the Lookout road another 1.5 miles to the top. The road undulates for a time and then climbs steadily to a parking flat. From here the lookout rises immediately in the west, and the highpoint (hidden by shrubbery) rises in the east. Follow a faint use trail through the brush for about 150 yards until you reach a large black oak backed by a crevice-laced boulder. Shinny up the crevice to find benchmarked summit rocks topped by a cement platform. The platform once supported a radio antenna and now provides a register nook.

The intriguing, time-worn tower, built in the 1930s by the Civilian Conversation Corps and manned by the Forest Service under an agreement with the Indians, closed down in 1976. The Forest Service planned to dismantle the lookout for public safety, but the Indians asked to let it stand, which it does to this day—barely!

The View: Superb. In the northwest Agua Caliente Canyon gapes below Hot Springs Mountain, backed by the Palomar Range. In the far north, on clear days, San Jacinto Peak and San Gorgonio Mountain rise above their surroundings. An impressive wall of mountains, the Santa Rosa Range, rises in the east, while the Laguna Range and the Cuyamaca Range extend to the south. In the west, past the foothills and the coastal plain, the low-lying profiles of several offshore islands—Los Coronados, San Clemente, and Santa Catalina—wrinkle the ocean horizon.

The Environment: Hot Springs Mountain is part of the granitic, fault-blocked Peninsular Ranges Province. Chaparral girds its lower slopes, while a verdant forest shades its upper reaches. The lush stands of oak, incense-cedar, white fir, and

Ice on window of old lookout, Hot Springs Mountain

pines (Coulter, Jeffrey, ponderosa, and sugar) surprise first-time visitors to Southern California. The mountain's height squeezes enough moisture from passing clouds (around 35 inches per year) to support the trees, and indirectly, the hot springs. Surface water percolates far underground, where its temperature increases (water reaches about 85° Fahrenheit at 1 mile and 212° at 2 miles below the earth's surface). The heated water resurfaces through rock fissures, such as the fault line at Warner Springs. The spring, now a private resort closed to the public, has a long history. It served as a refreshing stagecoach stop in the late 1800s, and, before that, Indians immersed in the pools to keep warm on cold nights. Prehistoric evidence suggests villagers enjoyed the hot springs for thousands of years.

Nearby Campgrounds: A developed campground 2.5 miles up the road from the entrance gate and scattered primitive campsites invite an overnight stay on the Reservation. Close by Anza-Borrego Desert State Park offers unlimited opportunities for camping.

The County: Spanish explorers named the area after Saint Didacus of Alcala, Spain. The county sprawls across 4255 square miles, including 76 miles of coastline and half a million acres of desert. In the spring, it's possible to splash in the ocean, throw snowballs in the mountains, and see wildflowers in the desert all on the same day. Such amenities and a mild climate have spurred spectacular population growth. During the last 40 years the city of San Diego jumped from the 31st to the 6th largest city in the nation. Of course, the expanding population adversely impacts the environment. Habitat destruction, combined with the great diversity of climate, topography, and geology, give the county a somber distinction: San Diego has the highest incidence of rare and endangered plants of any county in the continental United States.

Additional Sources of Information/Recommended Reading:

Los Coyotes Indian Reservation
P.O. Box 249
Warner Springs, CA 92086
(619) 782-3269

Pryde, Philip R., ed., *San Diego, an Introduction to the Region,* 3rd ed., Kendall/Hunt Publishing Company, 1992.
Schad, Jerry, *Afoot and Afield in San Diego County,* 2nd ed., Wilderness Press, 1992.

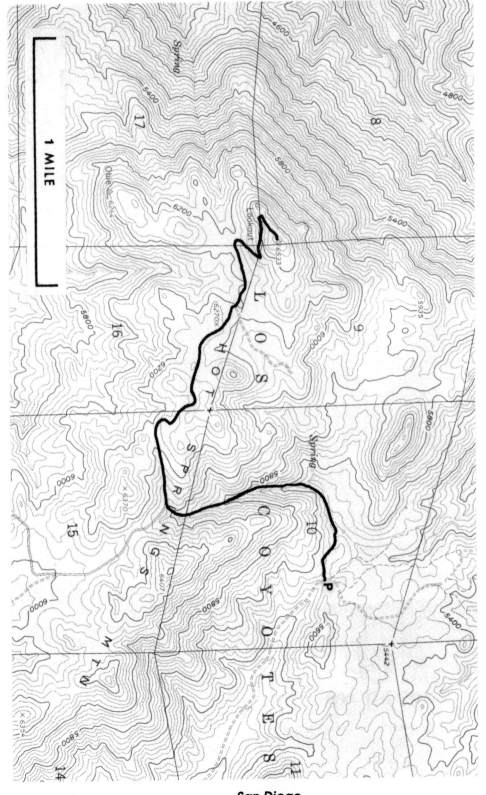

San Diego

San Francisco

Mount Davidson   927′   **#55**

Location and Maps: Slightly southwest of the center of the county
USGS 7½-minute *San Francisco South*
Distance: 0.5 mile round trip/150′ elevation gain
Grade: Easy/Class 1
Hiking Time: 20 minutes
Season: Year-round

Trailnotes: A short jaunt through a delightful urban hideaway, the only city-encircled county summit. Pleasant residential neighborhoods wrap around Mount Davidson Park, a 26-acre tree-filled hill, capped by a 103-foot concrete cross. The trees block a 360° vantage (as can be had at slightly lower Twin Peaks to the north), but much of the City and the South Bay come into view from a summit shelf. In the 1920s, when development threatened the crest, concerned citizens successfully campaigned to establish a park. Professor George Davidson (1825-1911) surveyed the mountain in 1862, which was later named in his honor. Davidson led a geodetic survey of the West Coast and later served as president of the California Academy of Sciences. Avoid San Francisco's rush-hour traffic by visiting the park during midday or, preferably on a quiet weekend morning.

Approach: From U.S. 101 near the Golden Gate, take SR 1 south about 4 miles through a gauntlet of traffic signals to Vicente Street. Turn left on Vicente, and ½ mile later turn left on Portola Drive. Follow Portola for almost ½ mile and then steer right on Marne Avenue, and right again on Landsdale Avenue, which soon intersects Dalewood Way. Go left on Dalewood and climb one of San Francisco's steeper streets to a four-way intersection with Myra Way, Sherwood Court, and Landsdale Avenue. Park along the parkside curb of Dalewood Way.

From I 280, 2 miles south of the junction with U.S. 101, take the Monterey Blvd. offramp west for a mile to Hazelwood Ave. Turn right on Hazelwood, right on Casitas Ave., and right again on Landsdale, which winds up to the four-way intersection. Public bus transportation serves Mount Davidson, and it's about a 1.5-mile walk from the Glen Park BART Station. From the station, go west on Joost Avenue to Hazelwood and follow the directions above or, using a street map, explore one of several meandering neighborhood routes to the park.

Directions to Summit: From the four-way intersection, find the bus-stop pole labeled TERMINAL and a sign that reads WALKING TRAIL TO MT. DAVIDSON. A moderately steep dirt road heads up the wooded slope. In 0.1 mile, one side trail and then another lead off to the left, but keep to the right, on the main trail, and circle an eastern knoll to gain the flat-topped summit. According to a City survey, this highest of San Francisco's famous hills measures 927 feet, followed by Twin Peaks South at 910 feet and Sutro Crest at 909 feet. On the east end of the summit clearing you will find a square vent from an underground pillbox built during World War II. On the west end stands the imposing cruciform. Return by way of the main trail that winds downhill west and then south to its terminus, across the street from 39 Dalewood Way. Finish the loop by walking east along Dalewood about 100 yards back to your starting point.

A maze of short cuts and side trails crisscrosses the park. For a steeper north-side approach (reached from Portola Drive), find the little stairway between 919 and 925 Rockdale Drive and wend your way to the summit.

The View: Mount Davidson overlooks one of the most beautiful urban environments in the world. Downtown San Francisco's glass towers scintillate in the sun, and beyond them the blue bay waters glisten. The San Francisco-Oakland Bay Bridge stretches toward faintly visible East Bay cities, the Oakland-Berkeley Hills, and distant Mount Diablo. Closer in, a part of Golden Gate Park, the Presidio, Sutro Towers, and Twin Peaks can be seen in the north, the Mission District and Bernal Heights in the east, and McLaren Park and San Bruno Mountain in the southeast. Due south, the Santa Cruz Mountains march down the peninsula.

Over the years, thousands of people have witnessed daybreak views from the hilltop, because Mount Davidson has since 1923 served as a site for Easter Sunrise services. In 1934 President Franklin D. Roosevelt pressed a gold telegraph key in Washington D.C. to switch on floodlights at the base of the cross for the first time. Illuminated at night, it can be seen for 50 miles.

The Environment: Little remains of Mount Davidson's natural environment; its lower slopes are covered with houses, its upper ones with mostly exotic vegetation. On the open north-eastern hillside, remnants of native blue wild rye and bunchgrass mix with alien wild oats and rabbit-foot grass. Blue brodiaea, golden poppies, violet phacelia and a few additional spring wildflowers somehow push up through the weeds. A forest of eucalyptus, cypress, and other trees shades an interesting understory, where native baby blue eyes and ferns grow alongside introduced ivy vines and berry bushes.

The Mt. Davidson trailhead

From this highest point in the city, observers have a front row seat to see the marvelous fogfalls. Particularly during the summer, moist marine air passes eastward over chilly coastal waters, where it cools and its water vapor condenses to form fog. The fog piles up offshore. Inland, hot air rises, generating a partial vacuum that sucks the cool, fog-laden air through a famous breach in the Coast Ranges, the Golden Gate. Sometimes modest fingers of fog encroach on lower parts of the Peninsula and stop there. At other times, a billowing avalanche of fog rolls up to engulf Mount Davidson itself.

Nearby Campgrounds: There are no public campgrounds within the coterminous City and County of San Francisco, but a number of youth hostels provide inexpensive lodging.

The County: Uniquely situated on a narrow peninsula, surrounded on three sides by ocean and bay waters, this smallest and most densely populated California county has a varied landscape on its 46 square miles. The name derives from the Mission San Francisco de Assisi. The county's hills consist of Francisco Formation cherts, sandstones, and shales, while the lowlands contain poorly consolidated sand, gravel, and mudfill. Structures built upon these unstable sediments suffer the most damage when earthquakes hit, inevitable occurrences because the San Andreas Rift is close by.

The maritime influence moderates temperatures and gives the city one of the most moderate climates in the country, with an average seasonal range of just 12 degrees. Brisk ocean breezes "air condition" the city and disperse pollutants to produce the cleanest skies of any metropolis in the state. The county's boundary also extends out into San Francisco Bay, incorporating Alcatraz, Yerba Buena, and Treasure islands. The bay ranks as one of the best natural harbors in the world. Its waters reach to a depth of 216 feet, but 70% of the bay is less than 12 feet deep. Since the mid-1800s, river sediments and fill projects have reduced its volume by one third.

Additional Sources of Information/Recommended Reading:

Bay Area Rapid Transit (BART)
(415) 788-2278

Municipal Railway of San
Francisco
(415) 673-6864
Call for Muni bus timetable
serving Mount Davidson

Doss, Margot Patterson. *San Francisco At Your Feet: The Great Walks in a Walker's Town,* 2nd revised and updated ed., Grove Press, 1980.
Whitnah, Dorothy L., *An Outdoor Guide to the San Francisco Bay Area,* 5th ed., Wilderness Press, 1989.

San Francisco

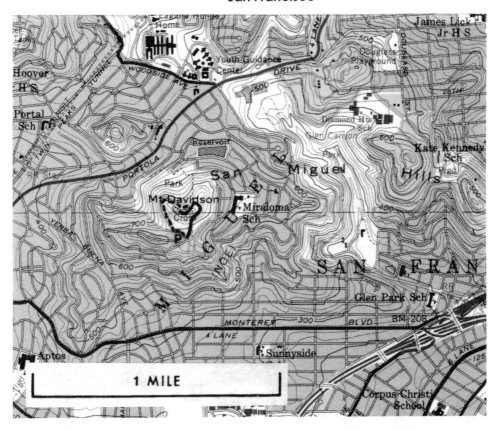

San Joaquin

Mount Boardman North   3626′   **#47**

Location and Maps: Southwest corner of the county
USGS 7½-minute *Mt. Boardman, Eylar Mtn.,*
Cedar Mtn., Lone Tree Creek

Private Highpoint Notes: Secluded among huge hills and isolated by private ranchland, this Diablo Range mountaintop goes little noticed except by surveyors—four county boundaries converge on the crest. Fittingly, the peak honors W. F. Boardman, surveyor of Alameda County and City Engineer of Oakland from 1864 to 1868. A gently sloping half-mile-long saddle connects Mount Boardman to a north summit 33 feet higher than Mount Boardman itself. The owner of a 40,000+ acre cattle ranch reaching from Mount Boardman to Discovery Peak in Alameda County gave a few highpoint seekers permission to hike to the peak. But the ranch manager, cool to increasing numbers of hikers and to liability release forms, no longer grants entry.

From a gate on Mines Road, ranch roads and steep trails push eastward to the ridgeline and then curve south to the peak. Hikers passed dwellings, irrigation ponds, and hunters' trailers along the route. The trek entailed a 10-mile round trip with 1800 feet elevation gain. Tarraville Canyon, to the south, affords more direct access, but several homesteads lie between Mines Road and the peak in this canyon. Chamise-chaparral predominates on Mount Boardman, interspersed with oak, Digger pine, and juniper. A cement survey cylinder lies atop Mount Boardman North, while a small rock cairn tops Mount Boardman proper. From the rounded summits, jumbled mountains and canyons fall off in all directions, with the Central Valley visible in the northeast. Mount Oso rises directly in the east, where the California Department of Forestry erected its first fire lookout in 1921. Far from forests the wood-framed lookout served to protect stock range from fire at the behest of local cattle ranchers.

The County: Spanish explorers named the San Joaquin River after Saint Joachim, Biblical father of the Virgin Mary, and the county derived its name from the river. The San Joaquin flows through the heart of the county's fertile flatland, bounded on the west by the Diablo Range and on the east by the Sierra foothills. The San Joaquin joins the Sacramento and Mokelumne rivers to create myriad waterways in the Delta, a magnet for houseboaters and anglers. A deep-water channel meanders from San Francisco Bay to Stockton, the county seat, creating a major "seaport" almost 80 miles from the ocean. Giant freighters ply the channel and carry California agricultural products worldwide. Major San Joaquin County crops include corn, tomatoes, asparagus, dry beans, sweet cherries, apricots, walnuts, table grapes, and wine grapes. Lodi, known for its Tokay vineyards, holds an annual nationally acclaimed Grape Festival and Wine Show.

Jeep trail to the summit of Mt. Boardman North

San Joaquin

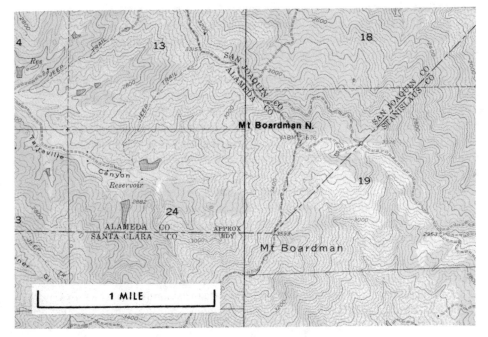

San Luis Obispo

Caliente Mountain   5106'   **#37**

Location and Maps: Southeast part of the county
USGS 7½-minute *Caliente Mtn., Painted Rock;*
BLM Access Map, Temblor-Caliente Range
Distance: 16 miles round trip/1600' elevation gain
Grade: Moderate/Class 1
Hiking Time: 8 hours
Season: Year-round, with limitations

Trailnotes: A fascinating, faraway highpoint. The mesa-topped mountain lies within an 18,122-acre Bureau of Land Management Wilderness Study Area. The BLM recommends the route described below, neither the shortest nor the longest of several approaches to the summit. A well-graded seasonal access road leads to the trailhead. The BLM normally opens the road gate from April through November, except when bad weather makes the road impassable. Call the BLM office in Bakersfield for current information. When the gate bars car entry, you can walk up the road to the trailhead, gaining 1000 feet in 3 miles. This option transforms the outing into a strenuous 22-mile round trip with a 2600-foot elevation gain. Dayhike or backpack. The route has no water and little shade. Ideally, visit Caliente Mountain, and the nearby Carrizo Plain Natural Area, in the spring. Hunters stalk game in the fall, rain and occasional snow muddy the course in the winter, and the sun bakes the peak in the summer. *Caliente* means "hot" in Spanish. However, the name stems not from the summer heat but from a hot spring, Ojo Caliente, located in the Cuyama Valley south of the summit.

Approach: From I 5, 4 miles north of the junction with U.S. 99, take SR 166 west for 32 miles to Reyes Station and a junction with Soda Lake Road. From U.S. 101 at Santa Maria, take SR 166 east for 68 miles to Reyes Station. Turn onto Soda Lake Road and drive over on-again-off-again pavement for 29 miles to a turnoff on your left. Proceed up the road 3.8 miles to a road gate. A spur to your left goes to the Shelby Parking Area. Follow the main road 3 more miles to the Caliente Ridge Parking Area.

From I 5 at Buttonwillow, take SR 58 west 45 miles to California Valley. From U.S. 101 at Santa Margarita, follow SR 58 east for 41 miles to California Valley. Turn south onto Soda Lake Road, go 13.3 miles to the aforementioned turnoff, and proceed as above.

Directions to Summit: Fence posts across the road from the parking area identify the trailhead. Sally forth down the roadbed. The eroding dirt track wends across an undulating ridgetop that tilts gently toward the summit, almost 8 miles to the southeast. Ignore the many road spurs. At about 2.5 miles, where a solar antenna appears out of nowhere, you can glimpse the highpoint far to the south and left of a rounded hill. Continue traversing a long series of rises and saddles. At last the road curves eastward to surmount the summit ridge. A dilapidated lookout and a lone telephone pole top the peak. Locate a benchmark outside the lookout's north wall and find a register and lawn furniture inside the structure. The observers who manned this World War II vintage lookout spotted fires, but their main duty was watching for enemy aircraft—to foil any sneak attack on strategic oil fields in the vicinity.

The View: Solitude and vast spaces surround you on Caliente Mountain. Steep canyons plunge toward the compact Cuyama Valley to the west and south, and toward the spacious Carrizo Plain to the north and east. Beyond the valleys, behold a vista-packed montane melange: the Sierra Madre and San Rafael mountains in the southwest, the La Panza and Diablo ranges in the north, the Temblor and Tehachapi mountains in the east, and a tumult of Transverse Ranges in the south.

The Environment: Geologically young, unmetamorphosed Miocene marine sandstone and shale underlie Caliente Mountain. The 25-30-million-year-old sediments weather into distinctive shapes, as at Shelby Rocks near the road gate. (Close-by Painted Rock displays some of the best Indian pictograph rock art in North America.) The buff-colored formations possess a high potential for oil and gas development. This potential, combined with current grazing and game-management practices, led the BLM to endorse a "no wilderness" alternative for the Study Area. But Caliente Mountain deserves wilderness status. In the spring, lush annual grasses soften a landscape replete with juniper, sagebrush, and scrub

Abandoned lookout and snow on Caliente Mountain

oak. The California Steppe and Grassland provinces, some of which we see here, remain unrepresented in the National Wilderness System. Wilderness status would complement the adjoining Carrizo Plain Natural Area. The newly established 180,000-acre Carrizo Preserve holds more rare and endangered vertebrates than any other place in California, including the blunt-nosed leopard lizard, the giant kangaroo rat, and the San Joaquin kit fox, the smallest fox in the United States.

Nearby Campgrounds: The BLM allows primitive car camping at the Shelby Parking Area and at the KCL Ranch, 13 miles south, off Soda Lake Road. The nearest developed campground with water lies 26 miles away at La Panza, in Los Padres National Forest, on Pozo Road off SR 58, northwest of California Valley.

The County: The Mission San Luis Obispo bequeathed the county's name, honoring Saint Louis, the Bishop of Toulouse. Mountains pervade the landscape, with the Santa Lucia Range in the west, the Machesna Mountain Wilderness and the Temblor and Caliente ranges in the east. Population clusters in coastal plains and valleys (Morro Bay, Arroyo Grande, and San Luis Obispo) and along the upper Salinas River Valley (Paso Robles and Atascadero). Picturesque hamlets perch between sheer ocean cliffs and mountainous uplands at Cambria and San Simeon. Opulent Hearst San Simeon State Historical Monument and scenic Montana De Oro and Morro Bay state parks draw thousands of visitors yearly. Famous Morro Rock once stood as an island at high tide. Over 1 million tons of rock quarried between 1880 and 1963 dramatically altered its shape. The 581-foot-high landmark now stands as a wildlife sanctuary (climbing prohibited) to protect endangered peregrine-falcon nests high on the rock.

Additional Sources of Information/Recommended Reading:

Bureau of Land Management, Caliente Resource Area
4301 Rosedale Highway
Bakersfield, CA 93308
(805) 861-4236

Bureau of Land Management, "Carrizo Plain Natural Area, An Endangered Species Management Showcase," brochure.
San Luis Obispo County Trail Guide, 2nd ed., Santa Lucia Chapter, Sierra Club, 1989.

San Luis Obispo

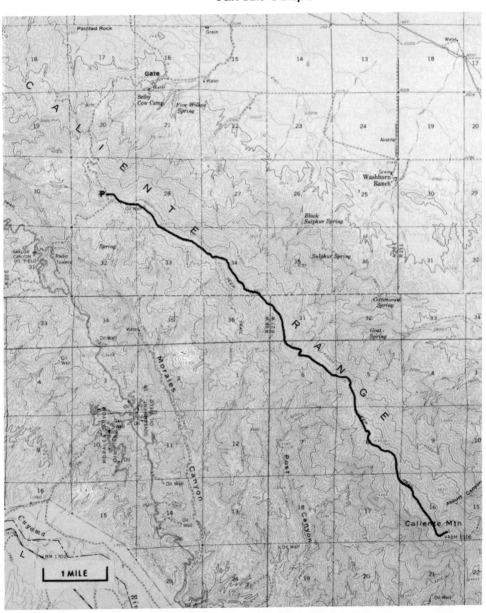

San Mateo

Long Ridge   2600+′   **#52**

Location and Maps:	South end of the county
	USGS 7½-minute *Mindego Hill;* MROSD *Long Ridge/Saratoga Gap Open Space Preserves* Map Brochure
Distance:	4.2 miles round trip/580′ elevation gain
Grade:	Moderate/Class 1
Hiking Time:	2 hours
Season:	Year-round

Trailnotes: This pleasing highpoint tops a grassy sward and forest-edged knoll on the fringe of Long Ridge Open Space Preserve in the northern Santa Cruz Mountains. The Midpeninsula Regional Open Space District manages the 1011-acre preserve. Established in 1972 as a tax-supported public agency, MROSD has acquired over 35,000 acres spread over 24 open-space preserves in San Mateo and Santa Cruz counties. The Long Ridge Preserve stays open 365 days a year, from dawn to dusk. A well-maintained and mostly tree-shaded trail extends close to the preserve boundary. The highpoint sits just 200 yards beyond the boundary. Although on private property, use trails from the boundary to the highpoint indicate that hikers routinely visit the site. Mountaineer Andy Martin located the highpoint in 1993. The name "Long Ridge" presumably refers to the relative length of the landform. Highpointers like to synchronize the Long Ridge climb with a brief trip to the nearby Santa Cruz County summit, Mount McPherson.

Approach: From SR 17 at Los Gatos, 7 miles south of San Jose and 20 miles north of Santa Cruz, take SR 9 for 10.5 miles to Skyline Boulevard at Saratoga Gap. Turn right on Skyline Boulevard and travel 3.3 miles to reach the Upper Stevens Creek County Park/Grizzly Flat parking area. Park on either side of the road. The trailhead is on the west side of Skyline Boulevard. From I 280, between Palo Alto and Mountain View, take the Page Mill Road exit, turn west, and snake upward 9 miles to Skyline Boulevard. Bear left on Skyline Boulevard and proceed 3 miles to the Upper Stevens Creek County Park/Grizzly Flat parking area. (To reach Mount McPherson, drive 6.4 miles south from the parking area on Skyline Boulevard, or from the junction of Skyline Boulevard and SR 9 at Saratoga Gap go 3.1 miles south. Park along the roadside near milepost 35 SCL 11.09, and by a black mailbox and a grey mailbox numbered 15717. A dirt road immediately south of the mailboxes marks the trailhead.)

Directions to Summit: Walk through the fence threshold and make a gradual 0.5-mile descent across grassy slopes to a tree-canopied creek bottom. Cross a footbridge and shortly bear right at a signed trail junction. Follow a moderately steep path through shady woods accented with flowers, ferns, and mossy rocks. The gradient eases as the trail parallels an asphalt road and makes a brief descent to a signed junction, 0.7 mile from the footbridge. (At this point, you may choose to take the slightly longer Peters Creek loop trail back to the junction by the footbridge on your return). Continue to the right and climb a gentle grade to reach dirt-surfaced Long Ridge Road in 0.8 mile. Here, a sign reads LONG RIDGE ROAD, TO WARD ROAD, TO SKYLINE BOULEVARD. To your right, the dirt road runs northwest to a locked gate, and an overgrown spur road (blocked by a log) heads west. Follow the spur road. Pass a small red PRIVATE PROPERTY AHEAD sign and presently reach a downed fenceline. This fence delimits the preserve boundary (a use trail continues west for 70 yards and then northwest upslope for 130 more yards to the highpoint at the forest's edge. A scrawny young oak growing in the grass among decaying logs and pieces of weathered lumber mark the summit).

The View: The heart of the Santa Cruz Mountains spreads to the south in verdant, layered ridges. Long Ridge overlooks Hickory Oak Ridge to the southeast, Castle Rock State Park to the south, and Portola State Park to the southwest. Trees impede vistas to the north. Walk a short ways southward from the top to see Mount Hamilton on the east and the Pacific Ocean on the western horizon.

The Environment: The outcrops on Long Ridge consist of mostly Tertiary-age buff-colored sandstone and conglomerate. Many minor faults lace the vicinity, and the major San Andreas Rift lies a few miles to the east. Steep, densely wooded canyons fall away from the ridgetop. Multibranched oak, sizable madrone, and tall Douglas-fir line the trail route, along with sycamore, bay, tanoak, and other species. Steller jays frequently squawk from tree branches and coyotes sometimes yelp from recesses in the forest. In season, wildflowers color grassy openings—poppies, violets, lilies, goldfields, and many more. Local Costanoan Indians collected flower and grass seeds for food and then set fire to the hills. The fires enriched the soil, improved the next year's harvest, and helped prevent more damaging wildfires due to greater fuel accumulation. The area's grassy swales may be partly due to the Indians' burning practices.

Nearby Campgrounds: Portola State Park, off Alpine Road, has 52 campsites. Nearby Castle Rock State Park, off Skyline Boulevard, offers primitive walk-in trail camps. Adjacent state parks at Butano, Big Basin Redwoods, and Henry Cowell Redwoods provide numerous campsites.

The County: *San Mateo,* Spanish for the apostle Saint Matthew, first appeared as a regional place name in 1776. The Santa Cruz Mountains rise between the ocean and the bay sides of the county. The cool and often foggy ocean side contains rocky headlands and beach terraces interspersed with truck farms and small communities. The warmer and milder bay side consists of foothills and a broad alluvial plain with a swelling population. Nurseries, retail stores, and electronics plants, among myriad other businesses, spur the economy. Early logging enterprises echo in county names like Redwood City, Page Mill Road, and Woodside. San Mateo boasts many elegant residential communities, including Burlingame, Hillsborough, and Atherton.

Additional Sources of Information/Recommended Reading:

Midpeninsula Regional Open Space District
330 Distel Circle
Los Altos, CA 94022-1404
(415) 691-1200

Rusmore, Jean, and Frances Spangle, *Peninsula Trails, Outdoor Adventures on the San Francisco Peninsula,* 2nd ed., Wilderness Press, 1989.

San Mateo

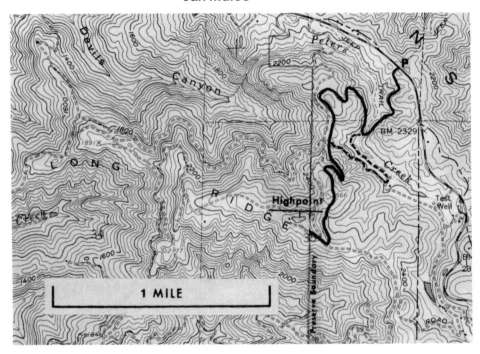

Santa Barbara

Big Pine Mountain   6800+´   **#31**

Location and Maps:	Central east side of the county
	USGS 7½-minute *Big Pine Mtn., Madulce Peak,*
	Fox Mountain, Salisbury Potrero; USFS *Dick*
	Smith Wilderness
Distance:	31 miles round trip/4200´ elevation gain
Grade:	Strenuous/Class 1
Hiking Time:	16 hours
Season:	Year round, with limitations

Trailnotes: Big Pine Mountain is the southernmost major peak of the South Coast Ranges. Big Pine crowns a vast, rugged wildland filled with steep ridges, sheer canyons and impenetrable chaparral. Fortunately for highpoint seekers, a dirt road and a jeep track forge to the summit, located within 64,700-acre Dick Smith Wilderness and near adjoining 149,000-acre San Rafael Wilderness. The standard hiking route follows the road. A slightly shorter, steeper trail makes a semiloop trip possible. Both routes are described. Madulce Spring, 6.5 miles up the trail, and Chokecherry Spring, 9.5 miles up the road, provide dependable water sources except in the driest years.

With an early start, strong hikers make the trek in a day. Others prefer to backpack. Black bears live in the area, including "problem bears" that have been captured along the Southland urban fringe and relocated in the Wilderness. Hikers seldom see bears and rangers report no problems, but backpackers should secure their food. The Forest Service requires no wilderness permit, but it does require a campfire permit between May 15 and October 31, even to use a portable stove. Rangers often impose long fire closures in the Wilderness, normally from about July 1 to November 15. Winter rains frequently wash out the access road, and high-country snowfall occasionally impedes hiking. Call the ranger station before your trip for the latest information.

Approach: From I 5, 4 miles north of the junction with U.S. 99, take SR 166 west 38 miles to an intersection with SR 33. From U.S. 101, 3 miles north of Santa Maria, take SR 166 east 65 miles to reach SR 33. Drive 2.7 miles south on SR 33 and then turn right onto Foothill Road. Foothill Road crosses the Cuyama River Wash and in 2.1 miles intersects Santa Barbara Canyon Road. (The wash has a ROAD CLOSED sign, applicable only at the rare times when water fills the channel; if necessary, circumvent the wash by traveling 4.7 miles west from the SR 166/SR 33 junction, then 2.4 miles south on Kirschenmann Road, and left on Foothill Road for 3 miles to join Santa Barbara Canyon Road. Go south on Santa Barbara Canyon Road 3.1 miles to a fork and turn right. Proceed 4.4 miles to a fork at Santa Barbara

Canyon Ranch. Bear right and cross a stream as the pavement ends. Follow the dirt road up Santa Barbara Canyon 5.1 miles to a locked gate, keeping right at junctions along the way.

Directions to Summit: From the gate hike up the dirt road, flat at first and then moderately steep. Views open up as you ascend. In about 3.5 miles you pass wooden gate posts, and in another 0.5 mile you reach a junction near a grassy plane called Santa Barbara Portrero. Go left (south) at the junction. The road rises and dips gently, drops to a drainage divide, and then climbs steadily to Chokecherry Spring, about 5.5 miles past the junction. Just above and below the water trough and tank, the road flattens out enough to make a suitable, if uninspiring, campsite.

Continue upward for about 2 miles to a saddle and a sign indicating the Madulce Trailhead. Shortly the road veers from south to west. Proceed west on the road, losing several hundred feet elevation in a long mile to another saddle. At the saddle a rusty sign proclaims the San Rafael Wilderness (the first wilderness designated under the landmark 1964 Wilderness Act). A trail to Bear Camp, ½ mile away, heads north. Water can usually be found there. Beyond the saddle the road forks, a spur to the left descending in 40 yards to Alamar Station, a good campsite but without water.

Advance on the main road, climbing moderately around the north flank of Big Pine Mountain. Approximately 2.3 miles beyond Alamar Station, where the road swings sharply from northwest to southwest, watch for an indistinct jeep road on your left marked by a triangular orange sign inscribed D73. The jeep road switchbacks to the conifer-covered, tablelike summit. A register rests on a boulder pile to the right of the jeep road, about 70 yards west from another triangular sign labeled D74. You may wish to mount other small boulder piles on the flat summit to guarantee reaching the topmost point. The old 15-minute topo marks a summit of 6828 feet, while the new 7½-minute map shows only a 6800-foot contour.

On your return you can take the trail route at the Madulce junction, better to descend than to ascend because of its steepness. From the saddle the trail descends continuously, passing a spur to Madulce Peak en route to a junction with the Santa Barbara Trail, about 2.6 miles from the saddle. Pass a trail camp, a spring, and the Madulce Ranger Cabin, complete with bunkbeds and a kitchen stove. Take the Santa Barbara Trail down a relentlessly steep grade for over ½ mile, then enjoy a gradual descent along a creek bed for about 6 miles to the access road. At the road, turn left (west) to shortly reach the parking area by the fence gate.

The View: Big pines block the view! Walk around the perimeter of the summit flat to enjoy eye-stretching vistas. In the west a sister peak, West Big Pine Mountain, fills the foreground, and ridge after ridge of the San Rafael Mountains pack the background. In the north Samon Peak pokes up boldly, a highpoint on the Sierra Madre Mountains' spine. Madulce Peak rises immediately to the east, backed by a crumpled procession of Transverse Ranges. Due south, the Santa Ynez Mountains line the horizon, with civilized Santa Barbara out of sight at their base, just 20 air miles but a world away.

The Environment: The wild, corrugated topography originated from weathered bits of ancient mountains washed down to the sea. Crustal-plate movement uplifted, folded, and faulted the ocean-bottom sediments. Granite-based particles formed hard sandstone ridges resistant to erosion, while mud-based particles formed siltstone and shale, easily carved by streams into deep canyons. Remarkably varied vegetation covers the slopes. Near the trailhead, willow, cottonwood, and sycamore border the creek, while sagebrush, pinyon, and juniper grow on adjacent dry exposures. Thick chaparral mats the canyonsides. A luxuriant live-oak grove canopies Chokecherry Spring. Big Pine Mountain harbors ponderosa, Jeffrey, and Coulter pine, white fir, incense-cedar, and big-cone spruce. Numerous footprints and droppings from deer, bobcats, and other creatures reveal that wildlife, too, travels the road in order to progress through the indented terrain. The hawks, falcons, and vultures have it easier, and condors once did. The Sisquoc Condor Sanctuary lies just north of Big Pine Mountain. The Wilderness honors Dick Smith, a Santa Barbara writer who championed the condor.

Nearby Campgrounds: This area in Los Padres National Forest has no developed campgrounds, but you may car-camp along the creek near the trailhead.

The County: Santa Barbara derives its name from the mission and commemorates Saint Barbara, a Roman virgin beheaded by her pagan father for accepting Christianity. Santa Barbara has a 109-mile coastline—the longest of any county in California. The coastal plain quickly gives way to rolling foothills, interior valleys, and a mountainous backcountry. The town of Santa Barbara shows a Spanish heritage: tile roofs and colonial adobe architecture grace government buildings, shopping centers, and residences. In the Santa Ynez Valley to the north, more than 30 wineries cover the hillsides with vineyards, while in Lompoc, flower growers blanket thousands of acres with poppies, marigolds, and other blossoms to supply a sizable part of the world's horticultural seeds. The county's boundaries incorporate several Channel Islands. On the largest island, Santa Cruz, Devil's Peak rises 2450+ feet above sea level, the highest *offshore* summit in California!

Additional Sources of Information/Recommended Reading:

Los Padres National Forest, Mt. Pinos District
HC1-400
Frazier Park, CA 93225
(805) 245-3731

Benkaim, Arthur, *Santa Barbara Trail Guide,* Los Padres Chapter, Sierra Club, 1986.
Gagnon, Dennis, *Hike the Santa Barbara Backcountry,* Western Tanager Press, 1990.

Santa Barbara

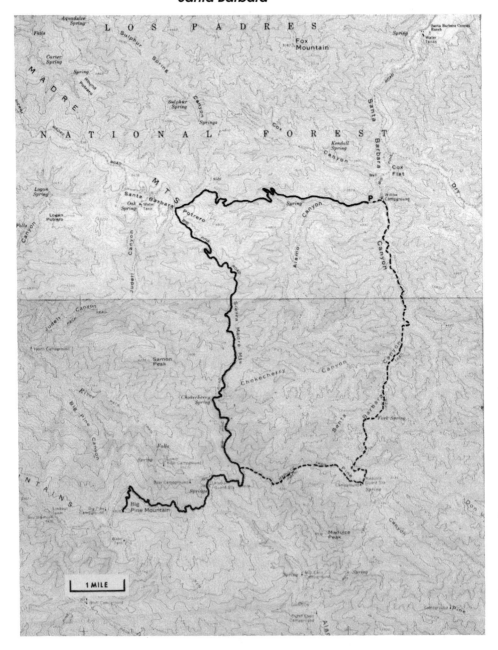

Santa Clara

Copernicus Peak 4360+′ **#41**

Location and Maps:	North-central part of the county
	USGS 7½-minute *Lick Observatory*
Distance:	0.7-mile round trip/180′ elevation gain
Grade:	Easy/Class 1
Hiking Time:	15 minutes
Season:	Year-round

Trailnotes: Copernicus Peak reaches toward the stars, 70 feet *above* the famous Lick Observatory on Mount Hamilton. The summit knob caps a 3762-acre scientific reserve owned by the University of California, which welcomes visitors every day of the year except Thanksgiving and Christmas. The main building is open 1 P.M. to 5 P.M. The building houses a telescope and photographic exhibits. A gift shop sells postcards, posters, and booklets. No food, gas, or other services are available. The hike amounts to a little leg-stretcher after a long scenic drive. Arrive in the late afternoon and stay until dark to observe scintillating city lights below and starlight overhead, from the second highest point in the nine-county Bay Area.

Early astronomers here named the highpoint in honor of the Polish physician Nicolaus Copernicus (1473–1543). Copernicus refuted the centuries-old belief that the sun revolved around the earth; his sun-centered theory formed the foundation of modern astronomy. California Geodetic surveyor William Brewer named Mount Hamilton after his friend, the Reverend Laurentine Hamilton. Brewer and Hamilton climbed the mountain in 1861. Hamilton led, and probably stood on the knob of Copernicus Peak when he waved his hat and called down to Brewer, "First on top—for this is the highest point!"

Approach: From I 680 in San Jose take the Alum Rock Avenue exit and proceed 0.8 mile to SR 130/Mount Hamilton Road. Turn right and drive 19 miles up an increasingly twisty road to Mount Hamilton. At the top of the road, a sign reads BEGIN SAN ANTONIO VALLEY ROAD. From the sign, continue 0.6 mile to a pullout on the left side of the road. Park here. To approach from I 580 in Livermore, take the North Livermore Avenue exit south to Mines Road, which becomes San Antonio Valley Road, and maintain course to Mount Hamilton, a distance of 50 miles from I 580.

Directions to Summit: From the pullout pass around the gate/fence signed PROPERTY UNIVERSITY OF CALIFORNIA, and walk up a moderately inclined asphalt road. Pass a power pole and a building, turn left (east), and follow a short footpath that winds up to the lookout steps.

The California Department of Forestry maintains the lookout, built during World War II for surveillance against enemy aircraft as well as for fire detection.

Budget cuts preclude regular staffing, but volunteers serve the tower during times of high fire danger. Despite smog that obscures the view, cellular phones that allow communication from vehicles, and overflying aircraft, the lookout remains useful, particularly to report lightning-caused fires in the remote backcountry. California, in fact, has more active lookouts than any other state, about 150, half in national forests and half operated by other agencies.

The View: Unlimited. A wild and rugged hodgepodge of Diablo Range ridges and valleys wraps around Mount Hamilton. The southern Santa Clara Valley opens out to the south, backed by the distant Santa Lucia Range. The Santa Cruz Mountains rise in the west, topped by 3791-foot Loma Prieta. South San Francisco Bay and the South Bay cities spread over the lowlands in the northwest. Farther north Mount Diablo and Mount Tamalpais project high above their surroundings.

The Environment: Although telescope domes and other buildings are scattered across the mountaintop, the surrounding native vegetation is largely undisturbed—chaparral, oak and pines, and grassy downslopes patrolled by an introduced herd of tule elk. Benefactor James Lick donated the world's first permanently occupied mountain observatory to the University of California in 1888. A horse-drawn wagon lugged the original telescope up the mountain, requiring a gentle, endlessly switchbacked grade. Mount Hamilton affords excellent "seeing conditions" for astronomers; still air currents abide above the lowland smog, and cloudless skies prevail approximately 250 nights a year. Graduate students and other researchers reserve viewing time on the six major telescopes. The astronomers study quasars, nebulae, and many other phenomena in our unfathomable universe. They peer several billion light years away and see hundreds of millions of galaxies with no end in sight.

Nearby Campgrounds: Joseph D. Grant County Park, 10 miles to the west on Mount Hamilton Road, has 23 drive-in campsites. It's open every day between Apr. 15 and Oct. 30; open Friday and Saturday in Nov. and Mar., and closed in Dec., Jan., and Feb. For information call (408) 274-6121.

The County: The county's name comes from the Mission Santa Clara, honoring Saint Clare of Assisi, Italy, who founded the first Franciscan order of nuns, called the Poor Clares. The broad Santa Clara Valley forms the heart of the county, sided by the Santa Cruz Mountains on the west and the Diablo Range on the east. The Valley's mild climate and rich alluvial soils favored orchard and vegetable farming. In the 1950s and 1960s, the local electronics industry, stimulated by research at Stanford University, experienced phenomenal growth. Computer chips replaced cherry orchards as "Silicon Valley" became a world leader in the microchip business, and San Jose surpassed San Francisco as the third most populous city in the state, behind only Los Angeles and San Diego. The surrounding uplands retain some of their natural beauty, thanks to the creation of numerous parklands. The largest by far, nearly 80,000-acre Henry W. Coe State Park, preserves ranchlands and wildlands little changed from a century ago.

Additional Sources of Information/Recommended Reading:

Lick Observatory, University of California, Observing Station
Mount Hamilton, CA 95140
(408) 274-5061.

Spangle, Frances, and Jean Rusmore, *South Bay Trails,* 2nd ed., Wilderness
Press, 1991.

Santa Clara

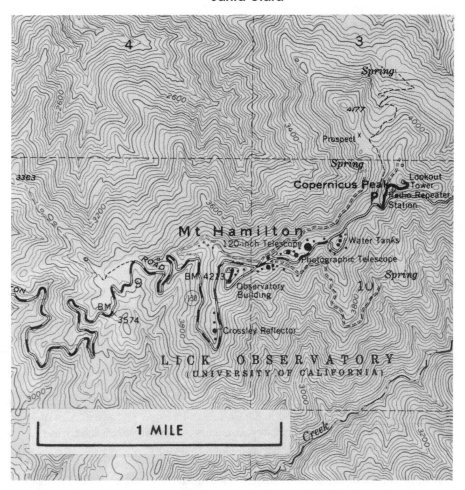

Santa Cruz

Mount McPherson   3231'   **#49**

Location and Maps: Northeast corner of the county
USGS 7½-minute *Castle Rock Ridge*
Distance: 0.5-mile round trip/110' elevation gain
Grade: Easy/Class 1
Hiking Time: 15 minutes
Season: The three weekends following Thanksgiving

Trailnotes: A short dirt road leads to the Bielawski Lookout on the crest of Mount McPherson. The access road and the lookout area are open to the public throughout the year. However, the actual highpoint lies on private property, about 200 yards northeast of the lookout. The fenced property contains a Christmas tree farm closed to the public except for three weekends after Thanksgiving. The owner graciously permits county-summit seekers to see the highpoint, without charge, during this period. Normally quiet and peaceful, the mountain bustles with Christmas-tree purchasers over the holidays.

Attorney, judge, and inventor Duncan McPherson, Jr., acquired the property around the year 1900 and named it after his father. Duncan, Sr., published the Santa Cruz *Sentinel* and pioneered in both the local timber industry and the forest-conservation movement. The California Department of Forestry erected the state's first steel lookout tower here in 1922. The tower's name honors Captain Casimic Bielawski, a Polish-born engineer who made most of the original township surveys in the Santa Cruz Mountains. Some cartographers extended Bielawski's name from the lookout to the mountain, as on the current USGS topo map. But the original and correct name remains Mount McPherson, as engraved on the U.S. Coast & Geodetic Survey summit marker.

Approach: Please turn to the Approach entry under San Mateo County.

Directions to Summit: From the roadside walk 30 feet up the dirt road to a gate (an access road to Castle Rock State Park descends on the right). Beyond the gate, the road climbs briefly to reach the Christmas-tree farm on the east edge of a flat. The flat holds the lookout tower, outbuildings, and antennas. Grapevines twine up the tower scaffolding, and a benchmark at the tower's base reads "Biel." The true highpoint benchmark lies on a wooded rise about 200 feet east of the Christmas-tree farm's entrance gate, off the lookout access road. Look for a tree-shaded four-foot-high metal pipe, and walk 12 yards east from the pipe to find it. In 1993 an orange ribbon hung from a tree branch by the benchmark.

The View: Trees surround the highpoint and block the view, but vistas open out from the lookout flat: Long Ridge in the north, Butano Ridge and the Pacific Ocean in the west, and Monterey Bay in the south. The lookout tower afforded wide-ranging views when CDF personnel formerly let the public climb the tower and sign the visitor's log. Budget constraints forced the lookout's closure in 1991.

The Environment: Weathered mudstone and shale underlie Mount McPherson. Adjoining Castle Rock State Park displays sandstone caves and honeycombed surfaces eroded by wind and precipitation that averages 40-50 inches a year. Earthquakes along the San Andreas Fault, located only 2 miles northwest, cause the lookout to sway dramatically. Douglas-fir, black oak, and madrone predominate on the mountaintop. Big band-tailed pigeons flock to the berries on manzanita bushes. Deer nibble on ripe apples and pears in the abandoned orchard west of the Christmas-tree farm. Tower observers have watched coyotes actually climb the trees to devour the fruit.

Nearby Campgrounds: Please see the entry for San Mateo County.

The County: *Santa Cruz,* named after a mission established in 1791, translates as "Holy Cross." From northern Monterey Bay, a coastal plain is backed by terraces and foothills that extend to the crest of the Santa Cruz Mountains. A noted University of California campus ensconced in the foothills sports an unusual school mascot, the banana slug. Santa Cruz leads all California counties in apple production, centered around Watsonville, the second largest town. Other important crops include mushrooms, raspberries, and brussel sprouts. Capitola, known as the Begonia Capital of the World, cultivates many kinds of flowers. Tourists support the economy as they explore the county's redwoods parks and play at the seaside resort town of Santa Cruz. A famous beach boardwalk in Santa Cruz has a Giant Dipper rollercoaster, which has carried over 25 million screaming riders since 1924.

Additional Sources of Information/Recommended Reading:

Santa Cruz Mountains Natural History Association
525 N. Big Trees Park Road
Felton, CA 95018
(408) 335-3174

Taber, Tom. *The Expanded Santa Cruz Mountain Trail Book,* Oak Valley Press, 1988.

Santa Cruz

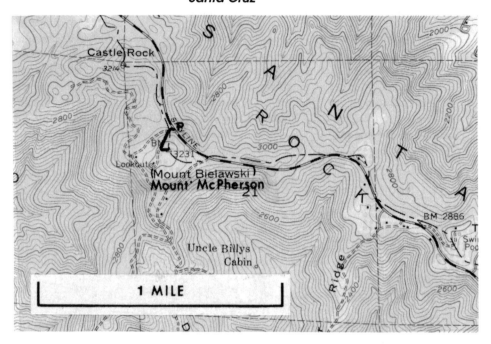

Shasta

Lassen Peak 10,457′ #12

Location and Maps:	Southeast corner of the county
	USGS 7½-series *Lassen Peak;* NPS *Lassen Volcanic National Park;* Wilderness Press *Lassen Volcanic National Park and Vicinity*
Distance:	5 miles round trip/2000′ elevation gain
Grade:	Moderate/Class 1
Hiking Time:	3 hours
Season:	Mid-July to October

Trailnotes: Lassen Peak, centerpiece of Lassen Volcanic National Park and one of the world's largest plug-dome volcanoes, dominates the skyline for miles around. A first-rate trail leads to the summit. In peak season, hundreds of hikers a day tramp the trail. Start early to avoid the crowd. (If you have the energy and the inclination, you can top two county highpoints in a day. After Lassen Peak, drive down the road a short distance to the trailhead for Brokeoff Mountain, highpoint of Tehama County.) If possible, acclimatize yourself to the altitude before the climbs. Use caution when crossing slippery snow patches on the trail. Dayhikers and campground users pay entrance fees. Backpackers need wilderness permits to overnight in the backcountry.

Danish blacksmith Peter Lassen (1800–1859), a northern California pioneer, may have been the first Caucasian to scale the peak, although evidence for the ascent is flimsy.

Approach: From I 5 in Red Bluff, take SR 36 east for 47 miles to a junction with SR 89. (You can also access the Park from Redding on SR 44.) From U.S. 395 south of Susanville, take SR 36 west 50 miles to the junction with SR 89. Turn north at the junction onto SR 89 and proceed 4.5 miles to the Lassen Volcanic National Park boundary. Drive another 0.5 mile to reach the trailhead for Brokeoff Mountain. Continue 0.4 mile to the entrance station, and another 6.8 miles to the large Lassen Peak trailhead parking lot.

Directions to Summit: The path begins with a straight stretch, doubles back through a mountain-hemlock grove, and then curves up the south shoulder of Lassen Peak. Signposts mark each half mile. A leg-tiring series of some 40 switchbacks climbs moderately steep slopes until the gradient eases near the top. The trail descends slightly to cross a snowbank, and then fades out among the rocks. Round the left side of the summit rockpile for an easy scramble to the top. Look for a register chained to a boulder. The 1914 eruption demolished a lookout perched on the peak. An intriguing pyramid sits there now, shaped and colored to blend with the surroundings. The pyramid holds a park communications device and a working seismograph.

Lassen Peak above Lake Helen

The View: Varicolored volcanic vistas. With an entrance-station map in hand you can pick out many Park landmarks including Cinder Cone, Chaos Crags, and Brokeoff Mountain. Lake Almanor sparkles in the southeast, one of many visible

Lassen summit rocks and seismograph shelter

lakes. Distantly, the Sutter Buttes jut above the Sacramento Valley floor. Mount Diablo and Mount Saint Helena rise in the south, Snow Mountain and the Yolla Bolly Mountains in the west, the Klamath Ranges in the northwest, and matchless Mount Shasta tops them all.

The Environment: Whitebark pines intermittently accompany hikers from the trailhead to nearly 10,000 feet before the last stunted tree surrenders to the alpine climate. Lupine, pussytoes, phacelia, butterweed, and other wildflowers soften the angular scree. Golden-mantled ground squirrels and perky pikas skitter about the summit crags. Lassen Peak, southernmost volcano in the Cascade chain, emerged from the vent of an extinct cone called Mount Tehama. Around 11,000 years ago a massive semisolid lava dome thrust up through the overlying rock. After several years of uplift, cooling debris plugged the vent. For thousands of years the peak remained essentially dormant. Then, in 1914, the volcano reawakened. Over the following year, 150 steam explosions piled debris and ash on the volcano's slopes. In 1915, a massive burst sent an enormous ash-laden mushroom cloud 7 miles high. Today only occasional whiffs of steam emit from the volcano. But a recent slight rise in temperature among the plug dome's associated geothermal fumaroles, hot springs, and boiling mud pots may presage future volcanic activity.

Nearby Campgrounds: The seven national-park campgrounds operate on a first-come first-served basis. Those closest to Lassen Peak include "Southwest" near the south entrance station, and Summit Lakes North and South, 9 miles up the road. Additional campgrounds can be found south of the park, along State Routes 36 and 32 in Lassen National Forest.

The County: Shasta County, named after Mount Shasta, encompasses the upper Sacramento Valley and an arc of mountains to the north, east, and west. Wood products, livestock, fruit and nut orchards, and nursery crops contribute to the economy. Redding, the major town, serves as a shipping and supply point for commerce and as a gateway to the surrounding recreation areas. Campers, boaters, and fishermen converge on Shasta Lake, the largest man-made lake in the state. The lake has 365 miles of shoreline, one third more than San Francisco Bay. The reservoir stores water from the Sacramento, Pit, and McCloud rivers for flood control, irrigation, hydroelectric power generation, and other purposes. Colossal Shasta Dam stands 602 feet high and has the world's highest overflow spillway, three times higher than Niagara Falls.

Additional Sources of Information/Recommended Reading:

Lassen Volcanic National Park
P.O. Box 100, Mineral, CA 96063-0100
(916) 595-4444

Harris, Stephen L., *Fire and Ice: the Cascade Volcanoes,* revised ed., The Mountaineers/Pacific Search Press, 1986.

Schaffer, Jeffrey P., *Lassen Volcanic National Park & Vicinity,* 2nd ed., Wilderness Press, 1986.

Strong, Douglas H., *These Happy Grounds, A History of the Lassen Region,* Loomis Museum Association, 1973.

Shasta

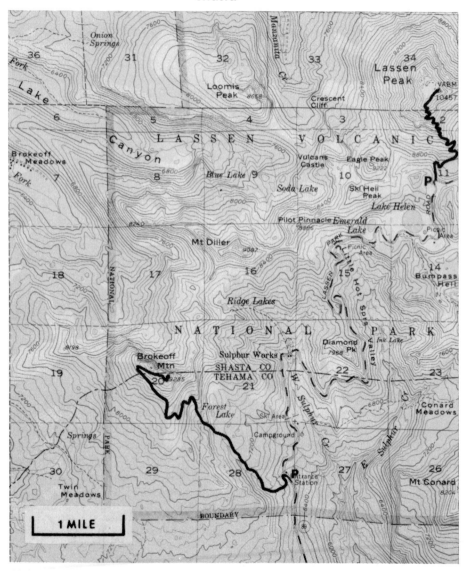

Sierra

Mount Lola North	8844′	#20

Location and Maps:	Southeast edge of the county
	USGS 7½-minute *Independence Lake, Webber Peak;* USFS *Tahoe National Forest*
Distance:	2.4 miles round trip/400′ elevation gain
Grade:	Moderate/Class 2 (Done in combination with Mount Lola; see explanation below)
Hiking Time:	1 hour
Season:	Mid-June to October

Trailnotes: The Sierra County highpoint tops off the Mount Lola climb like a delicious dessert after the main course. From Mount Lola's summit simply saunter north cross-country about 1.2 miles, along a lovely tree-scattered, flower-decked ridgetop. Traverse gentle downslopes to reach a minor saddle where you cross over the county line. From the saddle hike up to the modest but obvious highpoint knob, identified by Dinesh Desai in 1991. A register hides among the black and chartreuse lichen-encrusted rocks. Small boulders, grass, and sagebrush cover the hillock, intermingled with wildflowers like pennyroyal, pussy paws, and blue gentian. Mount Lola has the better view, but Mount Lola North has the wilder charm and untouched natural beauty that make this unsung county summit a joy. Please see the Nevada County description for all entries except the county.

The County: The Spanish *Sierra* translates as "mountain range," and also as "saw." Sierra Nevada means "snowy mountain range" or "snow saw," a poetic reference to the snowy, serrated skyline. Sierra County takes its name from the Sierra Nevada, which straddles the county, and/or from Sierra Buttes, a cluster of jagged granite peaks situated in the heart of the county. The county's mountains contain 45 mile-high lakes, abundant trout streams, and the main ranching basin in the Sierra Nevada, Sierra Valley. This 5000-foot-high valley has a short growing season, limiting crops to summer hay and grains. Livestock, lumber, tourism, and government jobs bring income to the lightly populated county. Little Downieville, the county seat, parades 19th Century buildings with overhanging balconies that harken back to Gold Rush days. Nearby Sierra City gained fame in 1869 with the discovery of a "Monumental Nugget" weighing 141 pounds!

Siskiyou

Mount Shasta   14,162'   **#4**

Location and Maps:	South-central part of the county
	USGS 7½-minute *Mt. Shasta;* USFS *Mt. Shasta Wilderness* and *Castle Crags Wilderness;* Wilderness Press *Mt. Shasta*
Distance:	11.6 miles round trip/7300' elevation gain
Grade:	Strenuous/Class 3
Hiking Time:	12 hours
Season:	June to September

Trailnotes: Mount Shasta, an unmistakable snow-clad landmark visible from 100 miles away, spellbinds all who see it. The mountain soars 11,000 feet above the surrounding plain, one of the highest plain-to-summit rises on Earth. Mount Shasta crowns a 38,200-acre wilderness area within surrounding Shasta-Trinity National Forest. The Forest Service requires no wilderness permit, but do register at a stand in front of the Mount Shasta Ranger Station before your climb, and sign out when you return.

The John Muir/Avalanche Gulch Route, described below, ranks as the most popular and the least difficult of many approaches to the summit. The steepest section of the route, by the Red Banks, has a Class 3 rating. Individuals in prime condition can scale Mount Shasta in a day. But climbers typically backpack to Horse Camp or Helen Lake to spend the night before tackling the summit. The trailhead-to-summit hiking time averages 7–9 hours for the ascent and 3–5 hours for the descent. Begin early—by 3 A.M. for the dayhike, or by sunrise from the trail camps. An early start assures maximum daylight and better climbing conditions; rockfalls occur more often later in the day as the warming sun melts the ice "glue" holding rocks in place, and the early hours' snow crust makes climbing easier. Many experienced Shasta climbers prefer walking over snow rather than loose talus and scree. Of course, more snow covers the ground in June and July than in August, the mildest month on the mountain. September trips entail a longer talus slog and more changeable weather. But weather requires constant vigilance throughout the climbing season. The ranger station posts the latest weather reports and also provides free instructive handouts on climbing Mount Shasta.

The Forest Service estimates that about 5000 people a year try for the peak. Less than half reach the top. In addition to cooperative weather, fine physical condition and keen planning are needed for success. Add an ice axe and crampons to your customary hiking gear. The Fifth Season and the House of Ski in Mount Shasta rent the equipment and answer questions about their proper use. (For an excellent primer on ice axes and crampons, see *Mountaineering, The Freedom of the Hills,* edited by Don Graydon.) Most first-time summit seekers have no previous snow climbing experience; most find the equipment a bother to procure but easy to use, and essential on the unavoidable snowfields.

The mountain's name has no clear origin. Possible derivations include the Russian fur traders' "tshastal," meaning white or pure; the French explorers' "chaste," also meaning pure; and the Native Americans' "sastise," the name of a local tribe.

Approach: From I 5, 61 miles north of Redding and 9 miles south of Weed, take the Central Mt. Shasta City exit which becomes West Lake Street. Proceed two blocks on West Lake, turn left onto Pine Street for two blocks, and then right onto West Alma. Drive up the street to find the Mount Shasta Ranger Station on your left. From the ranger station, continue on Alma Street 0.3 mile to Everitt Memorial Highway. Wind up the highway 10.9 miles to the Bunny Flat Trailhead, with a parking area and restrooms on the left (north) side of the road.

Directions to Summit: The route from Bunny Flat to Horse Camp traverses gentle slopes. At first, the path follows an old dirt road; then it joins a trail coming up from Sand Flat. The trail ascends a ridge to reach Horse Camp at 7900 feet, site of a rock-walled cabin built in the early 1920s. The Sierra Club owns the cabin and the adjacent grounds. The Club invites visitors to peruse the cabin library, fill containers at a spring-fed fountain (the last pure water source), and camp at sites near the cabin. The initial cabin custodian, Mac Olberman, spent nine years single-handedly building a flatstone "causeway" that extends over half a mile past the cabin. The summit lies only 4.1 miles beyond the cabin, but a heart-pounding 6,200 feet higher.

Walk up the causeway and then follow the main use trail in snow or scree up moderately steep slopes along the west side of Avalanche Gulch. (Snowline normally is at about 8000 feet in June; if snow covers the causeway, head up the wide main drainage behind the cabin to reach the upper slopes.) About 1.8 miles above Horse Camp, at an elevation of 10,400, you come upon a rock-strewn bench holding Helen Lake. The lake is usually concealed by snow. Backpacking climbers choose one of the campsites sprinkled about the bench to spend the night.

Above Helen Lake an intimidatingly steep snowfield angles at up to 35°, topped by the Red Banks, a geologically recent volcanic flow and a major source of rockfall. Ascend the snowfield, aiming toward the right side of both the Red Banks and a prominent outcrop called The Heart. Arduous effort brings you to an evident minor saddle between the Red Banks and Thumb Rock at 12,800 feet, a good place to catch your breath. From the saddle you have two options. You can trek *around* and behind the Red Banks, along the edge of the Konwakiton Glacier, to surmount the sloping plateau atop the Banks called Misery Hill. Alternatively, you can climb up *through* the Red Banks, using one of the very steep snow- and ice-filled gullies that cleave the Banks to reach Misery Hill. Although prone to rockfall, the shorter, steeper Red Banks option avoids the Konwakiton Glacier bergschrund (a crevasse formed where a glacier has pulled away from a headwall). Snow bridges across the narrow crevasse may become unstable as temperatures rise in midsummer. The well-trodden use paths of previous climbers will help to guide you up your chosen route.

Above the Red Banks, advance north over Misery Hill's easier gradient. Then cross a long, level snowfield and head for a discernible notch to the left of the summit pinnacle. Pass sulfurous fumaroles on your left before making a final easy scramble to the top. An elevated stand near the topmost crags holds an elegant oversized register.

The View: A blockbuster 360° panorama. To the north, Shasta Valley fills the foreground, while a number of volcanic cones rise in the background, notably Mount McLoughlin and Mount Thielsen. In the east, Mount Hoffman juts above the Modoc Plateau. In the south, Lassen Peak, the Sacramento River canyon, and Castle Crags stand out, as does a linear thread of concrete, I 5. To the west, the Eddys, the Trinity Alps, and a welter of Klamath Ranges unreel toward the Pacific Ocean. Only the curvature of the earth prevents seeing the ocean itself.

The Environment: A rich flora and fauna ring Mount Shasta, including the distinctive Shasta red fir, seen along the first leg of the route. Whitney Glacier, the largest in California, and six others gird the mountain's upper slopes. Four overlapping volcanic cones spewed eruptions over several hundred thousand years to create Mount Shasta, the largest volcano in the continental U.S. An eroding plug dome on the crater rim forms the highpoint. Shastina, the distinctive subsidiary cone, arose from a side vent about 10,000 years ago. Geologists classify Shasta as an "active" volcano, a "sleeping giant." They believe Shasta erupts every 250 to 500 years. Quake fissures beneath volcanoes allow molten lava to rise toward the surface. Based on the frequency and intensity of earthquakes in the region, a University of Washington seismologist lists Mount Shasta as fourth out of ten Cascade volcanoes most likely to erupt in the next 20 to 30 years. But nobody knows for sure.

Nearby Campgrounds: Small campgrounds at McBride Springs and Panther Meadows edge Everitt Memorial Highway. A KOA campground sits at the north end of Mount Shasta City. Bunny Flat and close-by Sand Flat have primitive campsites, but backpacking climbers prefer Horse Camp or Helen Lake.

The County: The word "Siskiyou" has a dim origin. It may stem from "Six Callieux" (six stones), the early French fur-trappers' name for an Umpqua River crossing. Many rivers drain the well-watered county, including the Klamath, the Salmon, the Scott, and headwater tributaries of the Sacramento. Mountain ranges interspersed with hills and valleys characterize the topography. Forest products, beef cattle, and field crops lead the economy. The county ranks first in the state in growing oats and fall potatoes. Yreka, the largest town and county seat, began as a Gold Rush camp in 1851. Mining-era buildings front the business zone, and Victorian homes beautify a nationally registered historic district. California's first successful fish hatchery, a century-old site in Mount Shasta City, has spawned rainbow trout by the millions for planting as far away as New Zealand.

. . . .

Additional Sources of Information/Recommended Reading:

Mt. Shasta Ranger District
204 W. Alma Street
Mount Shasta, CA 96067
(916) 926-4511
The ranger station sells books and
provides numerous free handouts
on Mount Shasta trails, wildlife,
and so forth

The Fifth Season, 300 N. Mt.
Shasta Blvd., (916) 926-3606,
and The House of Ski, 1208
Everitt Memorial Highway, (916)
926-2359, rent ice axes,
crampons, and boots

For climbing conditions on Mount
Shasta call a 24-hour recorded
message at (916) 926-5555

Selters, Andy, and Michael Zanger, *The Mt. Shasta Book,* Wilderness Press,
1989.
Zanger, Michael, *Mt. Shasta, History, Legend and Lore,* Celestial Arts, 1992.

Mt. Shasta

Siskiyou

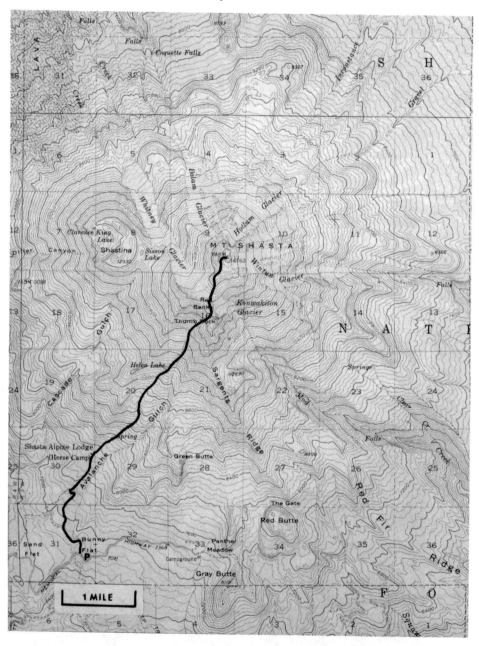

Solano

Mount Vaca   2819′   **#51**

Location and Maps:	Northwest corner of the county
	USGS 7½-minute *Mt. Vaca*
Distance:	1.8 miles round trip/250′ elevation gain
Grade:	Easy/Class 1
Hiking Time:	50 minutes
Season:	Year-round

Trailnotes: Rocky Ridge forms a 2000-foot-high wall along the east edge of Solano County and Mount Vaca caps the ridge. As one of several antenna-topped blips on the ridgeline, the highpoint captures little attention. A part-paved, part-well-graded dirt road reaches to within a mile of the top. The hiking route follows a firebreak and an antenna access road. According to the County Transportation Department, the public has a "prescriptive easement" to the access road, which means you can walk over it despite no-trespassing signs on adjacent transmitter-facility fences. The U.S. Government owns Mount Vaca proper and 23 acres surrounding an Army Signal Corps tower on the summit.

Mount Vaca memorializes Juan Manuel Vaca, an industrious colonist from New Mexico, who garnered a local land grant in the 1840s. He deeded part of his land to another settler with the stipulation that a townsite on the parcel be named Vacaville.

Approach: From I 80 between Vacaville and Fairfield (62 miles north of San Francisco and 30 miles south of Sacramento) take the Cherry Glen Road offramp. Drive north on Cherry Glen Road 1 mile to a junction with Pleasants Valley Road. Continue north on Pleasants Valley Road 5 miles to an intersection with Mix Canyon road. Signs read NOT A THROUGH ROAD, RESTRICTED ENTRY, HAZARDOUS FIRE ENTRY. Drive up sinuous Mix Canyon Road. After 3.7 miles the pavement ends, and in another 1.1 miles a gated road forks to the left. Park in a pullout on the right side of the road near the road fork.

Directions to Summit: Stroll up the steep left road fork. Cement pavement ends after a few yards, the steepness abates, and the road dips and rises gently south along the ridgeline. In about 0.5 mile take the right branch and continue another 0.4 mile to arrive at the highest point, topped by a multistoried tower signed number 20. Walk a few yards west of the fenced complex to enjoy unblocked views.

The View: Lake Curry and its chaparral-robed watershed lie at your feet to the west. Rocky Ridge, also known as the Vaca Mountains, and companion Blue Ridge extend to the north, backed by layers of adjoining ridges and valleys. Rectangular swatches deck the valley farmlands in the east, with state capital buildings discernible 35 air miles away. The Delta lands sprawl in the southeast. Storage tanks, mothballed ships, and waterfront buildings fringe Suisun Bay in the south, while Mount Diablo punctuates the far horizon.

The Environment: The huge Miller Canyon fire overswept Mount Vaca in 1989, evidenced by charred branches along the roadside. Vigorous, stump-sprouting chamise and manzanita exemplify how fire rejuvenates chaparral (from the Spanish word *chaparro,* meaning "scrub oak," a dominant species on Mount Vaca). Fast-moving brush fires seldom damage root systems, and within a few short months green shoots emerge from blackened burls. Ash nourishes the soil, and with more open space available after a fire plant growth abounds. Some species even *require* heat to crack or alter seed coatings to allow germination. Fire-following annuals like fire poppies, whispering bells, and golden eardrops flourish after a burn. Brushy shrubs eventually re-establish themselves, combustible and ready to repeat the cycle. During a fire, the chaparral's small birds take wing, the large animals flee, and many other creatures take shelter in insulated underground burrows to survive.

Nearby Campgrounds: Lake Solano County Park borders Putah Creek, 7.7 miles north of Mix Canyon Road on Pleasants Valley Road. This pretty park has 50 sites and takes reservations.

The County: In 1835 General Mariano Vallejo befriended a local Indian chief who led his tribe to protect a mission and settlers' properties from attacks by other Indians. In gratitude, Vallejo later asked that the county be named, in the chief's honor, "Solano," his baptized name, after the Mission San Francisco Solano at Sonoma. The Sacramento River floodplain covers the southern and eastern two thirds of the county, an important agricultural area. Farms specialize in fruits, tree nuts, and beef cattle. Food processing and natural-gas fields also aid the economy. South Solano edges the Delta lands, a labyrinth of waterways, islands, and mudflats embracing some 1000 miles of navigable channels. Grizzly Island State Wildlife Area, south of Fairfield, contains the nation's most expansive estuarine marsh, a home to waterfowl, river otter, and tule elk.

Additional Sources of Information/Recommended Reading:

Grizzly Island Wildlife Area
California Department of Fish and Game
2548 Grizzly Island Road (off SR 12)
Suisun, CA 94585
(707) 425-3828

Wayburn, Peggy, *Adventuring in the San Francisco Bay Area,* Sierra Club Books, 1987.

Solano

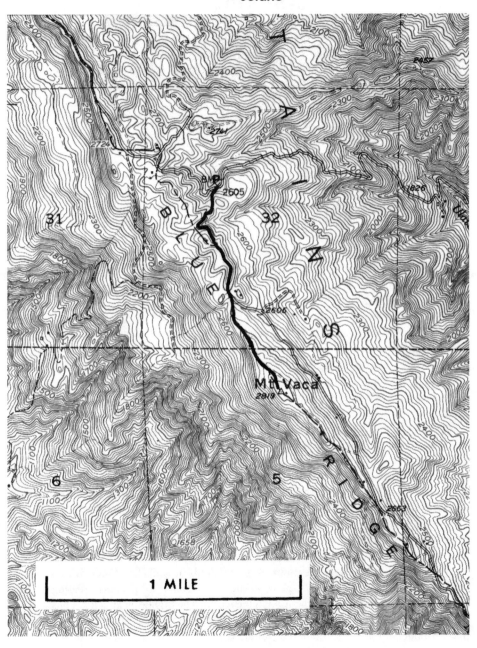

1 MILE

Sonoma

Cobb Mountain West Rim   4480+'   **#40**

Location and Maps: Northeast edge of the county
USGS 7½-minute *Whispering Pines*

Private Highpoint Notes: Mount Saint Helena, a regional landmark, was long considered the apex of Sonoma County. However, in 1993, local landowner V.K. Leary and experienced mountaineer Bill Hauser recognized a higher point on Cobb Mountain. The new highpoint lies about 10 air miles northwest of Mount Saint Helena, near the hamlet of Whispering Pines. Cobb Mountain forms the summit of an old volcanic crater. The Sonoma County boundary cuts across the west rim of the crater, at a point 137+ feet higher than Mount Saint Helena, making Cobb Mountain the highest point in the entire nine-county Bay Area!

The highpoint sits on private property. Nonetheless, for many years, members of the public have used an ungated dirt road to hike to the summit of Cobb Mountain (Cobb is the surname of an original settler in the region). The route begins at the Maple Shadows Road intersection with SR 175, adjacent to the Whispering Pines Tavern, 7.2 miles north of Middletown. Hikers park along the highway roadside. They then walk past vacation homes along Maple Shadows Road, Brookside Drive, and Pinewood Way to reach the dirt road. (NO TRESPASSING signs abound on cabin properties bordering the dirt road.) The road winds up through a forest of oak, pine, fir, and madrone in a moderately steep 2.5-mile ascent to antenna-topped Cobb Mountain. From this summit, another dirt road marked by orange "Truck Road" ribbons runs 0.2 mile south and then curves west, descending shortly to a saddle. From the saddle, a brief cross-country hike through brush and trees leads to the forested highpoint, designated by a rock cairn piled atop an andesite slab between two trees in a flat, relatively open area. The outing covers about 7 miles round trip and entails a 2500-foot elevation gain.

Trees—Douglas-fir, ponderosa pine, western white pine, and other species— limit the view. The perimeter of the summit affords vistas to the west overlooking The Geysers. Here, pioneers found natural steam shooting skyward through vents in the ground called fumaroles. Molten magma lies just 5 miles beneath the surface (instead of the normal 20 miles). The magma heats groundwater to steam and forces it up through faults in the mountains. Hundreds of wells have been drilled in the vicinity, tapping the steam to generate electricity and, in the process, creating the largest geothermal power operation in the world. The highpoint area itself has recently been leased for geothermal exploration. This occurrence, and the timber-harvest-boundary ribbons scattered about, presage imminent changes in the natural character of Cobb Mountain.

The County: Renowned horiculturist Luther Burbank considered Sonoma County "the chosen spot of all the earth as far as nature is concerned." Sea cliffs and coves etch a long Pacific shoreline. Rivers and creeks meander through forested coastal mountains. Orchards and vineyards accent rolling hills and valleys. The name "Sonoma" comes from an Indian word translated by some to mean "valley of the moon" and by others to indicate "land of chief nose," perhaps referring to a tribal leader's prominent facial feature.

In 1775 the first non-Indian to explore the area, a Spaniard named Francisco de la Bodega, dropped anchor in the bay now bearing his name. The first white settlers, a party of Russians, hunted sea otters and planted wheat on bluffs overlooking the bay in 1809. Farther north, they later built Fort Rossiya (Little Russia), complete with a governor's residence, a domed chapel, and many other structures. The settlers planned to grow crops to supply their Alaskan colonies, and even establish a Russian state. Concerned Mexican and American leaders sought to check their expansion, but the Russians left peacefully of their own accord in 1841. Overhunting, crop failures, and additional hardships led to their departure. Other immigrants took their place, and growth has continued to the present day. Santa Rosa, the county seat, is the largest city in Northern California north of San Francisco and west of Sacramento. Here, as well as in Petaluma, Sonoma, and smaller towns, residents work to preserve the region's physical charms in the face of relentless urbanization.

Additional Sources of Information/Recommended Reading:

Lorentzen, Bob, *The Hiker's Hip Pocket Guide to Sonoma County,* Bored Feet Publications, 1990.

Sonoma

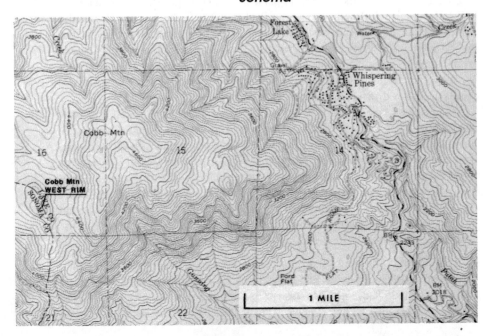

Stanislaus

| Mount Stakes | 3804' | #45 |

> **Location and Maps:** West edge of the county
> USGS 7½-minute *Mt. Stakes;* Henry W. Coe State
> Park trail and camping maps

Private Highpoint Notes: Mount Stakes caps a gently rounded ridgetop in a remote part of the Diablo Range. The highpoint forms a bump on the ridgeline, visible from backcountry San Antonio Valley Road, just before the road curves sharply from south to west. From the curve dirt ranch roads lead straight to the brush-covered peak, but NO TRESPASSING signs bar access. Cattle graze beyond the fence, and members of an exclusive hunting club stalk black-tailed deer, feral pigs, and waterfowl attracted to manmade hunting ponds on the property.

A "backdoor" to Mount Stakes opens through Henry W. Coe State Park. Park trails bring hikers to within 1.5 miles of the peak. But the landowner controlling the intervening 1.5-mile parcel denies access to the general public, so the summit remains legally inaccessible. Additionally, just to reach the Park boundary requires a herculean hike. The multiday backpack covers approximately 50 miles round trip, with rollercoaster relief that accrues a 9600-foot elevation gain, in contrast to the closed approach from San Antonio Valley Road, which covers about 10 miles round trip with an 1800-foot elevation gain.

To make the State Park journey, register at Park Headquarters and with a Park trail map in hand follow in order: the Pacheco Route, the Interior Route, the Hartman Trail, the Gill Route to the Rooster Comb Loop, and a spur road up to the highest point in the Park, along the northern boundary at 3560 feet. Other routes are possible. This destination lies 244 feet lower than Mount Stakes. The mountain's name derives from a well-respected Stanislaus County resident, Judge A. G. Stakes, a former district attorney and county surveyor who died in 1873.

Magnificent Coe State Park, to be almost 80,000 acres, is the largest state park in northern California. The park's plant and animal life includes chaparral, grassland, oak woodland, and ridgetop stands of ponderosa pine, as well as badger, bobcat, mountain lion, and reintroduced tule elk. The park grew from 13,000 acres to 68,000 acres in 1980, and will add 11,000 more in 1994. Other large parcels have been offered to the park, but the state lacks the funds to purchase them. Perhaps one day Mount Stakes will be acquired, or at least an easement established, to give the public an opportunity to enjoy expansive views of the Central Valley and the surrounding wildlands from the top of Stanislaus County.

The County: The word "Stanislaus" traces back to a mission-educated Indian chief baptized "Estanislao," after a Polish saint. Estanislao ran away and led other Indians in an 1829 battle with Mexican troops beside a river, subsequently named for the chief. The county took its name from the river. The Diablo Range rises along the west edge of the county, and the Sierra foothills border on the east. Three major rivers course through the county: the Stanislaus, the Tuolumne and the San Joaquin. The rivers and the state's largest groundwater basin irrigate bountiful floodplain farmlands. Peaches, melons, apricots, and walnuts head a long list of county crops. Poultry and livestock ranching also boost the economy. Modesto, the county seat, prospers with food-processing plants, dairies, and other industries, including a huge Gallo winery. The winery produces one fourth of all wine consumed each year in the United States.

Additional Sources of Information/Recommended Reading:

The Pine Ridge Association
Henry W. Coe State Park
P.O. Box 846
Morgan Hill, CA 95038
(408) 779-2728

Spangle, Frances, and Jean Rusmore, *South Bay Trails,* 2nd ed., Wilderness Press, 1991.

Stanislaus

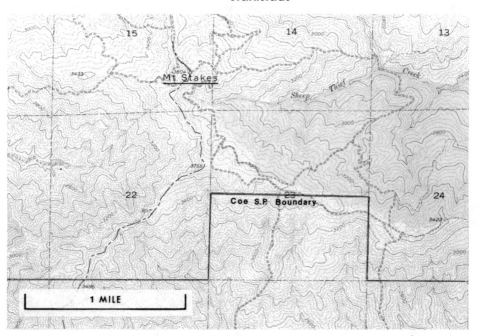

Sutter

South Butte   2120+′   **#54**

Location and Maps: North-central part of the county
USGS 7½-minute *Sutter Buttes*
Distance: 6 miles round trip/1850′ elevation gain
Grade: Moderate/Class 2
Hiking Time: 4 hours
Season: October through May

Trailnotes: The Sutter Buttes' startlingly sharp rise from the flat Sacramento Valley floor brings to mind a lovely fairytale illustration, too exaggerated to be true. Yet a circular cluster of peaks, dubbed "the smallest mountain range in the world," lofts above the lowland, and South Butte tops them all. In 1974 the State Parks Department identified the privately owned Buttes as their highest priority for acquisition but political opposition squelched the idea. In 1976 one private owner founded a public-access program guided by naturalist Walt Anderson. Colleagues Ira Heinrich, Joe Freeman, and others expanded the program through the years to form the Middle Mountain Foundation. The foundation offers an array of guided trips, including excursions to the South Butte area.

A gated 3-mile-long paved road winds up to a transmitting facility on the summit. The guided trip follows a more natural route from Moore Canyon; a dirt road, use trails, and cross-country travel lead to the top. Trip fees (around $30 per person) cover expenses. Additional contributions help support the Middle Mountain Foundation's education and preservation efforts. Call or write to request a program brochure. Outings take place throughout the year except during the hot summer months.

Approach: From SR 99 in Yuba City take SR 20 west 6 miles to Acacia Ave. Turn right and go 1.7 miles to an intersection with Pass Road/Butte House Road. Continue on Pass Road 3.5 miles to see excellent views of South Butte, near the access gate to the transmitting towers. From I 5 near Williams take SR 20 east 22 miles to West Butte Road. Turn left and after 5 miles intersect Pass Road. Turn right and drive down Pass Road along a segment of the "Sutter Buttes Scenic Route."

Directions to Summit: A guide from the Middle Mountain Foundation leads the way. Receive specific information about the trailhead departure point when you make your trip reservation.

The View: A benchmark lies among the highest brush-fringed crags just northwest of the antenna complex. From here a unique 360° view sweeps around the entire Sacramento Valley. A farmland patchwork carpets the valley floor. Snow Mountain crowns the interior Coast Ranges in the west. Blue Ridge and Rocky Ridge border the valley in the southwest. Green bands of remnant riparian woodland edge the Feather River in the east. Greenery also marks the twin towns of Yuba City and Marysville, backed by foothills rising to the Sierra Nevada.

Immediately to the north, West Butte, North Butte, and lesser pinnacles poke skyward, and Mount Shasta and Lassen Peak are visible on the far horizon.

The Environment: Volcanism created the Buttes. About 3 million years ago, magma formed an immense bubble some 100 miles below the surface. Upthrusting magma buckled surface sediments to form a mammoth fault-laced mound. Explosive gases breached the mound and lava gushed forth, building volcanic cones. Later, pasty molten material oozed upward and displaced the cones with high domes. The domes hardened as volcanic activity ceased around 1.4 million years ago. Further fracturing, avalanches, and weathering shaped the landforms we see today.

About half a dozen seasonal creeks and a dozen year-round springs flow in the Buttes. Cattle and sheep graze the hillsides, a reminder of the area's status as private ranchland. Commonly seen wildlife includes red-tailed hawk, turkey vulture, coyote, ground squirrel, and gopher snake. The sagebrush lizard, normally seen at elevations above 5000 feet, scurries about at 300 feet here. No chamise and little manzanita grow on the slopes, and many more anomalies occur within the otherwise typical chaparral and oak woodland. Fine blue-oak stands drew native Americans into the Buttes to harvest acorns. Mortar holes attest to their presence. Shamans came frequently, for the Indians considered the middle mountain a holy place, literally the center of the world.

Nearby Campgrounds: None. The Middle Mountain Foundation offers overnight backpack trips in the Buttes.

The County: The Buttes and the county take their name from John A. Sutter (1803–1880), an influential Northern California pioneer and the first white man to lay claim to the Buttes. Precious yellow metal discovered at Sutter's sawmill near Sacramento triggered the Gold Rush. Apart from the Buttes, Sutter County encompasses a broad plain between the Sacramento and Feather rivers. Floods long plagued the lowlands, but the resulting rich alluvial soils allow farmers to grow a cornucopia of crops, including beans, rice, walnuts, peaches, and prunes. Sutter National Wildlife Refuge harbors migratory waterfowl. Farmers lobbied for the refuge on the premise that birds would flock to the sanctuary for food, rather than feast on their crops. Today land speculators pose a more pressing threat. Between 1988 and 1992 speculation drove the value of farmland in south Sutter County from $2,500 to $16,000 an acre. As farmers sell out, rice fields become subdivisions. This process is gobbling up irreplaceable fertile acreage in farming areas throughout California.

Additional Sources of Information/Recommended Reading:

The Middle Mountain Foundation
P.O. Box 626
Sutter, CA 95982
(916) 343-0703

Anderson, Walt, *The Sutter Buttes, A Naturalist's View,* The Natural Selection Press, 1983 (available from the Middle Mountain Foundation).

**South Butte
above orchard**

Sutter

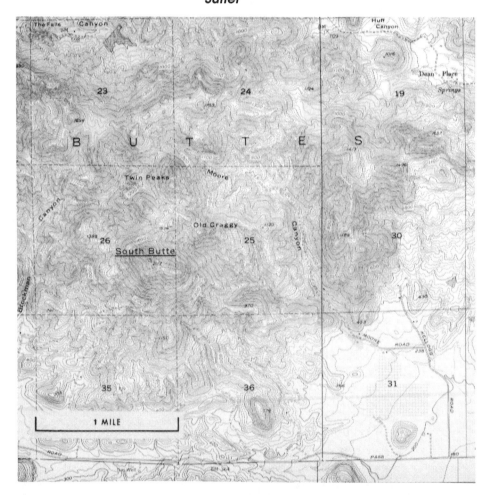

Tehama

Brokeoff Mountain   9235′   **#16**

Location: Northeast corner of the county (See below)
Distance: 7 miles round trip/2600′ elevation gain
Grade: Moderate/Class 1
Hiking Time: 5 hours
Season: Mid-July to October

Trailnotes: A distinctive summit, the remnant of an immense volcano that rose over 2 miles high. The mountain lies in the southwest corner of Lassen Volcanic National Park. An excellent trail, more scenic and less crowded than the one to nearby Lassen Peak, takes you to an arresting overlook. Highpoint seekers normally climb Brokeoff Mountain jointly with Lassen Peak, the apex of Shasta County. Please turn to the Shasta County Trailnotes for further details, and for the following paired entries: Maps, Approach, Nearby Campgrounds, and Additional Sources of Information.

Directions to Summit: A well-signed trail takes off by the west side of the road, across from the parking lot. Initially you delve into a damp, creekside alder thicket. Past the alders the trail swings shortly west and then northwest, crossing and recrossing babbling brooks in an open forest brightened by wildflower bouquets. At about 1.3 miles, an unsigned path on the right tags along a creek for 200 yards to log-laden Forest Lake. The main trail gradient steepens to ascend south-facing slopes covered with brush and thinning trees. A long straight stretch traverses a talus slope and gains the west ridge of Brokeoff Mountain. Now only about ½ mile from your goal, the trail veers east and climbs at a moderate incline to the top. The unnaturally flat area on the rugged summit plateau once held a lookout and still holds a benchmark. A use trail extends to the slightly lower far (west) end of the mountaintop.

The View: Brokeoff Mountain's precipitous north face leaves one breathless. Easily identified outlying landmarks include Mount Shasta and Black Butte in the northwest, and the Sacramento Valley and Sutter Buttes in the south. Lassen Peak captures the scene in the northeast, with Helen Lake on its shoulder. Southwest of Lassen Peak, Eagle Peak, Pilot Pinnacle, and Mount Diller arc toward Brokeoff Mountain; they all once formed flanks of enormous Mount Tehama.

The Environment: Mount Tehama arose some 600,000 years ago and grew to 11,000 feet in elevation during the next 300,000 years. But the volcano's genesis coincided with the Ice Age, and glaciers quickly—in geologic terms—began scouring the cone. Glaciers eventually ground the peak into oblivion, except for vestiges like Brokeoff Mountain, largest remnant of the former giant volcano. To early settlers, the mountain looked "brokeoff"—faulted from the surrounding landscape. The misnomer stuck, even after geologists understood that ice rather than earthquakes had created the escarpment. The sheer cliffs generate updrafts, which carry myriad insects aloft. Hikers often find the summit abuzz with flying bugs, buzzing bees, and flitting butterflies.

The County: An Indian tribe named Tehama may have inhabited the region. Other interpretations suggest that Tehama comes from an Indian word for lowland, or from the Arabic *tehama*, which means "hot lowlands." The latter term fits Red Bluff to a tee. This main town and county seat roasts in summertime with some of the hottest temperatures in the nation. The all-time high registered 121° in 1981. Red Bluff centers in the northern Sacramento Valley. The county boundaries extend to the Coast Ranges on the west and to the Cascade Range and the Sierra Nevada foothills on the east. Tehama ranks high in olive production. The Sevillano variety, grown for eating rather than for olive oil, flourishes in orchards around Corning, south of Red Bluff. Other important crops include hay, wheat, sugar beets and rice. Lumbering and livestock also add to the economy.

Brokeoff Mountain above Lake Helen

Trinity

Mount Eddy   9025'   **#18**

Location and Maps:	Northeast corner of the county
	USGS 7½-minute *Mount Eddy, South China Mtn.;*
	USFS *Shasta-Trinity National Forest*
Distance:	8.4 miles round trip/2800' elevation gain
Grade:	Moderate/Class 1
Hiking Time:	5 hours
Season:	Late June to October

Trailnotes: A pleasurable dayhike to a majestic mountaintop. Although Mt. Eddy is the highest point west of I 5 between the Canadian border and the Mexican border, it is almost totally eclipsed by skyscraping Mount Shasta, 15 air miles to the east. A paved road accesses the trailhead. Shasta-Trinity National Forest trails take you over lake-bejeweled terrain on the way to the summit. The mountain's name honors Olive Paddock Eddy, a Shasta Valley pioneer and the first woman to climb Mount Shasta.

Approach: From I 5, 3 miles north of Weed and 26 miles south of Yreka, take the Edgewood-Gazelle/Stewart Springs Road exit. Go west a few yards to a **T** junction and turn right. After 0.5 mile turn left onto Stewart Springs Road. Proceed 3.9 miles and then turn right onto Forest Road 17. Drive up it 10.4 miles to the Deadfall Meadows Parking Area, on the right side of the road.

Directions to Summit: From the parking area cross the road by the trailhead sign and enjoy a garden of rock pedestals. Cross and recross Deadfall Creek and little brooks in a gentle ascent through an open forest and a flower-filled meadow. In 1.5 miles you reach a four-way junction, where the Pacific Crest Trail intersects the Sisson-Callahan Trail. Continue southeast on the Sisson-Callahan Trail, climbing easy benches to the Deadfall Lakes. The trail skirts the lakes and then veers south to mount a ridge topped by Deadfall Summit, about 2.8 miles from the start. Just beyond the summit, a trail sign indicates the Mount Eddy Trail departure point. Turn northeast and head upslope between a rocky knob on the left and a clump of trees on the right. The path begins faintly, but after 0.1 mile you pick up a good trail. The trail switchbacks up the mountain at a comfortable 15% grade, scaling about 1000 feet in 1.4 miles. A small, dilapidated cabin sits atop the spacious summit flat, part of a lookout facility abandoned in 1931. A register nestles in a cairn next to a concrete foundation east of the cabin.

The View: Mount Shasta monopolizes the view, in all its jaw-dropping splendor. The Scott Mountains rise in the west behind Deadfall Lakes Basin. Shasta Valley spreads in the north, and the Eddy Range unfurls in the south. Look for the Trinity Alps in the southwest and Castle Crags in the southeast, with Lassen Peak in the background.

The Environment: Mount Eddy, the eastern climax to the Klamath Mountains, formed from intrusive igneous material between 400 and 65 million years ago. Gabbro, the common rock type here, looks similar to granite but has a higher percentage of dark minerals like magnesium and iron. The iron "rusts," giving Mount Eddy an ochre cast. The Eddy Range harbors an exceptionally rich flora. Trailside wildflowers include hulsea, penstemon, marsh marigold, buttercup, wild rose, yellow lupine, corn lily, and the unusual, carnivorous pitcher plant (seen in boggy spots along the first leg of the hike). A crowd of conifers grows between upper Deadfall Lake and Deadfall Summit: red fir, white fir, foxtail pine, lodgepole pine, western white pine, and whitebark pine.

Nearby Campgrounds: Shasta-Trinity, the largest national forest in California, has more than 80 campgrounds spread over its 2.1 million acres. But sites nearest the trailhead lie at least 15 miles west, off Highway 3 at Horse Flat, Eagle Creek, and Scott Mountain. Good backpacking sites ring Deadfall Lakes.

The County: Trinity County takes its name from the Trinity River, named by Major Pearson Reading in 1845, who mistakenly thought the river emptied into Trinidad Bay (Trinity is the English equivalent of Trinidad). In 1775 Spanish explorers named Trinidad Head, a promontory above Trinidad Bay in Humboldt County, for Trinity Sunday (the first Sunday after Pentecost). Mountains blanket Trinity County. The Klamath Ranges cover the northern two thirds of the county, and the Coast Ranges extend over the southern third. Pine and fir forests dominate the vegetation and underpin an economy based on lumbering and wood products. Livestock ranching and tourism also play a role. Recreation centers around the magnificent, glaciated Trinity Alps. Weaverville, the only town of consequence, had more residents during the Gold Rush than it has today. The entire county population numbers only about 15,000—too few to require traffic lights or parking meters.

Additional Sources of Information/Recommended Reading:

Mt. Shasta Ranger District
204 W. Alma St.
Mount Shasta, CA 96067
(916) 926-4511
The ranger office has a substantial collection of free handouts on trails, campgrounds, and natural history.

Linkhart, Luther, *The Trinity Alps,* 2nd ed., Wilderness Press, 1986.
Selters, Andy, and Michael Zanger, *The Mt. Shasta Book,* Wilderness Press, 1989.

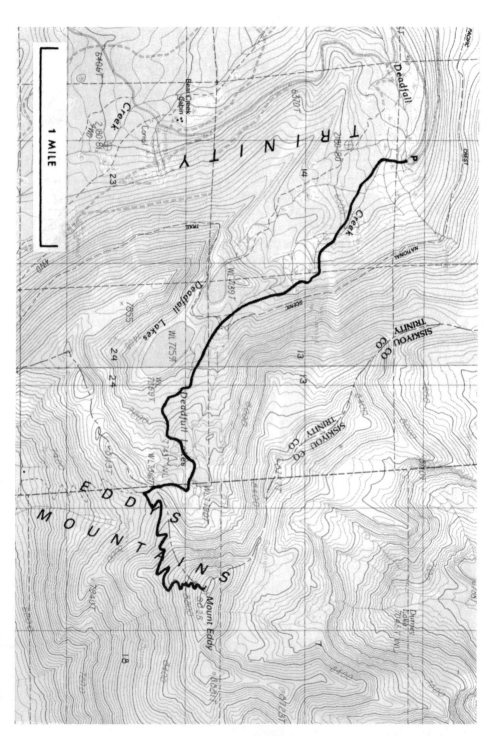

Trinity

Tulare

Mount Whitney   14,491′   #1

Location: Along the east border of the county. Mount Whitney is the highpoint of both Tulare County *and* Inyo County. Please see Inyo County for all entries except the County.

The County: "Tulare" comes from *Los Tules,* Spanish for "The Rushes," alluding to former widespread marshlands around Tulare Lake. County elevations range from 260 feet on the San Joaquin Valley floor to over 14,000 feet in the High Sierra. Level alluvial soils suited to agriculture cover the western third of the county. Tulare holds first place in the state for sorghum grain, kiwi fruit, olives, pomegranates, table grapes, and Valencia oranges. Such crops, as well as livestock, poultry, and dairy production give Tulare the second highest agricultural income of any county in the nation. Forested slopes, deep canyons, and high peaks suited to recreation comprise the eastern two-thirds of the county. Over 40 developed campgrounds dot the back country. Domeland Wilderness and Golden Trout Wilderness invite exploration. Sequoia National Park protects the world's largest Giant Sequoia: the General Sherman tree stands 275 feet high and about 33 feet in diameter.

Tuolumne

Mount Lyell   13,114′   **#6**

Location and Maps:	Southeast corner of the county
	USGS 7½-minute *Mt. Lyell, Vogelsang Peak;*
	Wilderness Press, *Yosemite National Park and*
	Vicinity (See Mariposa County for the first Mt.
	Lyell route map.)
Distance:	28 miles round trip/4600′ elevation gain
Grade:	Strenuous/Class 3
Hiking Time:	18 hours
Season:	Mid-July to late September

Trailnotes: The highest point in Yosemite National Park, a crown jewel set above the forest, lake, and meadow gems of Lyell Canyon. The peak's alpine grandeur has long enthralled artists and mountaineers. To reach the summit, you follow the John Muir Trail for 12 miles and then venture cross country for 2 miles on a popular climbers' route. The route traverses Lyell Glacier and ascends a short Class 3 section near the top. The glacier's surface changes seasonally (smooth to rough, soft to hard); an ice axe and crampons often make the glacier crossing easier. A skilled climber should lead the Class 3 stretch and use a rope to belay those less experienced.

The trail mileage calls for an epic dayhike or an overnight backpack. Dayhikes require no wilderness permit, but overnight trips do. If possible, write for a permit before your outing. The Park's Wilderness Office takes applications only between March 1 and May 31. Or you may apply in person at a kiosk in Tuolumne Meadows located along the spur road to the trailhead. The kiosk has extended hours from late June to Labor Day. You can get a permit a day ahead, and it's a good idea to do so, especially on summer weekends, when the trail quota fills up quickly.

The mountain's name commemorates an eminent English geologist, Sir Charles Lyell (1797–1875).

Approach: From U.S. 395 near Lee Vining, take SR 120 19 miles west and watch for a WILDERNESS PERMITS sign as you approach Tuolumne Meadows. Turn left (south) onto a spur road near the sign. After 0.1 mile on the spur road you pass a wilderness permits kiosk in a parking lot on your right. Proceed another 0.7 mile to arrive at the trailhead parking area. The trail begins on the right side of the road, immediately south of the parking lot.

From I 5 near Manteca, take SR 120 east for 150 miles, passing the Tuolumne Meadows Visitors Center on your right 2.0 miles before you reach the WILDERNESS PERMITS sign and the spur road to the trailhead.

Directions to Summit: From the trailhead sign, walk south a short way on a much-trodden path to find the John Muir Trail. Go left and soon cross a bridge over the Dana Fork of the Tuolumne River. Then you go right at a junction and pass over a rise to reach two bridges spanning the Lyell Fork of the Tuolumne River. About 70 yards past the bridges, you turn left on a trail coming from Tuolumne Campground, and ½ mile later you pass a trail to Vogelsang, near a ford of Rafferty Creek. Now follow a generally level, rut-riven tread for nearly 8 miles to unsigned Lyell Base Camp at the south end of the canyon floor, passing several meadow-edge backpack camps and a trail fork to Ireland Lake 5.8 miles from the start.

Beyond the long level stretch, switchback up the canyonside to reach a footbridge, near where Maclure Creek joins the Lyell Fork. Press upward to a bench with an unnamed tarn. Cross the outlet and ascend to a higher basin and tarn, about 2 miles above the footbridge. Here, on a rise where the trail veers dramatically from south to east, the climbers' route begins.

Leave the John Muir Trail and head south across the basin. Climb jumbo slabs to attain a grassy shelf just southwest of the basin. From the shelf surmount an extensive boulder field to reach the foot of the glacier, curving around the west side of a prominent rocky knob that temporarily hides Mount Lyell from view. Traverse the glacier diagonally, aiming for the saddle between Mount Lyell and Mount Maclure. Carefully cross the bergschrund (a crevasse formed where the glacier has pulled away from the headwall). Rope up at the saddle. (In years of light snow, and/or late in the season, you can avoid the glacier by hiking west and south around the ice, and up a scree slope to the saddle).

From the saddle work your way east a short distance between the rock face above and the ice below until you reach a narrow, steep chute slicing upward toward the summit. Clamber up the ledges west of the chute, or up the chute itself (the best route varies with snow and ice conditions from year to year). The ledges have ample solid handholds and footsteps, but, for about 100 feet, the sheer angle of ascent leaves climbers exposed to a dangerous fall. Past this crux, easy scrambling and a boulderhop across the tilted summit plateau bring you to the top. A register lodged in concrete sits on a boulder just north of the highest crag.

The View: A glorious, all-embracing northern Sierra panorama. Looking west, Mount Maclure fills the foreground, with the Clark Range off to the left and the Cathedral Range to the right. Lakes sparkle in granite basins all around you. Twin pinnacles Mount Ritter and Banner Peak jut skyward in the southeast. Mount Lyell's south face drops precipitously directly below, while a plethora of peaks fills the southern horizon. Lyell Canyon unrolls to the north, alongside the Kuna Crest, Mount Gibbs, and Mount Dana. The largest subalpine meadow in the Sierra Nevada spreads to the northwest, backed by a deeper recess, the Grand Canyon of the Tuolumne.

The Environment: Ancient metamorphosed slate tops the summit, underlain by a geologically younger granite base. Headwaters on Mount Lyell feed the Tuolumne River to the north, the Merced River to the west, the San Joaquin River to the south, and Rush Creek to the east. Ten thousand years ago, glittering ice rivers flowed down all these drainages. The glaciers formed during colder times, when snowfall exceeded snowmelt, and the heavy accumulation compacted to form glacial ice. A massive icefield high on Mount Lyell fed the largest glacier in the Sierra. This 60-mile ribbon of ice sculpted Lyell Canyon, Tuolumne Meadows, the Grand Canyon of the Tuolumne, and Hetch Hetchy Valley. Then warming temperatures melted the glaciers. The present Lyell Glacier formed during a cooling cycle around 2500 years ago. Longstanding cyclical changes in temperature suggest the glaciers will one day advance again.

Nearby Campgrounds: Several small Forest Service campgrounds line the road east of Tioga Pass. The Park's Tuolumne Meadows Campground has 330 spaces, half reserved through MISTIX and half available on a first-come, first-served basis (arrive early). The campground also has 25 sites for backpackers. Some Lyell Canyon trail camps have cables to secure food from the area's notoriously bold bears.

The County: The melodic Indian word *Tuolumne* has been given various possible meanings, including "people who dwell in stone houses" and "straight up steep." The entirely mountainous county extends from Sierra foothills to high peaks on the crest of the range. A small population clusters in old mining towns like China Camp and Sonora, the county seat. County commerce revolves around lumbering, cattle and poultry raising, and tourism, centered in Yosemite. Interestingly, Park visitation has increased by about a third since 1975, to around 3.5 million people per year, while backcountry use has dropped by half. The reduction reflects the impact of the wilderness-permit system as well as a demographic shift in the population, as aging baby boomers trade backpacks and trail camps for suitcases and country inns.

Additional Sources of Information/Recommended Reading:

Yosemite National Park, Wilderness Office
P.O. Box 577
Yosemite, CA 95389
(209) 372-0310 (recording)
(209) 372-0285 (for specific information)

Medley, Steven P., *The Complete Guidebook to Yosemite National Park,* Yosemite Association, 1991.

Schaffer, Jeffrey P., *Yosemite National Park, A Natural-History Guide to Yosemite and Its Trails,* 3rd ed., Wilderness Press, 1992.

Mt. Lyell from the south

Tuolumne

See Mariposa County map

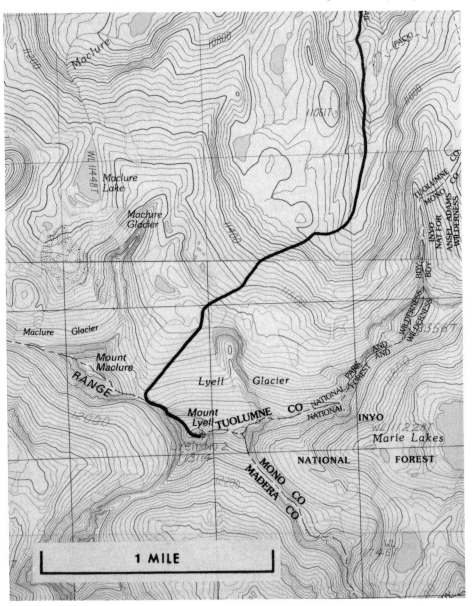

Ventura

Mount Pinos   8831'   **#21**

Location and Maps: Along the north border of the county
USGS 7½-minute *Sawmill Mountain, Cuddy Valley;* USFS *Los Padres National Forest*
Distance: 3 miles round trip/800' elevation gain
Grade: Moderate/Class 1
Hiking Time: 1.5 hours
Season: April to November

Trailnotes: Mount Pinos overlooks wild high country in Los Padres National Forest. A paved road reaches to within 1.5 miles of the peak, and a rough dirt road (usually open and passable by passenger cars) continues to the top. A trail then leads from Mount Pinos to Sawmill Mountain, highpoint of Kern County. This single outing lets you breezily attain a pair of county summits. Coincidentally, each of the climbs (assuming you begin the Sawmill Mountain hike at Mt. Pinos) entails a 3-mile round trip and a total elevation gain of 800 feet. No water available. Winter snow draws many cross-country skiers to the area; easy access and gentle terrain make winter ascents a possibility. *Piños,* Spanish for "pine," heralds the yellow-pine forest growing on the mountaintop.

Approach: Take the Frazier Park/Mt. Pinos Recreation Area exit off I 5, about 70 miles north of Los Angeles and 40 miles south of Bakersfield. Go 5 miles west to a junction with Lockwood Valley Road in Lake of the Woods. Keep right at the junction and proceed 5 miles to a junction with Mill Potrero Road. Bear left and drive up 9 sinuous miles to a spacious parking lot. Park here for hiking to the summit.

Directions to Summit: Walk up the dirt road 1.5 miles to reach a broad summit shelf. The road forks at the top. Go right to find the Ventura County highpoint benchmark, located just north of an Air Force microwave station. Go left to see the paved lot, walkways and benches of a defunct Condor Observation Site.
Continue on to Sawmill Mountain by taking a trail that begins just past the westernmost walkway and bench. You switchback down the west face of Mount Pinos, bottom out at a saddle, and then climb rather steeply up the east shoulder of Sawmill Mountain. The gradient soon eases and the trail tops out. At this point, leave the trail and head northwest over easy cross-country terrain to reach an open ridgetop and a faint path going west to a summit cairn. The off-trail travel covers about 0.3 mile.

The View: A jumble of windswept ridges and valleys surrounds Mount Pinos and Sawmill Mountain. Distantly, you may descry part of the San Joaquin Valley, the southern Sierra, and the Mojave Desert. The former Condor Observation Site benches serve as eerie reminders of a view removed—a view of giant black vultures with nine-foot wingspans soaring in the sky. Loss of habitat, shooting, and poisoning downed North America's largest bird. In 1987 authorities trapped the last free-flying condor south of Mount Pinos for a controversial captive breeding program. Condors have bred well in captivity. Over the next 20 years, officials hope to re-establish two geographically separate condor populations in the wild, with 100 birds each.

The Environment: The Sierra Nevada, the Coast Ranges, and the Transverse Ranges converge at the south end of the San Joaquin Valley in a mishmash of mountains termed "The Knot." Mount Pinos tops The Knot. The mountains consist of uplifted blocks, dissected by erosion and bisected by faultlines. The San Andreas Fault cuts across the north base of Mount Pinos and Sawmill Mountain. The 10-mile drive from I 5 to the turnoff for Mount Pinos takes you directly over the famous fault. Jeffrey pine and limber pine dominate the upper elevations. Descending vertical zones exhibit Douglas oak woodland, pinyon woodland, and chaparral. These plant associations serve as invaluable watershed cover for semiarid Southern California.

Nearby Campgrounds: Car campers may use Chula Vista Walk-in Campground adjacent to the trailhead parking area, as well as Mt. Pinos Campground, 2 miles down the road from the trailhead parking lot. McGill Campground offers more spaces, 1.6 miles farther down the road. Both campgrounds have water. Sheep Camp, a backpackers' site with a seasonal spring, lies about 1.5 miles west of Sawmill Mountain.

The County: Junipero Serra founded Mission San Buenaventura in 1782. The name commemorates a 13th Century Italian cleric. The local Chumash Indians surprised the Spaniards with their technical skills; the Indians built partitioned rooms in their homes, created beautiful pottery and basketry, and used asphalt to caulk canoes. The presence of asphalt, a crude form of oil, indicated deposits of petroleum, later to form a mainstay of the county's economy. Agriculture flourishes in the deltalike coastal lowland called the Oxnard Plain. Major crops include lemons, lima beans, lettuce, and cut flowers. Urbanization now competes with agriculture for land. Population clusters in the large towns of Ventura and Oxnard on the coastal plain, and in smaller towns like Ojai and Santa Paula, tucked in interior valleys. Forty-six percent of the county's land area lies within Los Padres National Forest.

Additional Sources of Information/Recommended Reading:

Los Padres National Forest, Mt. Pinos District
HC1-400
Frazier Park, CA 93225
(805) 245-3731

Darlington, David, *In Condor Country,* Henry Holt and Company, 1987.

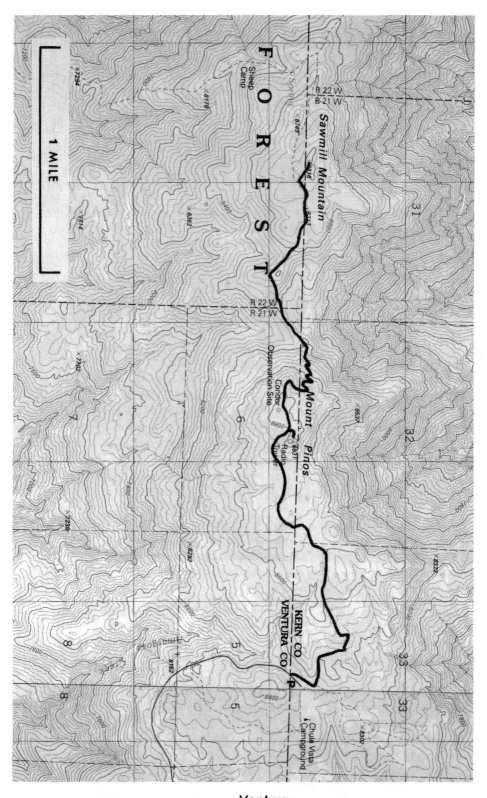

Ventura

Yolo

Little Blue Peak   3120+′   **#50**

Location and Maps: Central western edge of the county
USGS 7½-minute *Wilson Valley, Jericho Valley;*
BLM Surface Management Status Map
Healdsburg, Calif.
Distance: 8.5 miles round trip/1900′ elevation gain
Grade: Moderate/Class 2
Hiking Time: 5 hours
Season: Mid-April to November

Trailnotes: An out-of-the-way chaparral-covered ridgetop. The highpoint lies almost unnoticed among other rolling hills and ridges in the 33,582-acre Bureau of Land Management Rocky Creek–Cache Creek Wilderness Study area. A well-graded dirt road, closed during the rainy season, snakes to the trailhead. Call Yolo County Road Maintenance for the latest road conditions.

Two routes are possible. (1) An all-BLM land route follows a four-wheel-drive road 2 miles and then goes cross-country the rest of the way. You may be literally trailblazing—the BLM considers the area a likely site for a new trail. For now, the cross-country stretch requires *major* bushwacking and is recommended only for determined hikers. (2) A private-segment route necessitates crossing undeveloped private property for just over a mile. This course covers roughly the same mileage as the all-BLM land route, but entails less elevation gain (1500 feet), and very little bushwhacking. Of course, ask any landowner you encounter for permission to cross private property.

Little Blue Peak takes its name from the underpinning Little Blue Ridge. County highpoint pioneers mistook other peaks in the area for the Yolo summit until mountaineer John Sarna discerned the true highpoint on a topo map in 1991. Little Blue Ridge forms a prong of the larger Blue Ridge to the east, named for the bluish cast of its blue-oak woodlands and chaparral.

Approach: From I 5 at Woodland, 20 miles northwest of Sacramento, take SR 16 west 10 miles to I 505. From I 80 at Vacaville, take I 505 north 22 miles to SR 16. From the junction of SR 16 and I 505, go west on SR 16 33 miles to Cache Creek Canyon Regional Park. Bear left at a turnoff signed LOWER SITE, COUNTY OF YOLO, PICNIC AREA. The turnoff becomes dirt-graded Rayhouse Road/Road 40. Drive up the road 4.5 miles to a signed junction. From the junction take Morgan Valley/ Rayhouse Road/Road 40 west 6 miles, passing Davis Creek Reservoir en route to a street-sign-posted junction reading YOLO COUNTY LINE/ROAD 40. Park on the right side of the road. The hiking route begins a scant 0.1 mile west of the sign, where a four-wheel-drive road heads north. (The BLM plans shortly to close this road to vehicles, but it will remain open to hikers, horseback riders, and trailbikers.)

Directions to Summit: Amble up the flattish four-wheel-drive road. In about 1.2 miles, just after the road veers from north to east, look for a small cairn along the north side of the road. The private-segment route branches north at this point (see next paragraph). The all-BLM land route continues east down the four-wheel-drive road another 0.8 mile to reach a short ridge about 800 feet before the road ends. Descend the ridge, bushwacking your way 0.2 mile to Davis Creek. Cross the creek and ascend the steep minor ridge that rises northeast to the ridgetop. Traverse the ridgetop's dips and rises as you work your way northwest through thick brush about 1.8 miles to gain the roaded summit. An old wooden bench sits on the top, and alongside the bench a small rock cairn holds a register.

The private-segment route drops down from the four-wheel road into a shallow, brush-laden gulch. Press through the brush in a northwestward direction to the BLM boundary fenceline near a rock outcrop labeled "Twin Sisters" on the topo map. The fenceline passes a homestead to the west, and after 0.5 mile turns from north to west, only to bend north again in another ¼ mile. Nearby, a dirt road on the west side of the fence heads northwest, approximately following the Yolo County–Lake County boundary line up toward Butte Rock, a prominent landmark. Sheep graze on the grassy, oak-strewn hillsides, and signs posted in the area indicate parcels for sale. From the vicinity of Butte Rock, a faint tread climbs northeast to merge with a substantial firebreak road. The firebreak drops down to a saddle and then climbs to Little Blue Peak's north flank, from where a spur runs directly up to the summit.

The View: The unassuming summit offers surprisingly long-range views. Davis Creek wraps around Little Blue Ridge to drain canyons east and west of the ridge before emptying into Cache Creek. Cache Creek flows out of sight in the east, breaching the prominent gap between Cortina Ridge and Blue Ridge, with the Central Valley's Sutter Buttes visible in the distance. Lassen Peak rises in the northeast. Snow Mountain and Mount Konocti stand out in the northwest, and Mount Saint Helena holds sway in the west. Berryessa Peak tops the southeast horizon, prominent and higher-looking than Little Blue Peak, but lagging 63 feet below this county summit.

The Environment: Tan-colored sandstone, conglomerate, and other sedimentary rocks of the Knoxville Formation underlie Little Blue Peak. Detrital serpentine sediments foster a large Sargent cypress grove seen near the trailhead. A few Digger pines poke up through the chamise chaparral on Little Blue Ridge, joined by yerba santa, ceanothus, and California nutmeg. Hikers often see coyote, jackrabbit, and blacktailed deer on the ridge. The second-largest herd of tule elk in California, some 200 strong, roams through the Cache Creek region. Overwintering bald eagles feed and roost along Cache Creek. The BLM tallies around 50 bald eagles per year. The creek's ample food and natural seclusion attract the endangered bird. Its commoner cousin, the golden eagle, soars over the area throughout the year.

Nearby Campgrounds: The one campground in the vicinity lies off SR 16, a mile northwest of the turnoff to Rayhouse Road/Road 40. Cache Creek Regional Park contains 30 campsites, with grassy lawns and close proximity to Cache Creek, a popular rafting and fishing stream. This Yolo County campground operates on a first-come, first-served basis. For information call (916) 666-8115. The BLM permits primitive camping throughout the Wilderness Study Area.

The County: The word "yolo" most likely comes from a native Indian term *Yoloy,* meaning "a place abounding with rushes." Rush-filled marshlands once prevailed in low-lying eastern Yolo County. Flooding from the Sacramento River and from Cache, Putah, and Willow creeks created rich alluvial soils. Today, a flood of suburban housing threatens the fertile farmland. Major crops include alfalfa, barley, safflower, and sugar beets, as well as tomatoes, almonds, peaches, and honeydew melons. Woodland, the largest town and the county seat, supplies the area's farmers and has food-processing plants. The city of Davis, south of Woodland, has received awards for progressive energy-conservation programs. The town contains miles of bikeways, and hosts a University of California campus, considered one of the top 20 research universities in the country.

Additional Sources of Information/Recommended Reading:

Bureau of Land Management,
  Clear Lake Resource Area
555 Leslie Street
Ukiah, CA 95482
(707) 462-3873

Yolo County Road Maintenance
(916) 666-8032

Larkey, Joann L., and Shipley Walters, *Yolo County, Land of Changing Patterns,* Windsor Publications, 1987.

Little Blue Peak (far left) and hikers

Yolo

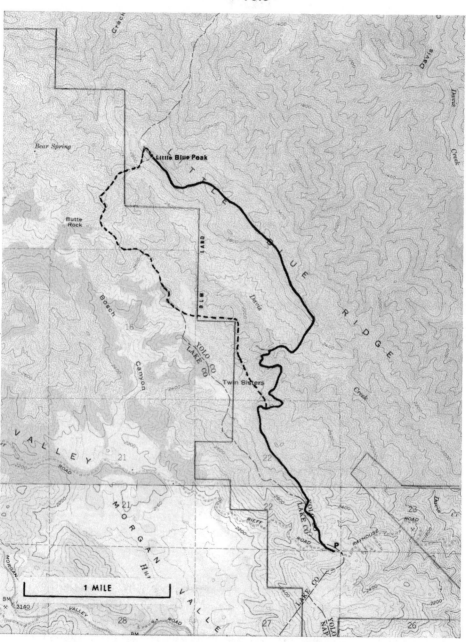

Yuba

Sugar Pine Peak   4825+´   #38

Location and Maps: Northeast edge of the county
USGS 7½-minute *Strawberry Valley, American House;* USFS *Plumas National Forest*
Distance: 1.4 miles round trip/375´ elevation gain
Grade: Easy/Class 1
Hiking Time: 40 minutes
Season: May to November

Trailnotes: The most obscure county summit, located on a thickly timbered hilltop in the northern Mother Lode country. Several stately sugar pines, standing out among other species on the summit, inspired the name. Loggers ply this section of Plumas National Forest, so watch for logging trucks as you negotiate the narrow paved and gravel roads that lead to the highpoint. Deer hunters roam the hills in the fall. The outing involves a long drive for a short hike; you may wish to extend your trip by visiting some of the old mining camps in the area.

Approach: From Marysville (37 miles east of I 5 on SR 20), take SR 20 east 12 miles to a junction with County Road E21. Travel 24.5 miles north on E21 to Challenge. Or, from Nevada City take SR 49 north 17 miles to Moonshine Road. Bear left on Moonshine Road for 5 miles, left again on Marysville Road for 4 miles, and then right on Oregon Hill Road for 12 miles to Challenge. From Challenge, continue east 8.5 miles to Strawberry Valley. Note the Strawberry Valley Fire Station on your left. Go 1.5 miles past the fire station to a turnoff on the right, signed FS04.

Follow FS04. The paved road displays occasional mileage markers as it descends into a canyon. After 5.5 miles, watch for a white-gravel road turnoff on your left. The turnoff is at a canyon bottom, just before the paved road crosses little Brushy Creek (the creek's name is posted on an inconspicuous sign). Take the white-gravel road. Pass side roads and go through a four-way junction en route to mileage marker 9.5. Go 0.3 mile beyond the mileage marker to reach a spur road on your right. This point is 3.6 miles from the paved road at Brushy Creek. Turn onto the spur and park along the roadside.

Directions to Summit: Hike the spur road (passable by four-wheel-drive vehicles). The road loops upslope at a moderate grade. After about 0.5 mile, watch for an unmaintained jeep road peeling off to the left (north). Take the jeep road 0.2 mile to the top. The road climbs very steeply at first and then eases near the summit flat. Just before the road begins to descend, look to the left (north) to find a pine-cone cairn stacked in the cleft of three closely growing tree trunks, about 10 yards from the road. A small register lies hidden in the pine cones. The topographic map designates the county boundary here "approximate," so the highpoint remains tentative. Lack of a benchmark and inadequate orientation due to the dense tree cover add to the uncertainty.

The View: An extremely close-up view of a mixed coniferous forest, period. The Forest Service plans no immediate timber sales in the area, but nearby logged slopes suggest a more expansive view may one day develop at the trees' expense.

The Environment: The region's favorable temperatures, soils, and precipitation create, in Forest Service parlance, "very high timber productivity." Douglas-fir and white fir dominate the overstory, joined by sugar pine, incense-cedar, black oak, and tanoak. Common understory plants include big-leaf maple, hazelnut, creeping snowberry, and wood rose. Fast-growing trees quickly reclaimed 19th Century mining camps scattered throughout the area, but some larger settlements endure. Poverty Hill, just north from the highpoint, yielded $2 million worth of gold in the 1870s. Strawberry Valley once bustled with mining activity, and nearby La Porte, with 7000 residents in its heyday, recorded $60 million in gold between 1855 and 1871. Modern miners, with metal detectors and portable dredges in hand, still seek the precious metal in these shadowed canyons.

Nearby Campgrounds: Forest Service campgrounds edge three lakes in the vicinity. Reach Strawberry and Sly Creek campgrounds at Sly Creek Reservoir near Strawberry Valley. Locate Running Bear and Red Feather campgrounds at Little Grass Valley Reservoir, north of La Porte, and find several other sites along New Bullards Bar Reservoir south of Challenge.

The County: The Yuba River gave the county its name. The river's name may derive from a local Indian tribe called variously "Yubu," "Yupu," and "Jubu," or from a Spanish word for grape, "uba," a reference to wild grapes growing in profusion along the stream banks. Western Yuba County spreads over the Sacramento Valley where rice, peaches, prunes, and other crops thrive in the fertile soil. Eastern Yuba County extends into the Sierra foothills and mountain slopes, culminating at Sugar Pine Peak. Marysville, the county seat, lies at the confluence of the Feather and Yuba rivers and serves as a major supply center for farmers in the lowlands and recreationists in the mountains. The sport of competitive skiing may have originated in the gold-mining camps along La Porte Road. Miners fashioned Scandinavian-inspired wooden runners to get about in the snow, and friendly rivalries developed among the fastest skiers. A ski club formed to organize downhill races for cash purses, which often included miners' golden nuggets.

Additional Sources of Information/Recommended Reading:

La Porte Ranger District
P.O. Drawer 369
Challenge, CA 95925
(916) 675-2462

Gordon, Marjorie. *Changes in Harmony, An Illustrated History of Yuba and Sutter Counties,* Windsor Publications, Inc., 1988.

Yuba

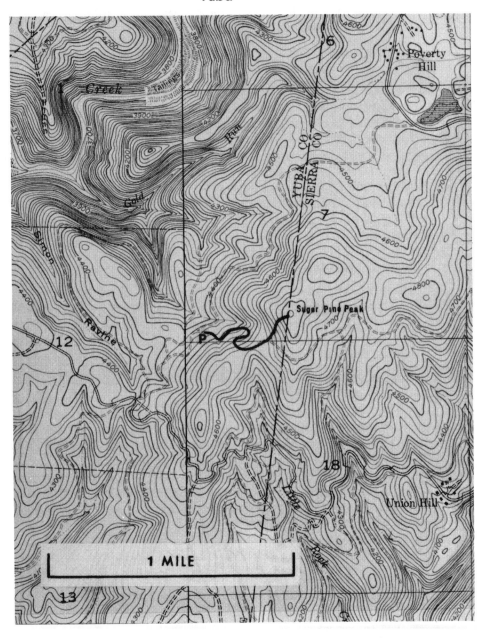

Appendix 1. Bibliography

A selection of general references and germane titles to supplement those listed at the end of the individual county descriptions.

Bakker, Elna, *An Island Called California: An Ecological Introduction to its Natural Communities,* University of California Press, 1985.

Barbour, Michael, *et al., California's Changing Landscapes: Diversity, and Conservation of California Vegetation,* California Native Plant Society, 1993.

Bernbaum, Edwin, *Sacred Mountains of the World,* Sierra Club Books. 1992.

Clark, Ginny, *Guide to Highway 395: Los Angeles to Reno,* Western Trails Publications, 1990.

Fay, James S., and Stephanie W. Fay, eds., *California Almanac,* 4th ed., Pacific Data Resources, 1990.

Graydon, Don, ed., *Mountaineering: The Freedom of the Hills,* 5th ed., The Mountaineers, 1992.

Hart, James D., *A Companion to California,* University of California Press, 1987

Hill, Russell B., *California Mountain Ranges,* Falcon Press, 1986.

Holing, Dwight, *California Wild Lands: A Guide to the Nature Conservancy Preserves,* Chronicle Books, 1988.

Holmes, Don, *Highpoints of the United States: A Hiking & Sightseeing Guide to the Highest Point in Each of the Fifty States,* Cordillera Press, 1990.

Hornbeck, David, *California Patterns: A Geographical and Historical Atlas,* Mayfield Publishing Co., 1983.

Irwin, Sue, *California's Eastern Sierra: A Visitor's Guide,* Cachuma Press, 1992.

Jenkins, J.C., and Ruby Johnson Jenkins, *Exploring the Southern Sierra: East Side,* 3rd ed., Wilderness Press, 1992.

Kreissman, Bern, *California, An Environmental Atlas and Guide,* Bear Klaw Press, 1991.

Krist, John, *50 Best Short Hikes in Yosemite and Sequoia/Kings Canyon,* Wilderness Press, 1993.

Lantis, David W. et al., *California: The Pacific Connection,* Creekside Press, 1988.

Lowe, Don and Roberta, *50 Hiking Trails: Lassen Tahoe Carson Pass,* The Touchstone Press, 1987

Muir, John, *The Mountains of California,* Sierra Club Books, 1989.

Palmer Tim, ed., *California's Threatened Environment, Restoring the Dream,* Island Press, 1993.

Porcella, Stephen F., and Cameron M. Burns, *California's Fourteeners,* Palisades Press, 1991.

Riegert, Ray, *California: The Ultimate Guidebook,* 3rd ed., Ulysses Press, 1993.

Robinson, John W., and Andy Selters, *High Sierra Hiking Guide to Mt. Goddard,* 3rd ed., Wilderness Press, 1986.

Sanford, Bill, *The San Joaquin, the Sierras and Beyond,* Western Tanager Press, 1993.

Schad, Jerry, and David Moser, *Wilderness Basics: The Complete Handbook for Hikers and Backpackers,* 2nd ed., The Mountaineers, 1993.

Schoenherr, Allan A., *Natural History of California,* University of California Press, 1992.

Shanks, Bernard, *California Wildlife,* Falcon Press, 1989.

Soares, John R., *Best Short Hikes In and Around the North Sacramento Valley,* The Mountaineers, 1992.

Stienstra, Tom, *California Camping 1993-94 Edition,* Foghorn Press, 1993.

Stratton, George, *The Recreation Guide to California's National Forests,* Falcon Press, 1991.

Sunset Magazine, *California Travel Guide,* Sunset Publishing Corporation, 1991.

Trzyna, Thaddeus C., ed., *The California Handbook: A Comprehensive Guide to Sources of Current Information & Action,* 6th ed., California Institute of Public Affairs, 1990.

Weir, Kim, *Northern California Handbook,* Moon Publications, Inc., 1990.

Whitehill, Karen and Terry, *Best Short Hikes in California's Southern Sierra,* The Mountaineers, 1991.

——, *Best Short Hikes in California's Northern Sierra,* The Mountaineers, 1990.

Winnett, Thomas, *Guide to the John Muir Trail,* 2nd ed., Wilderness Press, 1984.

——, *The Tahoe-Yosemite Trail,* 6th ed., 1994.

Winnett, Thomas, Jason Winnett, and Lyn Haber, *Sierra North, 100 Backcountry Trips,* 6th ed., Wilderness Press, 1991.

Winnett, Thomas, Jason Winnett, Kathy Morey, and Lyn Haber, *Sierra South, 100 Backcountry Trips,* 6th ed., Wilderness Press, 1993.

Yanker, Gary, and Carol Tarlow, *California Walking Atlas,* McGraw-Hill Publishing Co., 1990.

Zumwalt, Paul L., *Fifty State Summits,* Jack Grauer Publisher, 1988.

Appendix 2. Selected Conservation Organizations

California League of Conservation
Voters
965 Mission St., Suite 705
San Francisco, CA 94103

California Native Plant Society
1722 J St., Suite 17
Sacramento, CA 95815

California Oak Foundation
909 12th St., Suite 125
Sacramento, CA 95814

California State Parks Foundation
P.O. Box 548
Kentfield, CA 94914

California Wilderness Coalition
2655 Portage Bay East, Suite 5
Davis, CA 95616

Cenozoic Society, Inc.
P.O. Box 455
Richmond, VT 05477

Coalition for Clean Air
122 Lincoln Boulevard, Room 201
Venice, CA 90291

Defenders of Wildlife
1228 N St., Suite 6
Sacramento, CA 95814

Earth First!
P.O. Box 5176
Missoula, MT 59806

Earth Island Institute
300 Broadway, Suite 28
San Francisco, CA 94133

Environmental Defense Fund
5655 College Avenue, Suite 304
Oakland, CA 94618

Friends of the River
909 12th St., Suite 207
Sacramento, CA 95814

Greenpeace Pacific Southwest
139 Townsend St.
San Francisco, CA 94107

Klamath Forest Alliance
P.O. Box 820
Etna, CA 96027

League to Save Lake Tahoe
989 Tahoe Keys Boulevard, Suite 6
South Lake Tahoe, CA 96150

Mendocino Forest Watch
P.O. Box 1551
Willits, CA 95490

Mono Lake Committee
1207 Magnolia Boulevard, Suite D
Burbank, CA 90024

Mountain Lion Preservation Foundation
614 Tenth St.
Sacramento, CA 95814

National Audubon Society
555 Audubon Place
Sacramento, CA 95825

Natural Resources Defense Council
617 S. Olive St.
Los Angeles, CA 90014

The Nature Conservancy
785 Market St.
San Francisco, CA 94103

Pacific Crest Trail Association
1350 Castle Rock Road
Walnut Creek, CA 94598

Planning and Conservation League
926 J St., Suite 612
Sacramento, CA 95814

Sierra Club
730 Polk St.
San Francisco, CA 94109

Trust for Public Land
116 New Montgomery
San Francisco, CA 94105

The Wilderness Society
116 New Montgomery, Suite 526
San Francisco, CA 94105

Appendix 3. Map Sources

For a free California road map and a 196-page, full-color travel guide, write to the **California Office of Tourism**, 801 K St., Suite 1600, Sacramento, CA 95814, or call 1-800-TO-CALIF.

Raven Maps & Images, 34 N. Central Ave., Medford, OR 97501, 1-800-237-0798, sells handsome shaded-relief wall maps of California available in two sizes, 42"x64" and 39"x45".

The **United States Geological Survey** (see address below) offers a low-priced but very nice shaded-relief map of similar dimensions that includes county boundaries, an aid to locating county highpoints.

Hubbard, P.O. Box 760, Chippewa Falls, WI 54729-0760, 1-800-323-8368, makes raised relief maps, approximately 32"x21" covering all areas of the state.

The **National Geographic Society**, P.O. Box 1640, Washington, D.C. 20013 sells a detailed 29"x37" wall map of California.

DeLorme Mapping Company offers a *Northern California Atlas & Gazetteer* and a *Central and Southern California Atlas and Gazatteer* with metric contour lines and elevations.

The **California State Automobile Association** drafts excellent state, regional, and county maps for members, and the maps are now available at selected bookstores.

The **Forest Service** supplies fine low-cost topographic-contour maps of wilderness areas as well as national-forest maps (without contour lines).

Topographic maps may be ordered from: **USGS Map Distribution**, Box 25286, Building 810, MS 306, Denver Federal Center, Denver, CO 80225, (303) 236-7477, FAX (303) 236-1972. Ask for two free publications, *California, Catalog of Topographic and Other Published Maps,* and *California, Index to Topographic and Other Map Coverage* to select and order maps.

The **USGS Earth Science Information Center**, 345 Middlefield Road, MS 532, Menlo Park, CA 94025, (415) 329-4390 sells topos over the counter.

Private companies also provide quick service, including:

• **The Map Center**, 2440 Bancroft Way, Berkeley, CA 94704, (510) 841-6277

• **Map Express**, P.O. Box 280445, Lakewood, CO 80228, 1-800-627-0039

• **Timely Discount Topos**, Inc., 9769 W. 119th Drive, Suite 9, Broomfield, CO 80021, 1-800-821-7609

The USGS currently charges $2.50 per map, with a $1 handling fee applied to mail orders of less than $10, but no tax or postage fees. Private companies ask from $2.50 to $3.50 per topo, plus charges for tax, handling, and postage.

Appendix 4. Emblems of California

Flower—California Poppy

Bird—California Quail

Animal—California Grizzly Bear

Fish—Golden Trout

Reptile—Desert Tortoise

Insect—California Dog-face Butterfly

Marine Mammal—California Gray Whale

Tree—California Redwood

Mineral—Gold

Rock—Serpentine

Gemstone—Benitoite

Fossil—Sabre-tooth Cat

Artifact—Native American chipped-stone bear

Song—I Love You, California

Flag—Bear Flag

Colors—Blue and Gold

Motto—Eureka (I have found it)

Nickname—The Golden State

California derives its name from a 16th Century Spanish novel *Las Sergas de Esplandian,* by Garci de Montalvo. The book describes a mythical island called Califia, on which there was no metal but gold.

Source: James D. Driscoll, *California's Legislature, 1984,* State of California, 1984.

Appendix 5. Highpoints Accessible to People with Disabilities

Road access to a number of county highpoints gives people with limited mobility the opportunity to enjoy magnificent vistas. Furthermore, most of the county summits can be seen and photographed from public highways or byways.

Key

* = Paved road reaches to the summit or close to the top
+ = Dirt road reaches to the summit or close to the top
† = Road accesses the summit but unopen to public vehicle use
– = No road access

County	Summit	
Alameda	Discovery Peak	† Park maintenance road
Alpine	Sonora Peak	–
Amador	Thunder Mountain	–
Butte	Lost Lake Ridge	–
Calaveras	Corral Ridge	+ ORV road to within 0.3 of s.
Colusa/Lake	Snow Mountain East	–
Contra Costa	Mount Diablo	* Wheelchair trail on summit
Del Norte	Bear Mountain	–
El Dorado	Freel Peak	–
Fresno	North Palisade	–
Glenn	Black Butte	–
Humboldt	Salmon Mountain	–
Imperial	Blue Angels Peak	+ ORV road to within 0.6 of s.
Inyo/Tulare	Mount Whitney	–
Kern	Sawmill Mountain	–
Kings	Table Mountain	† Private ranch & jeep roads
Lassen	Hat Mountain	–
Los Angeles	Mt. San Antonio	–
Madera	Mount Ritter	–
Marin	Mount Tamalpais	* Road to summit parking lot
Mariposa	Parsons Peak Ridge	–
Mendocino	Anthony Peak	+ Good dirt road to summit
Merced	Laveaga Peak	-
Modoc	Eagle Peak	–
Mono	White Mtn. Peak	† Abandoned jeep road
Monterey	Junipero Serra Pk.	† Old lookout access road
Napa	Mt. St. Helena East	† Special van tour possible
Nevada	Mount Lola	–
Orange	Santiago Peak	+ Steep dirt road to summit
Placer	Granite Chief	–

Highpoints accessible to people with disabilities (cont'd.)

County	Summit	
Plumas	Mount Ingalls	+ Rough jeep road to summit
Riverside	San Jacinto Peak	–
Sacramento	Carpenter Hill	† Antenna service road
San Benito	San Benito Mtn.	+ Steep jeep road to the top
San Bernardino	San Gorgonio Mtn.	–
San Diego	Hot Springs Mtn.	+ Within 150 yards of summit
San Francisco	Mount Davidson	† Park road with chair route possible
San Joaquin	Mt. Boardman North	† Private ranch & jeep roads
San Luis Obispo	Caliente Mountain	† Abandoned lookout road
San Mateo	Long Ridge	† Park service road near s.
Santa Barbara	Big Pine Mountain	† USFS administrative road
Santa Clara	Copernicus Peak	* Within 0.4 mile of summit
Santa Cruz	Mount McPherson	+ Within 200 feet of summit
Shasta	Lassen Peak	–
Sierra	Mount Lola North	–
Siskiyou	Mount Shasta	–
Solano	Mount Vaca	† Communications service road
Sonoma	Cobb Mtn. West Rim	–
Stanislaus	Mount Stakes	† Private ranch & jeep roads
Sutter	South Butte	† Communications service road
Tehama	Brokeoff Mountain	–
Trinity	Mount Eddy	–
Tuolumne	Mount Lyell	–
Ventura	Mount Pinos	+ Dirt road usually o.k. for cars
Yolo	Little Blue Peak	† Ranch roads and firebreaks
Yuba	Sugar Pine Peak	+ Steep, rugged jeep road

Appendix 6. County Highpoints Graded by Physical Exertion and Difficulty

Key

† Drive-up alternative would, of course, place these peaks in the "easy" category

+ Tram alternative would place these peaks in the "moderate" category

* Ice axe, crampons, or other climbing equipment recommended; see individual descriptions for details.

The numbers in parentheses refer to the difficulty of the climb, based on the rating system described for "Grade" in the section "Explanation of Entries" in this book's Introduction.

Easy	Moderate	Strenuous
Anthony Peak (1)	Blue Angels Peak (2)	Bear Mountain (2–3)
Black Butte (1)	Brokeoff Mountain (1)	Big Pine Mtn. (1)
Carpenter Hill (1)	Caliente Mountain (1)	Discovery Peak (1)
Copernicus Peak (1)	Cobb Mtn. West Rim (2)	Eagle Peak (2)
Mt. Davidson (1)	Corral Ridge† (1–2)	Freel Peak (2)
Mt. McPherson (1)	Hat Mountain (2)	Granite Chief+ (1)
Mt. Vaca (1)	Hot Springs Mtn.† (2)	Junipero Serra Pk. (1)
Sugar Pine Peak (1)	Lassen Peak (1)	Laveaga Peak (2)
	Little Blue Peak (2)	Mt. Lyell* (3)
	Long Ridge (1)	Mt. Ritter* (3)
	Lost Lake Ridge (1–2)	Mt. San Antonio+ (1)
	Mt. Boardman North (1)	Mt. Shasta* (3)
	Mt. Diablo† (1)	Mt. Stakes (1)
	Mt. Eddy (1)	Mt. Whitney (1)
	Mt. Ingalls† (1)	North Palisade* (4)
	Mt. Lola (1)	Parsons Peak Ridge (2)
	Mt. Lola North (2)	San Gorgonio Mtn. (1)
	Mt. Pinos† (1)	San Jacinto Peak+ (1)
	Mt. St. Helena E. (1)	Santiago Peak (1)
	Mt. Tamalpais† (1)	Table Mountain (1)
	Salmon Mountain (2)	White Mtn. Peak (1)
	San Benito Mtn.† (1)	
	Sawmill Mountain (1–2)	
	Snow Mtn. East (1)	
	Sonora Peak (2)	
	South Butte (2)	
	Thunder Mountain (2)	

Appendix 7. Lists of Peaks and Highpoints

The enjoyment of mountains often dovetails with the human love to collect things. Individuals and groups compile lists of peaks; these peaks beckon hikers to highpoints. The Sierra Club and other sponsors offer patches, pins, and emblems to those who reach specified peaks and/or complete a list.

- *Hundred Peaks Section (HPS)*, 272 peaks above 5000' in Southern California. Sierra Club, Angeles Chapter, c/o Bob Thompson, HPS Peak Guide Mailer, P.O. Box 633, Montrose, CA 91121.

- *Sierra Peaks Section (SPS)*, 247 peaks in the Sierra Nevada and 1 in Nevada. Sierra Club, Angeles Chapter, c/o Ron Jones, 119 N. Helen Drive, Fullerton CA 92635, (714) 773-5570.

- *Desert Peaks Section Peaks List (DPS)*, 97 peaks in the western states and in Mexico. Sierra Club, Angeles Chapter, c/o Ron Jones, 119 N. Helen Drive, Fullerton, CA 92635, (714) 773-5570.

- *Lower Peaks Committee List (LPC)*, 49 peaks below 5000' in Southern California. Sierra Club, Angeles Chapter, c/o Bob Wheatley, 1409 Skyline Drive, Fullerton, CA 92631, (714) 526-5997.

- *San Diego Peaks List,* 107 peaks within a few hours drive of San Diego. c/o Paul Freiman, 4868 Austin Drive, San Diego, CA 92115, (619) 583-0266.

- *Coastal Peaks List,* 296 peaks between California's Central Valley and the Pacific Ocean. Send SASE to Bill Hauser, 148 Westridge Drive, San Jose, CA 95117.

- *Peak and Gorge Qualifying List,* 238 peaks and 58 gorges within a day's drive of Sacramento. Sierra Club, Mother Lode Chapter, P.O. Box 1335, Sacramento, CA 95812.

- *Tahoe OGUL Qualifying Information,* 63 peaks in the Lake Tahoe area. Sierra Club, Mother Lode Chapter, P.O. Box 1335, Sacramento, CA 95812.

- *The Mazamas Peak List,* 16 major peaks in the Cascade Range. 919 N.W. 19th Street, Portland, OR 97209, (503) 227-2345.

- *Cascade Peaks,* 6 major peaks in Washington, 20 volcanic and 18 nonvolcanic peaks. The Mountaineers, 300 Third Ave. W., Seattle, WA 98119.

- *Colorado Rocky Mountains,* 53 peaks over 14,000'. The Colorado Mountain Club, 2530 W. Alameda Ave., Denver, CO 80219

- *National Forest Highpoints,* 155 national-forest highpoints. Send $1 for list to Roy Schweiker, 12 Chapel St., Concord, NH 03301.

- *The 50 State Highpoints,* Highpointers Club c/o Jack Longacre, P.O. Box 327, Mountain Home, AR 72653. Send $5 for membership and a year's subscription to *Apex to Zenith,* a lively, information-packed quarterly newsletter.

- *State 2nd Highest Points,* send SASE to David W. Olson, 5967 S. Gallup #307, Littleton, CO 80120.

• *California County Highpoint Club*, c/o Dinesh Desai, 870 Highlands Circle, Los Altos, CA 94024, (415) 969-2695. Club members lead group outings to county summits throughout California.

• *County Highpoint Lists,* 25 western and northeastern states, send $4 for 1994 orders to Andy Martin, 3030 N. Sarsaparilla Place, Tucson, AZ 85749, (602) 760-0337.

Yes, beyond California's 58 counties, over 3000 counties spread across America, offering unlimited *high* adventures . . . .

Index

. . . .

Personal Climbing Record

Date	County	Summit	Eleva-tion*	Comment
	Alameda	DISCOVERY PEAK	3840+	
	Alpine	SONORA PEAK	11,459	
	Amador	THUNDER MOUNTAIN	9410	
	Butte	LOST LAKE RIDGE	7120+	
	Calaveras	CORRAL RIDGE	8170	
	Colusa	SNOW MTN. EAST	7040+	
	Contra Costa	MT. DIABLO	3849	
	Del Norte	BEAR MOUNTAIN	6400+	
	El Dorado	FREEL PEAK	10,881	
	Fresno	NORTH PALISADE	14,242	
	Glenn	BLACK BUTTE	7448	
	Humboldt	SALMON MOUNTAIN	6956	
	Imperial	BLUE ANGELS PEAK	4548	
	Inyo	MOUNT WHITNEY	14,491	
	Kern	SAWMILL MTN.	8818	
	Kings	TABLE MOUNTAIN	3473	
	Lake	SNOW MTN. EAST	7056	
	Lassen	HAT MOUNTAIN	8737	
	Los Angeles	MT. SAN ANTONIO	10,064	
	Madera	MOUNT RITTER	13,143	
	Marin	MT. TAMALPAIS	2571	
	Mariposa	PARSONS PEAK RIDGE	12,040+	
	Mendocino	ANTHONY PEAK	6954	
	Merced	LAVEAGA PEAK	3801	
	Modoc	EAGLE PEAK	9892	
	Mono	WHITE MOUNTAIN PEAK	14,246	
	Monterey	JUNIPERO SERRA PEAK	5862	
	Napa	MT. ST. HELENA EAST	4200+	
	Nevada	MOUNT LOLA	9148	
	Orange	SANTIAGO PEAK	5687	

*In feet.

Personal Climbing Record (continued)

Date	County	Summit	Elevation	Comment
	Placer	GRANITE CHIEF	9006	
	Plumas	MOUNT INGALLS	8372	
	Riverside	SAN JACINTO PEAK	10,804	
	Sacramento	CARPENTER HILL	828	
	San Benito	SAN BENITO MTN.	5241	
	San Bernardino	SAN GORGONIO MT.	11,502	
	San Diego	HOT SPRINGS MTN.	6533	
	San Francisco	MT. DAVIDSON	927	
	San Joaquin	MT. BOARDMAN N.	3626	
	San Luis Obispo	CALIENTE MTN.	5106	
	San Mateo	LONG RIDGE	2600+	
	Santa Barbara	BIG PINE MTN.	6800+	
	Santa Clara	COPERNICUS PEAK	4360+	
	Santa Cruz	MT. MCPHERSON	3231	
	Shasta	LASSEN PEAK	10,457	
	Sierra	MOUNT LOLA NORTH	8844	
	Siskiyou	MOUNT SHASTA	14,162	
	Solano	MT. VACA	2819	
	Sonoma	COBB MTN. WEST RIM	4480+	
	Stanislaus	MT. STAKES	3804	
	Sutter	SOUTH BUTTE	2120+	
	Tehama	BROKEOFF MTN.	9235	
	Trinity	MOUNT EDDY	9025	
	Tulare	MOUNT WHITNEY	14,491	
	Tuolumne	MOUNT LYELL	13,114	
	Ventura	MT. PINOS	8831	
	Yolo	LITTLE BLUE PEAK	3120+	
	Yuba	SUGAR PINE PEAK	4825+	